Phyllis Court

Club and Manor

A History by Jason Tomes

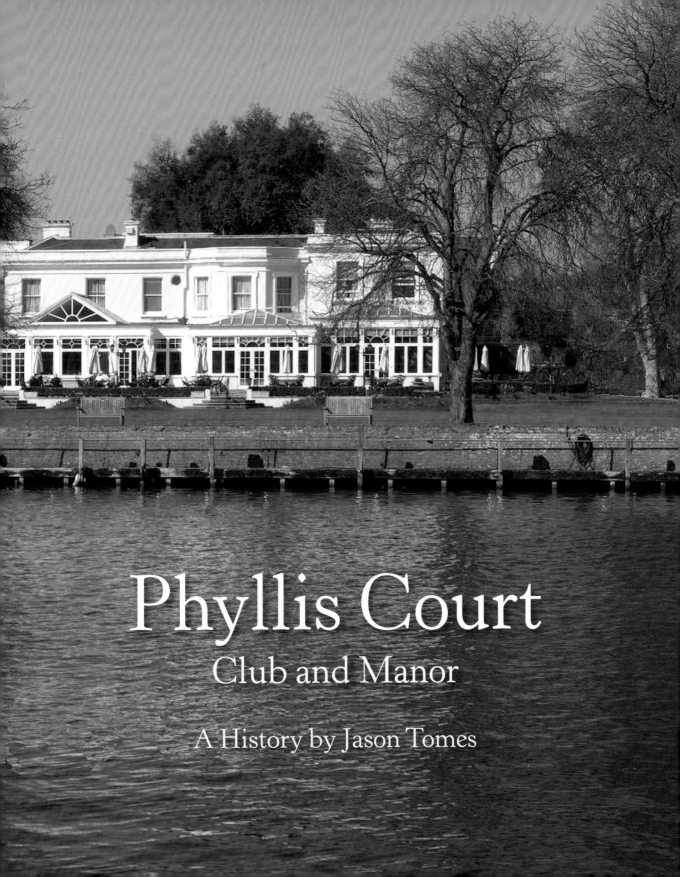

Phyllis Court

Club and Manor

A History by Jason Tomes

Published by Phyllis Court Members Club Ltd

© Phyllis Court Members Club Ltd 2012

ISBN 978-0-9573229-0-5

A CIP catalogue record for this book is available from The British Library.

Designed by Paul Barrett
Design, editorial and production in association with
The Cambridge Book Group, 9a Homerton Business Centre, Cambridge CB2 8QL
Printed and bound by Butler, Tanner and Dennis, Frome

Contents

List of Illustrations

Birth of a Club
1905–1906

The want of a really select Riverside Pleasure Club has long been felt. Many have been started, and many have been failures, partly because of their position, and partly because the choice of members has not always been judicious; and so the pleasure river of the world is still without *the Club* for which it has so long been waiting. As the Club which is now being formed will have its membership as jealously guarded as that of the best London Clubs, and the position and arrangements are such as will afford the maximum of comfort, convenience, and entertainment, there can be no doubt of its success. There is only one 'Henley' in the world, and but one Phyllis Court.

So began the prospectus, published in the final days of June 1905. Its timing was not a matter of chance. The following week a mass of potential applicants would be coming to the Henley Royal Regatta, and they were certain to see Phyllis Court. Who could fail to notice so prominent a property beside the winning post of the world-famous rowing course? Regatta regulars knew it already, and they were the prime targets of the publicity. The proposed Phyllis Court Club aimed 'to provide a headquarters for social and sporting life on the river for those of good social standing.' Such people appeared at Henley-on-Thames in thousands each July, since the Royal Regatta was as important a fixture of the English Season as Royal Ascot in June or Cowes Week in August.

The prospectus invited original members to invest in a promise at Phyllis Court:

The possibilities as a Riverside centre are admittedly unrivalled, and the building and decoration of the house as it stands lend themselves admirably as the nucleus of a Club of this description. The chief requisite to equip it fully for the purpose is a building suitable for use as a Restaurant, Ball and Concert Room, together with a band-stand and some improvements to the river front, and these will be added as soon as possible. In the meantime meals will be provided in the existing Club Dining Room, and there are several private rooms which can be engaged for luncheon, dining, and supper parties on notice being given to the Secretary. The grounds will be laid out eventually with such tennis courts, croquet lawns, bowling greens, &c., as may be found necessary for the entertainment of the members and their guests, and a billiard room will be provided in the Club-house. The Club is intended for both ladies and gentlemen. At present the bedroom accommodation is extremely limited, but by the River Season of 1906 it is

intended to have bedrooms built for members, an entirely separate building being provided for ladies, and a special feature will be made of week-end entertainments.

The Phyllis Court Club – for, at the start, people did say 'the Phyllis Court Club',
with the article only omitted later – faced the classic problem of all new social
clubs, which is the suspicion that it might be catering for persons who could not
gain admission to existing clubs. 'It is intended to make the club as select and
exclusive as possible', asserted the prospectus, 'and to this end the committee will
have full power to refuse undesirable applicants, whether from a social or moral
point of view.' Originally, the plan was to compile a list of the reputable gentlemen's clubs of St James's, Piccadilly, and Pall Mall, and to invite their members to
join the Henley venture. (When the prospectus said that the Phyllis Court Club
was 'intended for both ladies and gentlemen', it did not mean that women were eligible for full membership, but they could become 'lady guest members' if nominated
by a male relative.) By the time the election process began, however, this idea of
an approved list of London clubs had already been jettisoned. All applications
would be subject to ballot and, excepting candidates personally known to members
of the Committee, each 'MUST be accompanied by a reference from a personal
friend of a member of the Committee or a gentleman whose position will of itself
endorse his reference.' Not till February 1906 was the composition of the Founders'
Committee announced. Its ten members, alphabetically, were Lord Churchill,
Colonel Douglas Dawson, R.E. Finlay, Lord Gosford, Major Egerton Green, Lord
Lonsdale, Major-General Arthur Paget, Lord Ronaldshay, the Hon. Edward Stonor,
and Lord Valentia. They merit individual attention.

The Founders' Committee

The founding Chairman of the Phyllis Court Club was Victor Spencer, 1st Viscount
and 3rd Baron Churchill. Queen Victoria was his godmother. Winston Churchill
was his second cousin twice removed. Though highly traditional in some respects,
he might be seen in the context of his time as a new type of aristocrat. In 1896, he
had shocked relatives by selling off his heirlooms and ancestral acres at Cornbury
Park, Charlbury, Oxfordshire in order to lead a fashionable fox-hunting life in
Leicestershire. But Lord Churchill was not feckless. He combined the careers of
businessman and courtier. Companies initially invited him onto their boards on
account of his title and then discovered his abilities. He became a director of the
Grand Union Canal, the British India Shipping Line, and P&O, and went on to chair
the Great Western Railway for a quarter of a century. Meanwhile, as a Tory Whip in
the House of Lords, Churchill held corresponding Court posts under Conservative
Governments. His promotion to Viscount in 1902 arose from his standing in as Lord
Chamberlain at the Coronation of King Edward VII. The Civil List Act (1901)
abolished his position as Master of the Buckhounds, but he retained for life the

3

Viscount
Churchill,
Chairman of
the Founders'
Committee
1906–7, as
caricatured
by 'Spy' in
Vanity Fair, 21
January 1904.

Hugh Lowther, 5th Earl of Lonsdale, a member of the Founders' Committee.

role of His Majesty's Representative at Ascot. This helps explain his chairmanship of the Founders' Committee of the Phyllis Court Club. Everyone in Society stood a little in awe of the 'Ascot arbiter', who policed admission to the Royal Enclosure at the racecourse. His verdict on questions of 'social standing' was final. It seems likely that the Founders' Committee used the same method as the Ascot Office at St James's Palace and categorised applicants under the headings of 'certainly', 'possibly', and 'certainly not'. The Viscount held especially firm views on the inadmissibility of divorced persons – which is ironic, given the ultimate fate of his own first marriage. Lady Churchill, a recent convert to theosophy in 1906, liked to steer conversation towards such esoteric topics as reincarnation, automatic writing, Atlantis, and the astral plane.

The Earl of Lonsdale was her brother. He was also one of the richest men in Britain with an income of almost £4,000 per *week*, the royalties of the coal mines of West Cumberland. He spent it on horses, hunting, racing, motoring, coursing, yachting, and self-advertisement, all with such childlike *joie de vivre* that a sizeable section of the public heartily admired him. 'My life is lovely fun', he would say. He had run away to join the circus in his youth, and the showmanship never ceased, so everybody knew from the papers that 'Lordy' always wore a white gardenia, drank brandy and soda at breakfast, tipped £5 notes, smoked 6½-inch cigars (latterly called Lonsdales), and had his carriages and cars painted canary yellow. His club memberships were many, but they did not include the most highly prestigious, for he had no patience with waiting lists. Establishments that appealed to him often had a raffish flavour – the Pelican Club (boxing), the Shikar Club (big-game hunting), the Happy Club (being happy) – and he usually only interested himself in clubs that elected him President. The Automobile Association was one such; founded in 1905, it adopted his livery as its own. In 'The Yellow Earl', Phyllis Court had a celebrity.

Lord Gosford, a senior Anglo-Irish peer, was less controversial. Fondly regarded at Court as a *raconteur* and a crack shot, he had long served Queen Alexandra as Vice-Chamberlain of the Household, and his social gifts made him a welcome addition to functions of all kinds. The Travellers' and White's were his principal clubs. 'An old-fashioned gentleman, the flower of high-bred courtesy', recalled his obituarist in 1922, 'he did not fail to win the affection of the younger generation, for whom he had a large tolerance, though preserving a naïve regretfulness for the traditions of the past.'

Colonel Douglas Dawson, a grandson of the Earl of Dartry, likewise hailed from Ireland and held a position at Court, as Master of Ceremonies to His Majesty and Secretary of the Order of the Garter. Previously, as a soldier, he had fought in Egypt and the Sudan. 'As handsome as one of Ouida's guardsmen', according to journalist Stephen Bonsol, 'in addition he was endowed with brains and with charm.' Dawson performed well as a British military attaché, first in Vienna and the Balkans and then in Paris at the time of the Dreyfus Affair and the war-scare over Fashoda. A stalwart of the Guards' Club and the Turf Club, he also belonged to the Bachelors' Club till 1903, when he married at the age of forty-nine and settled at Medmenham Abbey, three miles east of Henley.

The Hon. Edward Stonor belonged to an Oxfordshire dynasty that had owned Stonor Park, four miles north of Henley, ever since the twelfth century. Although the mansion was rented out to Americans, his nephew, young Lord Camoys, remained the grandee of the district (and the Phyllis Court Club granted him honorary membership). Stonor's work entailed contact with nobility in profusion: he was a Clerk of the House of Lords. In addition, his closeness to royalty matched that of the courtiers on the Committee. He and his siblings had in childhood been the playmates of the princes and princesses at Marlborough House and Sandringham, and only the previous year he had accompanied King Edward to Marienbad.

Local eminence also accounts for the presence of Lord Valentia, chairman of Oxfordshire County Council and Conservative MP for Oxford (since, as an Irish peer, he could sit in the Commons). 'The Viscount', who lived at Bletchington Park, near Kidlington, had been a Government Whip until 1905, with the sinecure of Comptroller of the Household, and he raised volunteers for the Imperial Yeomanry during the Boer War, serving as their Assistant Adjutant-General. The customary link between Yeomanry service and fox-hunting held good in his case. Also, as a young hussar in the 1860s, he had helped bring polo to England.

Polo dominated the life of Major Francis Egerton Green, formerly of the 12th Lancers, a celebrated player and organiser of regimental matches who had since 1898 been manager of the Hurlingham, the riverside club in Fulham that operated as the headquarters of the sport within the British Empire. Lord Valentia was one of its senior members.

Major-General Arthur Paget, soon to be knighted, belonged to the same close-knit group as most of the Committeemen. Churchill, the Chairman, was his first cousin once removed, their common ancestor being that Marquess of Anglesey who was wounded beside Wellington at Waterloo ('By God, sir, I've lost my leg!' 'By God, sir, so you have!'). Nearly all the Pagets had been military men and courtiers. 'Arthur Paget was possessed of the true Paget manner which unkind people described as swagger', recalled George Cornwallis-West. 'His officers and men adored him.' Having fought in several colonial wars, he was at the time in command of the First Division at Aldershot, but his latter-day fame or notoriety dates

Major-General (Sir) Arthur Paget, member of the Founders' Committee 1906–10.

from his term as General Officer Commanding Ireland, where he so misrepresented Government policy in March 1914 that fifty-seven officers threatened to resign in the so-called 'Curragh mutiny', calling into question the loyalty of the army during the Ulster crisis. Consequently, Paget has gone down in history as at best 'gallant but impulsive' and at worst 'a stupid, arrogant, quick-tempered man'. There is no doubting his popularity with the Edwardian officer corps, however, or the favour shown him by Edward VII, who liked his American wife's repartee.

Much the youngest member of the Committee was Lord Ronaldshay, aged twenty-nine, whose extensive Anglo-Indian connections comprised his particular qualification. A slightly dandified figure, he had just stood unsuccessfully as a Conservative parliamentary candidate after five years in Calcutta as aide-de-camp to the Viceroy, Curzon, who was plainly his role model. Ronaldshay, later Marquess of Zetland, went on to be Governor of Bengal, Secretary of State for India, and chairman of the National Trust.

There is left only the sole member of the Committee who had neither aristocratic title nor military rank, namely, R.E. Finlay. Phyllis Court was to be a proprietary club; its prospectus emphasised the point that its members would not 'incur any financial liability whatsoever beyond their annual subscriptions'. Finlay was the nominal proprietor and, along with his elder son, the initiator of the enterprise.

The Finlays

Reginald Edmund Alexander Finlay, to give him his full name, was a Scot who had spent half his life in Australia. His father taught modern languages at the Glasgow Academy (and reputedly spoke fifteen of them), but Reginald chose to traverse the English-speaking world, emigrating first to the United States and then to New South Wales. By 1876, aged thirty, he was working for Scott, Henderson & Co., a Sydney shipping firm. That year he joined the commercial élite of the colony when he married Laura Mary Gedye. Her grandfather, Charles Michael Gedye (1799–1885), had left Cornwall in the 1830s to work with his cousin, Henry Dangar, initially as a surveyor and then as manager of a meat-processing factory, the first in Australia to utilise practical tinning methods. Their sons subsequently formed a partnership, trading in agricultural supplies, notably shearing equipment and corrugated iron. With the profits, Dangar, Gedye & Co. diversified as merchants, stock and station managers, wool exporters, shipping agents and financiers. The *Cutty Sark* was one ship carrying their cargoes.

Charles Townsend Gedye (1833–1900) became a wealthy man, and his wife, Mary (1834–76), gained some local renown as an amateur landscape watercolourist. Having three daughters and no son, Gedye took a close interest in the career of his son-in-law, Finlay, who duly advanced from auditor of the New South Wales Marine Assurance Company to general manager and director of the Queensland Investment & Land Mortgage Company. This last appointment involved a trip to the head office in London in 1889, and Finlay took with him his wife and three children, Laura Lucie, Mildred, and Reginald junior (known as Roy), then aged seven. Alan, a second son, was born in 1890. After their return to Australia, the Finlays moved to Brisbane, where they occupied one of the grandest houses in the city, Palma Rosa (later the clubhouse of the Queensland branch of the English Speaking Union).

In June 1896, the entire family again sailed for England, as Charles Gedye, on reaching retirement, had decided to settle in London, the better to indulge his passion for classical music. His influence was such that his daughters, son-in-law, and grandchildren did so too, sharing his home at 17 Craven Hill Gardens, Bayswater, when not following him around the musical venues of continental Europe. Finlay set up as a mining agent, seeking investors for Australian firms.

After Gedye's death in 1900, the Finlays (while keeping the London property) spent part of their inheritance on a portion of the Bolney Trevor estate at Lower

The Finlay family and friends at Shiplake in 1903–4. Reginald Finlay stands on the right. His wife Laura sits in the centre, holding their granddaughter, Jacintha. Roy Finlay is seated in the front row, left, with his sister Laura Buddicom on his left. His second sister, Mildred (Mimi) Finlay, stands at the back.

Phyllis Court
advertised 'To
Let' in 1905.

Shiplake, two miles south of Henley. The land was marketed as building plots, and
they did indeed build three houses: Quaint Cottage served as a second home for
Reginald and Laura Finlay, Roy lived at Trevone, and Laura Lucie lived at Quarry
House with her husband, Robert Buddicom, a science graduate. However, they
also planted orchards and erected glasshouses, because Roy intended to make a
living from fruit growing. He had spent most of 1901 in training at a market garden
at Brentwood, and his friend Frederick Norsworthy and brother-in-law Buddicom
came into the business with him. The site was very near Shiplake railway station,
so fresh produce could be transported to London.

    By 1903, the Thames Valley Horticultural Company was trading, but it did not
seem to thrive, and it may be doubted whether Finlay, Buddicom and Norsworthy
were truly green-fingered. The first time they took their fruit to Covent Garden
market, they wore their conventional city attire: top hats, morning coats, and
striped trousers. 'Look out! 'Ere come our college chums!' roared the Cockney porters. Roy had a liking for good clothes; his family nickname was 'Dudie' (presumably from 'dude'). Market gardening can scarcely have enhanced his self-image
as a man about town. Marital problems in the Buddicom household, meanwhile,
created awkwardness. Robert Buddicom (in the estimation of his daughter) was
a talented scientist who suffered from the delusion that his true *métier* was business. Over a lifetime, he left several failing enterprises. Initially keen on fruit
farming, by 1905 he had practically abandoned it in favour of lecturing on physiol-
ogy. Roy Finlay also wanted out.

    Observing the sign 'To Let on Lease' outside Phyllis Court, Roy came up with the
idea of turning it into a river club and enthusiastically canvassed his parents. If his
father felt any reservations, he evidently did not press them. After all, it would be

the Gedye legacy, not his personal money, which funded the project. He assented to support his son by overseeing the finances and leasing the property in his own name. A solid middle-aged gentleman with a grey moustache and business experience would clearly carry more credibility in negotiations than a twenty-three-year-old. It was envisaged, however, that Roy would attend to the day-to-day running of the Club; the prospectus named him as Honorary Secretary (using the style that he currently preferred: R. Gedye Finlay). On 7 June 1905, the family held a party to celebrate the purchase of the lease from the Fawley Estate. Reginald handed round a tinted postcard of Phyllis Court, depicting the ivy-clad mansion with the river in the foreground, and two dozen friends and relations showed their approval by signing the back.

The Cult of the Thames

The following month the Finlays welcomed a lady journalist from the *Sydney Morning Herald*. Her report combined jottings on the history of Phyllis Court (too garbled to bear quotation) with an eager appreciation of its setting:

> The only place at the present moment worth living in is the Valley of the Thames. There one tastes the sweets of riverside existence to the full…. The trees of Phyllis Court fascinated me. They are far older than the house, great of girth, majestic, with a depth of shade I have not seen equalled…. Then the river, smooth like glass mirroring the trees on either side with a range of low hills in the foreground, crept silently past down the straight reach which makes the Henley course so wonderful a site for racing. It was all so wondrously quiet; the regatta was over, the crowd had gone away. There remained only those living on this enchanted stream. Here and there a young laugh seemed to raise a ripple on the silver surface of the river, but for all the hours I was there, and saving those occupied by sleep, I remained by the river-side loving the coolness and the quiet, wondering why one should have to come back to town to dust, to work, to glare, and to crowds, when there are miles of this enchantment so near to hand.

This is a sample of an extensive body of Late Victorian and Edwardian writing in praise of the River Thames. During the preceding quarter-century, its upper reaches had gained extraordinary popularity as a place of resort for Londoners, conveyed there by railway and pleasure boat, and latterly also by motor car. Tranquillity and natural beauty were only two of its attractions. The multifaceted appeal of the river is reflected in the differing approaches of the topographical authors. Some invoked patriotism:

> There has never been a country of note in whose history some important river did not play a striking part. The famous Tiber dominates the annals of Rome; the wonderful Nile is the predominating factor of Egyptian lore; German story is bound up with the Rhine; America has its Potomac and its Hudson. But the glory of all these must pale

before the story of the Thames, whose history, from the days of Julius Caesar to the time of Edward VII, has been a part, and that no small one, of the great history of the Anglo-Saxon race.

So wrote George Wade in 1904, conveying the oft-expressed idea that this particular waterway was *the* river of England. It was also commonly reckoned '*the* River of Pleasure':

> Go where you will across the globe, nowhere shall you find so much merrymaking, so much sport, so much pastime, so much social pleasure all the year through as you will find on the Thames between Putney and Oxford. There is no conceivable sport or delight that can be obtained upon such a river that the Thames does not provide for English Society and its followers.

For the active, the Thames offered rowing, punting, sailing, swimming, fishing, and walking along the towpath. Hallton East, contributor to *The Idler*, preferred to sit back and observe:

> A great part of the charm of the River lies in its distinctive and varied humanity. The house-boat parties, the fishermen and punters, the skilled and unskilled scullers and sailors, Canadian canoeists and pseudo-Venetian gondolieri, with their varied craft and bright costumes, make up a kaleidoscopic mosaic of sunny, vivid life. The spirit of cheerfulness, the combination of easy familiarity with a perfect recognition of class distinctions, the supplanting of ordinary English etiquette by a version modified to meet the special circumstances of the river all tend to make even the newest comer feel at home.

Wade was candid enough to specify another attraction:

> A pretty, graceful girl never shows off to more advantage than when she is wielding the pole on a punt. Certainly the sight, a common one all the way from Kew to Oxford, is indeed exhilarating and beautiful…. The sterner sex usually rest and smoke while their fair companions make the craft glide along amidst charming scenery, past tree-fringed islands, down shady backwaters, which afford splendid scope for the lovemaking that has been so long anticipated. What the guid Scotchman thinks, who comes south 'fra Glasca' (where couples row decorously on the Clyde, the lady sitting at one end of the boat and the gentleman at the other!), when he first views the punts on the Thames… with fine ladies lying full lengths, their heads resting on the laps of the gentlemen lying ditto, words cannot describe! But the way he opens his mouth and eyes is sufficiently expressive of his astonishment.

Good Scotsman R.E. Finlay, having come south from Glasgow via Sydney and Brisbane, was probably not quite so easily shocked. These paeans to the Thames – and there are many more like them – can only have confirmed his belief in the potential of his handsome early Victorian riverside villa. Henley is not actually a very good place for proper punting (as the depth of the water requires too much use of the paddle rather than the pole), but it enjoyed unique distinction as the 'special site which fate reserved for the most brilliant and widely known of the social functions of the Thames'. As soon as he stated his intentions for Phyllis Court, the *Manchester Guardian* commented, 'The new club should be a success. It would always be able to get members who would join simply for the privilege of using it during Henley Week.' Several London clubs since the 1880s had rented a site on the river bank and erected a marquee for members attending the Regatta. The Phyllis Court Club aimed to offer far superior facilities. But would it be able to sustain itself after the races finished? What of the commercial competition?

Although the most celebrated gentlemen's clubs all clustered together in the West End, a fair few others already combined the usual facilities (food, drink, comfortable surroundings, congenial company, venue hire) with outdoor recreation in the vicinity of the Thames. Of these, the best known were in south-west London. Both occupying mansions by the river, the Hurlingham Club dated from 1869 and the Ranelagh Club from 1884. There was also the Roehampton Club, since 1901. Over thirty miles separated Phyllis Court from these three, all of which focused primarily on polo matches. Equestrian sport was hardly an option for the eighteen-acre Henley site, and the absence of any direct rivalry is underlined by the presence of Egerton Green and Valentia of the Hurlingham on the new Club's Committee.

More seriously, lack of space also ruled out golf at Phyllis Court. Its publicity material in 1906 could only draw attention to the proximity of the Huntercombe Golf Club, five miles away. The centre of attraction at Henley was obviously the river, but Putney, Richmond, Kingston, Twickenham, Maidenhead and many smaller places also counted as river resorts, boasting fashionable social venues, be they hotels or private clubs. The Richmond Club had been in existence since 1880. The Vernon Club of St James's had set up the Vernon River Club at Thames Ditton in 1885. The Datchet River Club started in 1892. All provided facilities for boating, croquet, tennis, and bowls, along with music at weekends.

A location further from London was not necessarily a disadvantage for Phyllis Court. Rail improvements had reduced the travel time between Paddington and Henley to as little as fifty minutes, and about twenty trains ran each day. Roy Finlay also assured his father that the key to the future was the motor car. (He had one of the first in Shiplake.) Cheap rail excursions, steamers, and charabancs were causing river resorts nearer the capital to cater to the type of tripper labelled 'Arry and 'Arriet by Edwardian journalists. The further up-river, the higher the social tone in respect of visitors. Pressing competition to the Phyllis Court Club would most likely come from Maidenhead, nicknamed 'Mayfair on the Thames'. The renown of Skindles and the Riviera Hotel was tinged with notoriety, however – 'patronised chiefly by dudes and ballet girls', according to Jerome K. Jerome. The Riverside Club there had closed in 1904 after fifteen years, though its impressive premises had soon been acquired by the Brigade of Guards' Club, whose own former clubhouse re-opened as the River Club. This offshoot of the Atlantic Club of Piccadilly was already in financial trouble. Riverside clubs were proverbially risky business; many came and went in the space of just a few years. Even well-established ones could fall out of favour. George Tagg, proprietor of the Hampton Court Club, had gone bankrupt in December 1904. Finlay hoped to assemble a less fickle membership. Phyllis Court (like Henley) would not be so 'fast' as some places downstream – and it had the Regatta.

The Opening

From original members, limited to five hundred, the Club required a subscription of five guineas per annum, then a sum equivalent to the cost of four high-quality shirts, a dozen bottles of champagne or the quarterly rental of a cottage. The going rate for London clubs was ten guineas, but a riverside club might close for the winter. For the present, the Phyllis Court Club did not levy an entrance fee. It relied on the Founders' Committee to ensure exclusivity. How the middle-class Finlays recruited so many courtiers, officers, and racing-men to it is a matter for surmise. Proximity to Windsor and Ascot might have helped, and some names on the celebratory postcard autographed in 1905 offer clues. One is Lettice V. Knollys; her uncle was the King's Private Secretary, her aunt the Queen's Private Secretary. Another is F. Paget, probably Fitzroy Paget, who later sought a role at the Club; his first cousin was Major-General Paget. Then there are the signatures of Robert and Isabel Baillie, two Scottish Australians. Sir Robert Baillie, Bart.,

A postcard autographed by the Finlays and their guests as a souvenir of their first party at Phyllis Court on 7 June 1905.

...llis ....ames, The Main Staircase.

commanded the Australasian Squadron of the King's Colonials, a Yeomanry regiment raised in London in 1902 yet composed of men from the Dominions. Roy Finlay was one of its 2nd Lieutenants, and the Imperial Yeomanry was dear to Viscount Valentia. Reginald Finlay's brother-in-law, Major Arthur Savage, also at the party, had fought in the Boer War on secondment from the Royal Australian Artillery. Connections to the British élite were plainly there to be cultivated.

The original main staircase of the Phyllis Court Club (replaced in 1928).

The Phyllis Court Club Company Ltd was incorporated under the Companies Acts on 3 April 1906. By then, preparations were well advanced for opening the Club at Whitsun. An arrangement had been made with Waring & Gillow to furnish the premises on hire purchase, and they supplied everything, from three dozen pairs of nutcrackers to the grandfather clock (with choice of Westminster or Whittington chimes) that still graces the entrance hall today. A local firm, Butler Brothers, was renovating the exterior and the grounds, though plans to build additional sleeping accommodation had to be postponed. The prospectus instead stated, 'Camping under canvas is to be a special feature, and waterproof tents suitably furnished will be pitched on the camping green'; twenty-four were available to rent for a night, a weekend, a month, or the whole summer. Catering was entrusted

D'Amato's
Neapolitan
Singers, who
performed at
the Phyllis
Court Club on
its opening day,
2 June 1906.

to Messrs. George of Cheltenham, a firm of repute. Only one unforeseen event
dealt a heavy blow to the enterprise: R.E. Finlay contracted pneumonia and died
at his London home on Good Friday, 13 April 1906, aged only fifty-nine. Full
responsibility thereby devolved on young Roy Finlay, who had to cope with launch-
ing a new business at the same time as grieving for his father. His mother and
sisters rallied round, perhaps finding welcome distraction in pressing practical
demands. The Founders' Committee went ahead with its first formal meeting at
the Savoy Hotel on 18 April and elected two hundred members. 'Owing to the
recent death of one of the principal founders of the Club there will be no opening
ceremony', the press was told.

The Phyllis Court Club accordingly welcomed members and guests to its
inauguration on Saturday, 2 June 1906 without speechifying or the cutting of
ribbons. Specially reserved carriages brought many from Paddington on trains
at noon and mid-afternoon. Luncheon and tea were offered, accompanied by
music, initially on the lawn from the band of the 1st West Yorkshire Regiment
and then indoors from D'Amato's Neapolitan Singers (six Italians with mandolins
performing the likes of 'O Sole Mio!' and 'Funiculì funiculà'). Despite indiffer-
ent weather, some three hundred people attended, about a tenth of whom were
listed in the local papers. Lord Churchill, Paget, and Dawson represented the
Committee. Robert and Laura Buddicom lent family support. From neighbouring
Fawley Court came Dalziel Mackenzie, owner of the freehold of Phyllis Court. He
was accompanied by his son Roderick, his brother Edward, and two of his sisters,
Aimee and Marie, with their husbands, Sir William Clayton of Harleyford House
and J.W. Rhodes of Hennerton House, plus his son Colonel John Rhodes. Baron

Saye and Sele, a leading Oxfordshire aristocrat, held honorary membership. Two other peers present were Viscount Massereene and Ferrard and Admiral of the Fleet Earl Clanwilliam, tenant of Badgemore Park, whose owner, Richard Ovey of Hernes, came with his wife. Invitations had clearly been sent to all the great houses of the district. Frank Crisp, the wealthy City lawyer, came from Friar Park, his neo-Gothic chateau on the western edge of town. Henry Pinnock, George Eyre, and W. Douglas Jones also lived nearby. H.T. Steward chaired the Committee of Management of the Henley Royal Regatta, and Harry 'Chunky' Willis was a rower, winner of the Silver Goblets in 1899. Sir William Shipley had lately been Mayor of Windsor. A name that stands out is Princess Duleep Singh, the British-born daughter of the last independent ruler of the Punjab, deposed and pensioned-off by the British in 1849. She lived in a grace-and-favour house at Hampton Court. Mr and Mrs Sidney Hoffnung Goldsmid had links to Australia via S. Hoffnung & Co., traders in opals and diamonds. (Unlike some clubs of the era, Phyllis Court did not exclude Jews.) The only foreigner listed was Bradley Martin, an American social-ite, whose masquerade ball in New York in 1897 is often cited by social historians as one of the excesses of America's 'Gilded Age'; on hearing that it cost $369,000, the New York state authorities had doubled his tax assessment, and Martin moved to Britain. A.R. Watney, J.G. Conrad and Sir Charles Adam, a Scottish baronet, were also at Phyllis Court that afternoon. 'Applications for membership were very numerous', observed the *Henley Standard*. 'The Club has been magnificently fur-nished by Waring's and is the last word in luxurious clubland.'

The First Season

So far, so good, but Finlay knew that the crucial test was still to come. The Phyllis Court Club would stand or fall according to the satisfaction experienced by its members during 'the great water carnival' next month. The intervening four week-ends provided opportunities to discover and resolve any outstanding problems. All the bedrooms were booked for the week of Royal Ascot, when the Club also hosted its first ever corporate function, a dinner for top executives from three railway companies seeking closer co-operation (the Great Central, the Metropolitan, and the London, Brighton & South Coast). Rivalry meanwhile intensified in the Henley hospitality trade, as a new establishment, simply called the River Club, opened its own 'charming old house and garden' and an erstwhile impresario called Sherrington Chinn advertised the 'The Clubs Lawn', a new tented Regatta enclo-sure on Swiss Farm Meadow for members of a consortium of London clubs. In past years, the Stewards of the Regatta had themselves rented Phyllis Court for a week each July and admitted spectators to its grounds by ticket. Finlay informed them that this would no longer be possible, as the Club planned a visitors' enclosure of its own, though he did offer free entry to Regatta subscribers in return for permission to run a ferry across the course (an arrangement that lasted till 1908).

Phyllis Court Club, Henley on Thames, The Ballroom.

The Ballroom during the opening season became the Card Room the following year; today it is called the Thames Room.

By late June, the crews were starting to arrive. As usual, the Mayor requested residents to put up bunting and flags. A row of steam launches took up their moorings directly off Phyllis Court. Behind *Nirvana*, nearest the winning post, came *Zingara*, *Chantet Mavis* (hired by the Sultan of Johore), *Sodona*, *Marian*, *Florence* and *La Valentine*. Beyond them, decorated barges and houseboats stretched a mile downriver. Motor vans brought crates of provisions to the Club, followed by a throng of additional maids and waiters to serve them. A torrential downpour on Thursday night raised concerns about the state of the lawn. The river was going to be brimming. Optimists declared it an excellent portent: if a month's worth of rain had fallen in one go, there should not be much more to come. Publishing the longest list of entries yet (sixty-nine all told), the Stewards announced the extension of the Regatta from three to four full days. That might be good for business. Rowing men were agog at the news that the Leander Club would not contest the premier event, being 'unable to make up as good an eight as they wished'. Leander had won the Grand Challenge Cup a dozen times in fifteen years. Did its refusal to defend the trophy betoken modesty or arrogance? Serious attention turned at once to the Argonaut Rowing Club of Toronto, very powerful but maybe too heavy.

The races began at noon on Monday 2 July. The Argonauts swept aside First Trinity, Cambridge, with ostentatious ease, so sporting pundits had plenty to discuss. Other people remarked that this extra day of heats seemed to lack the real Regatta ambience, as so many fashionable folk had given it a miss. Henley as a social occasion burst forth triumphantly the following day. On the river, skiffs, dinghies, punts and canoes lined the booms four or five boats deep all along the course. They wedged together in a good-tempered traffic jam, with the sound of cracking wood and unnerving creaking running up and down the juddering mass of timber. The wash from *Maritana*, the umpire's steam launch, surged into the press as the races went by, amplifying the groaning of the boats, and setting the crowd of standing spectators swaying like a cornfield in the wind. Excitable young ladies emitted little yelps as they struggled to keep their balance, and somebody somewhere was bound to start grumbling that everyone would see the rowing just as well if only they all had the sense to sit down. When the pressure eased, 'it was like the breaking up of an ice-field. Skiffs and punts shot here and there in a violent hurry, and brought up against others with resounding cracks, and in ten minutes the floating fragments had thickened and jammed again.' Viewing the Regatta afloat had its drawbacks. *Punch* included in its 'Henley Hints' this mordant observation: 'Six hours of enforced company is a strong order for the best of friends.'

The ladies and gentlemen at Phyllis Court were literally on a higher plane, with many of the former neatly displayed in a continuous row along the river-bank, lying back in hammock chairs with individual awnings. 'Nature and art

A typical scene at Henley Royal Regatta before the First World War. (River & Rowing Museum)

Regatta fashions

To Edwardian eyes, a Henley crowd had a very particular appearance:

> Black, so characteristic of conventional English crowds, was absent or so rare as to be conspicuous. The top hat of Piccadilly would, in such a scene, be an anachronism that would mark the wearer as signally as if he attempted to enter the Royal enclosure at Ascot in a bowler. The black coat and hat of Society and Respectability are banished – straw hats, linen and flannel suits of white or delicate shades of grey... distinguish the smart men. The women are a dream of dainty muslins, laces, and flowers.

By Wednesday, when the sun shone down with almost tropical heat, it was generally evident to fashion writers that 1906 was proving an exceptionally 'white Henley'. Gentlemen sought permission to shed their blazers, and ladies favoured white muslin or serge with elaborate flounces of *broderie anglaise*. Parasols provided spots of vivid colour, as did men's ties, hat-ribbons, and socks. ('At regattas you tell a girl by her parasol, a man by his hose – especially club colours.') 'Joli Coeur' of the *Henley Chronicle* regretted one innovation:

Bare arms were also a feature of this year's Regatta. Young girls had for arm-covering a dainty puff of lace or embroidery, so diminutive that it left their brown arms free for all the world to gaze upon.... At Henley, if anywhere, the bare arm may perhaps be permissible, but as a day-time fashion and from the modish point of view it has very little to recommend it.

Indeed, some ladies had taken to bandaging their red and sore forearms with chiffon scarves. There was only one five-minute shower all week, and twelve hours of sunshine on Thursday.

'Joli Coeur' was pleased to notice the reversal of one other trend:

> A young girl who sat the whole of Wednesday on the lawn of Phyllis Court with an ardent escort with whom she became every hour more skilled in the ogle of a 'roguish eye' was one of the very few who were out 'in their hair'. As a rule, in striking contrast to last year, hats were general, river hats in white embroidery threaded with wide coloured ribbons being the accepted head-gear for everyone under thirty-five, while ladies beyond forty provided a kindly refuge for their features by crowning themselves with hats in that middle shade of mauve which is the almost exclusive copyright of the matron.

united', remarked the *Henley Chronicle*. 'A truly delightful scene', said the *Henley Standard*. Occasionally, through the perpetual babble of a thousand conversations, the distinctive noises of the Royal Regatta made themselves heard: the ringing of bells for the clearing of the course, the cannon at Temple Island starting a race, the strident cries of the vendors of programmes, sunshades, and postcards. Over on the Berkshire bank, hawkers and buskers were legion, a spill-over from the adjoining fairground, complete with conjurors, fire-eaters, and fortune-tellers. This year the fastidious also complained of the vulgar notes of that modern curse, the portable wind-up gramophone. The loudest noise was, of course, the shouting of rival supporters that accompanied close finishes. Students from Oxford roared them-selves hoarse as Pembroke College and the Kingston Club rowed a dead heat (only the third in the Regatta's history).

An estimated fifty thousand people came to witness the eight finals, and more of them than ever before arrived by motor car. 'An observation taken on Henley bridge yielded the astonishing information that over 500 cars passed in the hour. There were 200 at Phyllis Court, and all over the town the garages were full to the utmost capacity.' To those who really cared about the fortunes of English rowing, the morning brought a jarring result, as the Belgian crew, Club Nautique de Gand, defeated Trinity Hall by three lengths to win the Grand Challenge Cup. For the first time in sixty-eight Henley Royal Regattas, that coveted trophy would be going overseas, and not even staying in the Empire. Of course, the foreigners deserved their victory, but it had to be said that their short jerky stroke was 'not half so graceful as the long swinging stroke adopted by Englishmen'. Others declared that the unforgettable moment of this year's racing actually came in the afternoon, when Harry Blackstaffe, the oldest rower in the Regatta, won the Diamond Sculls at the eleventh attempt. The ovation from Phyllis Court was deafening: 'Good old Blackie!'

The presentation of the trophies by Lady Esther Smith did not mark the end of festivities. Indeed, there were always some prepared to argue that the true enchantment of Henley began when the races were over for the day. 'Did you ever see Venice in England?' asked George Wade rhetorically. 'Processions of illu-minated and decorated boats; banks alight for a mile with coloured fire; houses and trees… picked out with lanterns; gaiety and pleasure everywhere.' Thanks to a myriad of little lamps, 'Phyllis Court looked like Fairyland.' Each evening, in pom-pom suits and white-face make-up, 'The Follies' took to a dais on its lawn to escalate the revelry. Britain's most ambitious pierrot troupe had risen from end-of-the-pier pitches to performing at the Queen's last birthday party. People loved their 'Potted Plays', the dainty dancing of Effie Cook, and the lugubrious comedy of Lewis Sydney. Performer-director Harry Pélissier composed many of their songs himself, including such hits as *Zulu Lulu, Tiddle-y-pom,* and *The Toothbrush and the Sponge.* Then, at ten o'clock, the thirty blue-uniformed bandsmen of the Royal Marine Light Infantry (Portsmouth Division) came out for their second concert of the day: some stirring marches, an operatic overture, extended selections from musical comedies, a concert waltz, and their signature tune, *A Life on the Ocean Wave.* Early nights were not an option within earshot of the river in Regatta Week, least of all on Thursday, when C.T. Brock & Co. displayed their pyrotechni-cal ingenuity in a programme of fifty items, beginning with the usual salvo of big rockets. Looking across the water to the Lion Meadow, members of the Club saw 'a colossal portrait in flame of King Edward, which naturally touched the patri-otic instinct, and tremendous cheering ensued.' Each explosion of 'Electric rain',

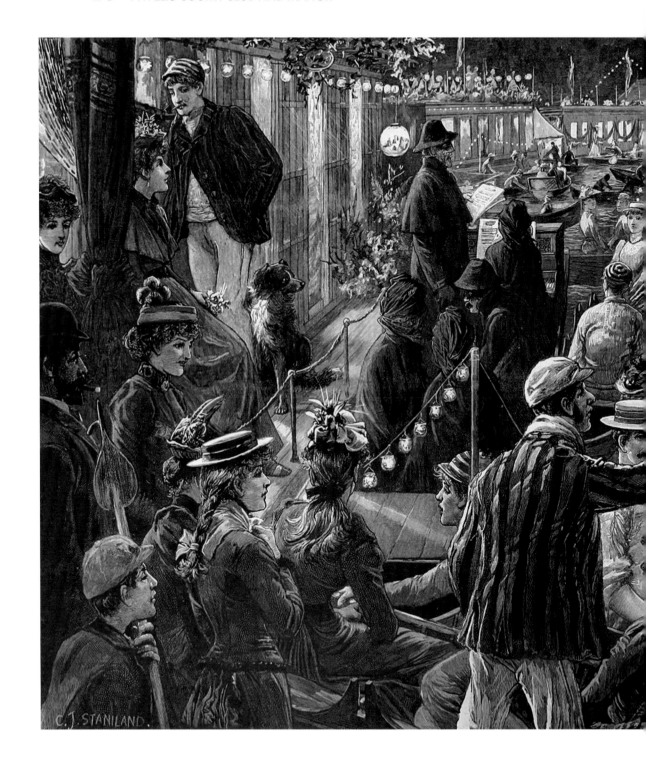

'Henley Regatta:
The Illuminations
after the Day's
Racing' by C.J.
Staniland. (River &
Rowing Museum)

'Diamond dust' and 'Liquid radium' cast glints of bright fantastical colour on the multitude of upturned faces. Even after hundreds of simultaneous fireworks signified the climax, a reluctance to return too abruptly to reality kept determined carousers by the river, postponing the end of the party. 'Words are heard dimly', wrote Clive Fenn, describing the final hours, 'there falls on the ear the snatch of some triumphant song or the plaintive note of "Come Back to Mandalay", the appealing echo of a tune, and all else is enfolded in the grey mantle of the soft summer night.'

Meanwhile, wave upon wave of humanity surged towards Henley station, where Mr Lock and his special staff (seconded from all outposts of the Great Western Railway) did their best to ensure the safe despatch of a train every eight or nine minutes.

> And long after… Henley's aftermath can be seen at all the intervening stations in women derailling with their white dresses soiled from a long day in the boats, and the lace of their petticoats hanging in strips to show where a high heel has got entangled. Often, too, there is the toll usually exacted by the goddess Pleasure from her votaries – their mouths are peevish and their eyes tired. But, at least, they will brighten up to tell you that they have had one glorious hour of crowded life.

Back at Phyllis Court, the uniformed chauffeurs cranked their masters' cars, while tired footmen stacked folding chairs and swept the tiled veranda. Indoors a mountain of dirty crockery tested the endurance of scullery maids. Roy Finlay, though likely exhausted himself, had the satisfaction of a job well done. The Club, now truly up and running, had in the space of just four days produced a profit of about £1,000.

Prospective members were already queuing to join, there having been some nine hundred applications for the original five hundred places. No membership list survives from 1906, but, in addition to the Committee and honorary members, it evidently included at least one viscount (Massereene & Ferrard), half-a-dozen earls (Buckinghamshire, Chesterfield, Clanwilliam, Kilmorey, Kinnoull, Orford) and eight barons (Braye, Castletown, Dunsandle & Clanconal, Elphinstone, Joicey, Knaresborough, Leigh, Newlands). A first-rate Regatta had silenced silly talk about the waning popularity of Henley. Even the agreeable weather continued. The last military band of the season played on 26 August, but members kept on coming. One syndicated women's columnist explained:

> The week-end craze has grown to be a society epidemic. It is as much as your social reputation is worth to be seen in London on a Sunday. Thus London on the Sabbath is dull and deserted. Every second person you meet has a bungalow, houseboat, or cottage of some kind, or a country club, which he or she religiously frequents for those week-ends. The few people who are unfashionable enough not to have places in the country

seek refuge at Ranelagh, Hurlingham, etc. One of the immediate results of the week-end craze is that the riverside clubs are flourishing as never before. The magnificent river house of the Phyllis Court Club, at Henley, has just opened its doors. It is intended to be the ideal week-end club. It has within its grounds almost everything that the most fastidious week-ender can want.

The Club had planned to shut on 8 October, but demand was such that the Committee decided to keep a part of it open throughout the winter. Finlay informed the press:

> After a season's working, which was necessarily more or less a trial one, it may be recorded that the Phyllis Court Club venture has been on the whole most satisfactory. Many things, not forgetting the remarkably fine summer and the successful regatta, have been material in establishing the club on a sound basis and its future prosperity and progress seem well assured.

That said, he must have known full well that not every summer would be so fine nor every Regatta so successful, and novelty might be a significant factor. The Phyllis Court Club had started well and demonstrated its appeal but, in truth, it remained an open question whether that appeal would prove transient or enduring. More than a century on, we know the answer.

2

The Manor of Filettes
To the Seventeenth Century

'The charm of the Thames, as of England, is the fusion of a shadowy past with an actual present. The mere name of the royal river summons up ghostly pageants.... Down all its two hundred flowing miles – from Thames' Head to the Nore – it is an open scroll of history and legend, which he may read who will.' These words of Vance Thompson from 1908 convey a notion sufficiently compelling to have received repeated expression, though probably never more frequently than in the Edwardian heyday of Thames tourism. Writers of guidebooks and excursionists by river boat evinced a keen appetite for historical anecdotes and, thanks to the course of the famous Regatta, few houses on the upper reaches were known to a wider public than Phyllis Court. The building was less than seventy years old when it was first turned into a clubhouse, yet an article about the property by Ernest Dormer appeared in *The Antiquary* in 1905. It explained, 'Phyllis Court is the present successor of a once historic manor house, silvered over with many faded memories of Old England. The ancient fabric, which has long disappeared, is now but a dim recollection of sun-browned walls, mullioned windows, and trailing roses, red-tiled roof, and terraced walks.'

Accordingly, when promoting his Club, Roy Finlay responded to popular expectations:

> Historically, Phyllis Court provides more events of interest than can be described here. It is mentioned in the Doomsday book as far back as 1347, when it was a Royal Lodge within the (then) boundaries of Windsor, and the grounds contain ancient foundations of great interest. The old wall along the river bank which is one of its beautiful features, was built by Cromwell from the remains of the old house which had been burned by the Royalists. Queen Anne paid a visit of several days to Phyllis Court, and Prince William of Orange held his first Court there in 1688.

A conscientious historian in a less romantic age cannot let all this pass. The 'Doomsday book', compiled in 1086, includes no mention of Phyllis Court (or of Henley). The property did not form any part of Windsor, nor was it burned by Royalists. The reference to a royal lodge is not quite right, the personal involvement of Cromwell is decidedly questionable, and the links to Queen Anne and William of Orange require some clarification. Even so, there is no disputing that this riparian site in south-east Oxfordshire has a documented history of considerable richness. Phyllis

A Roman Road?

With regard to the early centuries, there remain (unsurprisingly) many questions that only future archaeology may possibly resolve. Among them is whether a Roman road lies beneath the croquet lawns. The Fair Mile, northwest of Henley, has long been envisaged as part of a Roman route from Dorchester-on-Thames. Did it veer to the east at its southern end? The idea was advanced in the 1950s by H.P. Wiggins, a member of the Berkshire Archaeological Society, who reported signs of a buried roadway in the grounds of the Club, leading towards the Thames at a point where old piles had been seen in the river bed. These might have either carried a bridge or simply marked a ford. F.J. Malpas, in 1987, perceived evidence to support this theory in surrounding property boundaries. On the other hand, the strikingly straight line of the Fair Mile, if extended without deviation, would itself meet the river at Henley Bridge. Has the principal crossing always been there? If so, why did the later street plan ignore the ancient approach to it? Exactly where the Romans crossed the Thames in this vicinity is still debatable (and there might not have been a significant crossing at all), but supporters of the Phyllis Court theory will draw encouragement from the recent discovery of a shard of second-century pottery near the Club's front door during the excavation of new storm-water drains; found two metres down, it might have lain in the river gravel when the Thames was shallower and wider.

Court had demonstrably existed as a distinct entity for nearly six hundred years before the Club came into being, and the stories of its successive owners and residents naturally intertwine with those of Henley, the Thames Valley, and England.

From Saxon times, much of southern Oxfordshire belonged to the important royal manor of Bensington (latterly Benson), one of the estates attached to Wallingford Castle after the Norman conquest. A subsidiary manorial centre is thought to have stood on the site named Countess Gardens (just south-west of Phyllis Court Club) before the town of Henley existed. Given that its land stayed with the Crown till 1199, this may indeed have been a small royal lodge.

King Henry II is credited with founding the town of Henley in the 1170s. It soon established itself as a thriving market centre and river port, but the very success of urban development, combined with a redrawing of manorial boundaries around 1340, seems to have rendered the original lodge or manor-house redundant. By 1381, it was 'spoiled and dilapidated'. Just to the north, a new manor of several hundred acres had been carved out of the Bensington demesne. It lay beyond the limits of the town of Henley (till those limits were extended in 1892) while nevertheless forming a part of the parish. Its administrative centre, actually located in its far south-eastern corner, may have incorporated some of the northerly outbuildings of the older complex. The name of this new manor was Filettes.

'Was there some sort of a convent for girls [*fillettes*] on the site of our present Phyllis Court?' wondered Finlay's sister, Laura, in 1932. 'Or was it a place where the fishermen laid their nets [*filets*] to dry?' Neither, according to modern experts, who suggest that Filettes is derived from 'filiþe' (pronounced 'filith'), an Old English word for hay. Certainly, hay was a highly valued crop from riverside meadows. Over the next half-millennium, with numerous additional variants, Filettes became Fillets became Fillis became Phillis became Phyllis.

Sir John Molyns

The earliest surviving reference to the manor by name is found in one of the close rolls of chancery correspondence preserved in the National Archives. On 4 June 1341, an order went out from the Palace of Westminster to the collectors of wool in Oxfordshire 'to supersede the assessment and levying of wool of the manor of Filettes near Henley which belonged to John Molyns, knight, in that county… so long as the manor remains in the king's hand, as the king caused the lands which belonged to John Molyns to be taken into his hand.' In other words, Filettes need pay no wool tax, because it was once again royal property, confiscated by Edward III. But who was the expropriated John Molyns?

Medieval documents are mostly administrative and legal records. An unusual amount can therefore be discovered about Molyns, who was not only a knight but also an administrator of the royal household and a notorious criminal. Apparently the younger son of a Hampshire landowner, he began his ascent by marrying Egidia (or Gille), a relative of the lord of the manor of Stoke Poges. He then murdered her uncle and cousin so that she would inherit the property and contrived his own acquittal of the crime by rigging the jury. Joining the retinue of William Montagu, a trusted friend of Edward III, Molyns took part in the celebrated coup of 19 October 1330, when the teenaged King assumed full power by arresting his undesired 'protector' Roger Mortimer. This was a desperate life-or-death operation effected by twenty-odd armed conspirators who crept into Nottingham Castle via a secret passage at midnight. Afterwards, King Edward rewarded his supporters with grants of land and positions at court. Molyns became a shield-bearer (1330), a King's yeoman (1331), a knight (1336), a Steward of the King's Chamber (1337), the Keeper of the King's Goshawks and Birds (1338), and a member of the King's Council (1339). Filettes and Henley were just two of the manors given him as recompense for loyal service; by fair means and foul, he acquired a total of twenty-nine in Buckinghamshire, Oxfordshire, Surrey, Wiltshire, Northamptonshire, and Somerset.

As knight and courtier, Molyns moved in the classic medieval milieu of hunts, heralds, tournaments, and troubadours. Edward III was a devotee of pseudo-Arthurian lore. Molyns, however, provides a reminder that the cult of the warrior, while chivalrous in ideal form, could turn downright thuggish in reality. The

The Rose Rent

Strictly speaking, it was not the King but his eldest son (later nicknamed the Black Prince), who, as Duke of Cornwall and holder of Wallingford Castle, conferred the manor of Filettes. The Prince, though, was only nine years of age when, on 12 February 1340, 'at his father's request', he waived an annual rent of 33s 10d and confirmed that Molyns and his heirs could hold lands of the manor of Bensington 'on condition of their rendering a service of a rose every Midsummer.' At the time, a rose was a common token rent for privileged tenants. It is more picturesque than a peppercorn. Five hundred and sixty-five years later, Finlay would adopt an heraldic double rose, barbed and seeded, as the emblem of the Phyllis Court Club.

A fourteenth-century manuscript initial depicting King Edward III and the Black Prince.

more wealth he obtained, the more he sought. To some extent, this meant perfectly legitimate development of his estates, but it also led to robbery, extortion, and perverting the course of justice. Buckinghamshire, in particular, suffered his despotism. While Molyns proved a capable soldier and official, excesses were overlooked. He fought in the Scottish campaign of 1337, conducted diplomatic missions, raised contingents of archers and cavalry, and accompanied the King to Flanders as a military commander preparatory to the invasion of France. His duties extended to organising finance for the war, and this proved his undoing – when bankruptcy forced an English withdrawal, King Edward directed his fury against his treasurers. Sent to the Tower of London in December 1340, Molyns escaped within five days and passed the next five years as an outlaw, charged with rebellion, murder, kidnap, and misappropriation. Hence the seizure of his lands and the mention of Filettes in the close roll.

This was not the end of the avaricious knight. All charges were dropped and all properties restored in 1345, when Edward III perhaps felt need of his martial abilities again, for Molyns took part in the Crécy campaign of the following year. The Black Death may have been ravaging England, but his private fortunes flourished anew. Sir John Molyns became Baron Molyns and assumed the stewardship of all the Queen's lands south of the River Trent. The House of Commons soon protested about his abuses. Filettes meanwhile, in 1353, was leased to Thomas Galian, a cousin of Egidia Molyns, in exchange for his share of Bampton manor. Inability to resist opportunities for embezzlement then brought about a second downfall. Put on trial for fourteen felonies, including burglary, cattle-rustling, horse-theft, and harbouring murderers, Molyns avoided a death sentence in 1357 by the ludicrous legal ploy of claiming benefit of clergy. Literacy was then accepted as sufficient proof that a man had entered holy orders. The robber-baron died in prison in 1361.

Filettes stayed in the Molyns family for a further five generations. Based at Stoke Poges, fourteen miles away, and possessed of manors in five or six counties, Sir William Molyns (died 1381), Sir Richard Molyns (died 1384), Sir William Molyns (died 1425), and Sir William Molyns (died 1429) were all fighting knights of the Hundred Years' War. The first served in Brittany under John of Gaunt and represented Buckinghamshire in the Parliament of 1378. The second had to be ransomed from the Scots. The third can be seen in a memorial brass (at the parish church, Stoke Poges), dressed in full armour with a lion at his feet and his wife in a wimple beside him. The fourth lost his life at the Siege of Orléans, where Joan of Arc rallied the French. It seems unlikely that any of these men spent much time at the Henley manors, which were leased (with others) in the early fifteenth century to their former steward William Wyot.

In this respect, Filettes was typical, for only a minority of manors had a resident lord. A knight normally employed a steward to administer his lands as a whole, and each manor (if not farmed out to a single tenant) was managed by a resident

The memorial brass to Sir William Molyns (d. 1425) and his wife Dame Margery in the Church of St Giles, Stoke Poges.

bailiff. Periodically, all tenants would meet at the manorial court, where the steward, on his tour of inspection, would settle disputes and formalise changes of occupancy. This may explain why the chief premises of the manor came to be called Filettes Court. Over time, the land administered *from* Filettes Court became known as the manor *of* Filettes Court. Some information about its agriculture survives from the time of confiscation in 1341–42, when the crops were wheat, rye, barley, oats, and small amounts of vetches and pulses. Tenants were already paying rent in cash, not in kind or in labour, while the in-hand lands of the manors of Henley and Filettes were being farmed together by a single bailiff with a permanent staff of seven (a three-man plough team, two shepherds, a cowman, and a dairy hand), aided by much casual labour at harvest. The stock comprised four plough horses, a farm horse, thirteen head of cattle, and 264 sheep. It is likely that most of the produce was sold and shipped sixty-eight miles downriver to feed Londoners. The distance as the crow flies is only about half as far, but river transportation cost a fraction of land haulage. Wharves and granaries lined the Thames in Henley, where goods were loaded onto broad flat-bottomed boats (called 'shouts') with sails to supplement the natural flow. The city relied on the Chilterns for firewood as well as foodstuffs. Although upstream traffic was far more expensive, as boats had to be rowed or hauled, imported items included iron, fruit, wine, and herrings, some for removal to Oxford by packhorse (for mills, weirs, and toll-charging flash-locks discouraged navigation further inland).

Access to trade made Henley and Filettes two highly desirable manors. Being a co-heiress made Eleanor Molyns (1426–76) a highly desirable bride. Orphaned at three, by the age of fourteen she was married to Robert Hungerford, heir to the 2nd Baron Hungerford. This family had risen high in the service of the House of Lancaster, and Robert was poised to become the foremost magnate of central southern England, with scores of manors yielding a total income of £2,000 per year. Henry VI revived the barony of Molyns for him in 1445, so he need not wait to sit in the Lords. Then war and political turmoil intervened. Taken prisoner in 1453 at Castillon, the final battle of the Hundred Years' War, Hungerford spent the next seven years in French captivity, while his family mortgaged land to pay a ransom of £7,966. Next he plunged into the Wars of the Roses, fighting on the losing side at Towton and Hexham. Hungerford backed the Lancastrian cause to the end – in his case, 18 May 1464, when victorious Yorkists beheaded him. His widow and mother then struggled to pay off debts and regain confiscated properties. Overall, they eventually succeeded, but Filettes was sold or forfeited in the process, coming under separate ownership from Henley.

In 1462, Filettes was tenanted by Peter Marmyon, Edmund Rede, and Thomas Waldyene. By 1470, William Marmyon was the proprietor. The Marmyons were an established landed family in southern Oxfordshire, active in county affairs. Little Stoke, near Cholsey, was then called Stoke Marmyon. Their tenure of Filettes lasted less than two generations. A younger William Marmyon (not a son) and his wife Isabella sold it for £100 in 1493, subject to the life interest of Amys Mantell, presumed to be the re-married widow of William Marmyon the elder. The Latin conveyance records that the manor consisted of '7 messuages, 300 acres of land, 60 acres of meadow, 300 acres of pasture, 200 acres of wood, and 4 pounds of rent in Henley on Thames and Assendon.'

Thomas Hales

When dividing England's past into ancient, medieval, and modern, historians sometimes regard 1485 as the end of the Middle Ages. Innovations in warfare, such as artillery, were reducing the utility of knights. The new Tudor dynasty aimed at centralisation. Commerce was becoming more extensive and sophisticated. Filettes fits this schema rather neatly. It was not one of those manors, dear to the conservative imagination, which stayed in the hands of a single family for umpteen generations. Its pattern of ownership can instead be seen as a register of social change. At this point the warrior yields place to the merchant.

Thomas Hales was probably kin to the landed family of Hales Place, Tenterden, Kent, but he made his fortune as a member of the Company of the Staple at Calais, that is to say, as a wool exporter. Wool was a bedrock of England's trade, and, primarily for ease of taxation, most supplies of it sent abroad had by law to pass through the port of Calais, the last remaining English territory on the continent. (In this context, 'staple' means an exclusive market.) The merchant staplers, mainly Londoners, led a largely peripatetic existence, visiting country towns as buyers during the shearing season. Sheep farming formed a major sector of the economy of Oxfordshire in the fifteenth century, so it is easy to guess what first brought Hales to Henley, where raw wool was graded, packed into bales, and sent down the Thames to warehouses in London. Twice a year, when stocks had accumulated, the wool fleet of the entire Company crossed the Channel under armed escort. Different currencies and systems of weights, along with intricate credit arrangements, made trade at Calais a complicated business. Much of the wool found its way to the looms of weavers in Bruges and Ghent. Profits were good around 1500, and staplers occupied the first rank of English commerce.

Hales does appear to have inhabited Filettes Court. A royal pardon in 1509, for some unspecified offence, describes him not only as a merchant, but also as former bailiff of the neighbouring manors of Rotherfield Greys and Remenham. Filettes had a manor house of some kind from at least the 1350s, perhaps a fairly functional one, but the advent of an owner-occupier may have initiated a series of improvements during the sixteenth century. In 1502, a dispute over tithes between Hales and the Rector of Henley went all the way to the Vatican. Ecclesiastical court records from 1518, translated by P.J.P. Goldberg, also shed some light on his private life:

A copy lodged with the Court of Common Pleas of the Latin document conveying the Manor of Filettes from William and Isabella Marmyon to Thomas Hales on 6 October 1493.

William by God's grace bishop of Lincoln sitting in judgement in the chapel at the Old Temple, London, ordered Thomas Hales of Henley on Thames in the diocese of Lincoln and Agnes his wife, who were appearing in person there before him and who for some time previously had separated from bed and board contrary to the rules of canon law, that they should forthwith live together as man and wife, that Thomas should treat Agnes in a proper way as his wife, and that Agnes should obey Thomas as her husband. He further ordered Thomas to remove one Margaret Fuller his servant from his service, his home, and his society, and henceforth provide and employ to help him respectable servants of good standing and honest behaviour.

After Thomas Hales died in 1520, inheritance of Filettes was contested by his sons-in-law, with James Hales, husband of Mary, emerging as the victor. A surname in common suggests a marriage of cousins. James, being one of the Kentish Hales, owned a number of properties elsewhere and pursued a legal career, advising both the Corporation of Canterbury and Archbishop Thomas Cranmer. Knighted by King Edward VI, he became a Justice of the Court of Common Pleas in 1549 before falling foul of the fierce religious conflicts of the mid-Tudor era. First he refused to approve the accession of Lady Jane Grey to the throne and upheld the rights of Queen Mary, regardless of her Catholicism. Then, however, he opposed the repeal of anti-Catholic laws. This landed him in prison, where he yielded to pressure to renounce his Protestant faith. Troubled in his conscience, Sir James Hales drowned himself in a shallow stream on 4 August 1554. *Foxe's Book of Martyrs* recounts his 'lamentable and pitiful history', and the gravediggers in *Hamlet* are thought to allude to a subsequent lawsuit when discussing the suicide of Ophelia. It is doubtful that this Hales ever resided at Filettes. Three years prior to his death, he sold a 99-year lease of the manor at an annual rental of £48 9s 4d. Inflation, a feature of the century, made this a poor deal for his heirs, but at least their head rent stayed only a rose. This was paid at the time to Princess Elizabeth, since Wallingford Castle had in 1540 been transferred from the Duchy of Cornwall to the royal manor of Ewelme, which Edward VI subsequently granted to his half-sister.

Elizabethan Merchants

Here begins a complex phase in the annals of Filettes Court, for the lease changed hands almost a dozen times. Most of the holders were London merchants, a clear reminder of the close commercial links between Henley and the capital. However, the initial lessee, John Venner, was sufficiently rooted in the town to hold the civic office of Warden. Other definite sightings of him in the historical record are few. From the diary of Henry Machyn, a London clothier, we know that he attended a feast with music in January 1556:

> The twelfth evening was at Henley on Thames a Mistress Lenthall, widow, made a supper for Mr John Venner and his wife and I and divers other neighbours. And as we were at supper and ere we had supped, there came a twelve vessels with maidens singing with their vessels. And after came the chief wives singing with their vessels. And the gentlewomen had ordained a great table of banquet dishes of spices and fruit (as marmalade), gingerbread, jelly, comfit, sugar-plate, and divers others.

Venner seemingly encountered financial difficulties, for in 1560 he transferred the lease of Filettes to Henry Mansfield and John Frost for the benefit of his creditors. They in the same year conveyed it to John Wayte. Eight years later, the manor was occupied by somebody called Foster, maybe William Foster, who owned property in Henley in partnership with John Frost. It is tempting to posit a link between this instability and a general downturn in English trade, due to a glut of wool, the loss of Calais, and Spanish rule in the Netherlands. The prosperous merchants in possession of Filettes Court from the 1570s onwards were ones who branched out from the traditional business of exporting to the Low Countries.

On 24 May 1574, John Byrd assigned the lease of the manor to Philip Smyth. These two men in their thirties were brothers-in-law and business partners, active in the trade guilds that controlled commercial life in the capital. Byrd belonged to the Drapers' Company and Smyth to the Haberdashers' Company, but, even in Elizabethan times, liverymen did not necessarily engage in their nominal trades. Both were interested in shipping, money-lending, exporting grain, and importing sugar, dried fruit, and spices from the Spanish colonies. The worsening of Anglo-Spanish relations to the point of undeclared war might be thought to have impeded this line of business. In fact, it provided exceptional opportunities, as stolen cargoes could be far more profitable than purchased ones. Byrd and Smyth financed privateers. Several of the ships in which Byrd had a stake (*Golden Noble, Bark Burr, Moonshine, Minion*) were later mobilised against the Spanish Armada. It is uncertain whether John Birde, a Bridgeman of Henley in 1568, was the same person; the difference in spelling signifies nothing, only it was a very common name. Byrd the merchant lived mainly in Southwark and died at a great age in 1622. Smyth, however, had the longer connection with Filettes. Born in Wiltshire around 1540, he was related to Thomas 'Customer' Smyth, the influential collector of import duties.

It is hard to gauge how far these businessmen viewed Filettes Court as a home as distinct from an investment. Rich merchants routinely bought and sold land, yet many liked a house in the country as a refuge from the fatal plagues that so often afflicted London. In this regard, Henley was far from ideal, though, as boatmen brought infections up the Thames. The town suffered fearful outbreaks in 1581, 1603, and 1625. Smyth acquired other Oxfordshire lands at Nettlebed and Nuffield, and also the manor of Battles Hall at Stapleford Abbotts in Essex. He was not resident there, so the chances are that he did use Filettes as a second home (while keeping his base in Barking). His wife, Martha Byrd, married in 1568, bore him two sons and five daughters. The celebrity of the family (especially in the eyes of posterity) was the youngest of her three brothers, William Byrd, organist of the Chapel Royal, considered the greatest composer of the English Renaissance. He quite possibly stayed at Filettes Court, and it is certainly not unduly fanciful to think of its halls resounding to his galliards and pavans, performed on the viols or virginals. All the Byrds were musical; even John the merchant had been a choirboy at St Paul's. The dedicatee of *My Ladye Nevells Booke*, the compendium of William Byrd's keyboard music, is thought to have been the mistress of the nearby manor of Greenlands. Things latterly went badly wrong for Philip Smyth, who parted with the lease of Filettes in 1593. Four years on, the Fleet Prison was his residence, presumably because of debt or financial malpractice. He died there in 1604.

Smyth had been a warden of the Haberdashers' Company in 1591, but the new owner of Filettes Court climbed even higher in the City of London hierarchy. William Masham of the Grocers' Company was an Alderman, first for Aldgate and then for Cordwainer ward. He had taken his turn as a Sheriff in 1583–84, when his duties included hunting out 'Papists' in hiding (notably the Earl of Kildare). Aldermen were supposed to

A presumed likeness of William Byrd, the Elizabethan composer, whose brother and sister lived at Filettes Court.

serve for life, but Masham paid £600 'to godly and thankable uses' in January 1594 in order to secure his discharge. He described himself as 'grievously tormented with gout, colic, and stone, unwieldiness and disability of body', yet he managed to survive almost seven more years in semi-retirement at Henley. Had he not stood down from the Court of Aldermen when he did, seniority would probably have made him Lord Mayor of London, an honour strenuously avoided by all but the most ambitious businessmen, as it entailed entertaining on the grandest scale at personal expense (about £4,000 for the year). The second son of gentry from Badwell Ash in Suffolk, Masham had initially sold woollen cloth at Antwerp. His wife was a Dutchwoman. Later he switched to the importation of luxury goods as a founder member of the Spanish Company (1577), Turkey Company (1581), and Levant Company (1592). His son, another William, credibly claimed to have 'travelled in all Christendom'. At his death, late in 1600, Masham senior left £100 to the Corporation 'towards the setting of the poor of Henley on work, that they might learn to live by their honest labour'. Masham junior then quickly sold Filettes after getting arrested for involvement in the Earl of Essex's failed coup of 8 February 1601. A one-time employee of the rebel nobleman, he swore that his presence was accidental – he 'came to see what the matter was' – and denied drawing his sword. Essex was executed; Masham escaped with a fine.

Sir John Swinnerton

The next lessee came from much the same background but did consent to be Lord Mayor of London. This was John Swinnerton (1564–1616), a liveryman of the Merchant Taylors' Company, who traded principally in wine, although tax farming became his most lucrative business after he successfully tendered in 1593 for the right to collect the import duties on wines from France and the Rhineland. In 1599, for instance, while obliged to pay the Crown £15,000 annually by the terms of his contract, Swinnerton actually raised £35,000 and made a net profit of £14,000. His purchase of Filettes in 1601 was only one of many investments in land. Within two years, he had also bought the manors of Belhouse, Dagenham, and Stanway in Essex, plus a considerable slice of the London parish of St Mary Aldermanbury, including a house leased by the Countess of Shrewsbury. Fulke Greville, the poet, sent her a letter of commiseration, as 'your Ladyship would not willingly become the tenant to such a fellow'.

Swinnerton entered Parliament, sitting for Petersfield in 1601 and East Grinstead in 1604. More importantly, given his City interests, he was selected as Alderman for Cripplegate in June 1602 and (by custom) at once took his turn as Sheriff for a year. This meant that he was in office when Queen Elizabeth died, so it fell to him to lead the great ceremonial procession of civic dignitaries that welcomed her successor, King James I, on 7 May 1603 at the end of his journey from Scotland. The speech delivered at Stamford Hill on behalf of the Sheriffs of London and Middlesex floridly eulogised 'the bright star of the North', who reciprocated with knighthoods.

The new Queen stayed at Filettes Court briefly in the following year. Such a visit added to the prestige of Sir John Swinnerton, as royalty normally lodged with nobility. Evidently, the manor house had now attained some grandeur. Judging by the surviving depictions, it comprised a large two-storey, twin-gabled building of typically Tudor appearance, lit by mullioned and transomed windows. Abutting its eastern end was a slightly lower range with dormer windows, probably built at a different time. If a projection on the western side is reckoned to be a porch, the main elevation faced the Marlow Road. Directly to the north of the mansion stood an extensive barn, aligned on the same east–west axis and every bit as long. Other structures included a malthouse and brewhouse, dog kennels and an artificial rabbit warren. In a period when chimneys were a sign of wealth, Filettes Court looked prosperous. Sixty years later, hearth tax assessors recorded seventeen fireplaces, the highest rating in Henley. The rest of the interior can be conjectured: oak panelling, tapestries, decorative plasterwork, and ornately carved furniture. Swinnerton and his teenaged sons probably came to Filettes for sport. When renting out land, he retained the game and fishing rights. Deer-hunting with a crossbow was especially fashionable.

Anne of Denmark

An entry in the royal accounts for 1604 reads:

> To Giles Phettiplace, gentleman usher, daily
> waiter to the Queen, for the allowance of
> himself, one yeoman usher, three yeomen, two
> grooms of the Chamber, two grooms of the
> wardrobe, and one groom porter, for making
> ready a house at Henley, called Phillips [sic]
> Court, by the space of eight days in the month
> of August 1604. As appeareth by a bill thereof
> signed by the Lord Chamberlain – £7 17s 4d.

Thus the manor house accommodated
Queen Anne during her summer progress
(the Anne in question being Anne of Denmark,
Queen consort). Royal travel was intended to
impress, so the retinue very likely exceeded a
hundred people; Ladies of the Bedchamber,
Drawing Chamber, and Private Chamber all had
servants. The court liked to use its own linen,
tableware, and kitchenware, and the routines
were well established; although the Queen had
arrived in England only fourteen months earlier,
she journeyed from Edinburgh to London by road
and then toured Surrey, Hampshire, Wiltshire
and Oxfordshire. Anne has gone down in history
as an uninteresting woman, chiefly because her
husband found her so, but it may be questioned
whether his idiosyncratic judgment is entirely
to be trusted. They had married in 1589, when
he was already James VI of Scotland, and the
austerity of the royal court in Edinburgh led her
to react with gleeful extravagance to becoming
Queen of England. She adored clothes and
jewels and sometimes gave diamond rings as
tips. Dancing, masques, and music delighted her;
so too did childish games. Anne was twenty-nine
(and in the first month of her ninth pregnancy)
at the time of her stay at Filettes Court, but it

Anne of Denmark, Queen of England, painted by
(or after) John de Critz, c.1605. (National Maritime
Museum)

is quite conceivable that she and her ladies ran
around the garden in their farthingales playing
'One penny, follow me' and 'Rise, pig, and
go'. For her, the great event of the summer was a
reunion with her four-year-old son, Prince Charles,
who had hitherto stayed behind in Scotland, as
he was considered too frail to travel. Meanwhile,
peace with Spain after decades of war topped the
political news. The Queen herself was in London
on 14 August 1604 to see the Spanish delegation.

Swinnerton, son of a merchant, is said to have passed some of his formative years in Spain, 'there acquiring the character of an accomplished gentleman'. As Master of the Merchant Taylors in 1607, he invited the King to dine at their livery hall and engaged Ben Jonson to write the oration. Other recipients of his literary patronage (Anthony Munday, Wentworth Smith, Bishop Joseph Hall) all praised his learning and taste. Thomas Dekker, author of the pageant that marked his taking office as Lord Mayor in 1612, even held out the prospect of immortality:

Go on nobly, may thy name,
Be as old, and good as fame.
Ever be remembered here
Whilst a blessing, or a tear
    Is in store
    With the poor
So shall Swinnerton ne'er die,
But his virtues upward fly
    And still spring
    Whilst we sing
In a chorus ceasing never
He is living, living ever.

Further highlights of his public life in London included opening the New River, a man-made water supply, and presiding at a ball for the Elector Palatine. The low point was possibly a comedy entitled *The Hog hath lost his pearl*. Its villain is a usurer named Hog (hence swine, hence Swinnerton), who plots to wed his daughter to a nobleman. The Lord Mayor arrested the actors but could not prevent publication.

In 1611 Swinnerton had wed one of his daughters, Mary, to John Meller, son and heir of Sir Robert Meller of Little Bredy. Three years later, this elder Meller took over the lease of Filettes Court. Perhaps it was part of the marriage settlement, or maybe the Alderman needed to economise after his mayoralty. When Sir John Swinnerton died in 1616, his will disclosed that he was 'not altogether so great or rich a man as he was held and made show of'.

The Mellers were Dorset gentry whose forebears had 'made purchases of abbey lands in villages, and were remarkable for depopulating most of them'. Sir Robert was probably the fourth generation of his family to own the manor of Winterborne Came. His father acquired Little Bredy, and he himself bought Upcerne from Sir Walter Raleigh and built a new manor house there. His knighthood dated from 1603, after his year as High Sheriff of Dorset and before his election as MP for Bridport. He owned shares in the Virginia Company of London that financed early colonies in North America. Filettes Court does not appear to have played any great part in his life. Much of its land was sub-let in 1621 to Thomas

Freke, probably the nephew of his second wife and heir to an even larger Dorset patrimony.

John Meller, on the other hand, did frequent Filettes, being in residence in 1622, when violence erupted over disputed rights of way. Educated at Cambridge, he inherited from his father in 1624 at the age of thirty-five and followed a very similar public career as a knight (1625), MP for Wareham (1628), and High Sheriff of Dorset (1630). However, he also served as High Sheriff of Oxfordshire three years later, and the duties of the office in respect of law enforcement remained substantial in the seventeenth century. His political sympathies were Royalist.

The Freehold

The preceding pages have tracked the 1551 lease of Filettes Court through eight decades, from John Venner to Sir John Meller. The freehold also changed ownership during this time. It stayed within the Hales family till 1575, held first by Humphrey Hales (died 1571), son of the judge, and then by a second Sir James Hales (died 1589). The latter was High Sheriff of Kent and took part in Drake's expedition to Lisbon, but by then he had conveyed the reversion of Filettes through a trustee, Thomas Hawten, to Robert Rokes.

Question: Who would want to buy an estate that paid an unattractive rent without vacant possession for seventy-five years? Answer: The owner of the neighbouring estate. The Rokes family had acquired the manor of Fawley (to the north of Filettes) by marriage around 1477. The two manor houses were less than a mile apart, though in different counties, the property boundary forming the frontier between Buckinghamshire and Oxfordshire. The opportunity for territorial expansion seemed too good to miss. However, Robert Rokes did not have a son to succeed him at Fawley, and the ordering of his affairs became extremely complicated. For one thing, he mortgaged part of the freehold of Filettes in order to raise 500 marks (£333) for Phyllis Lovelace, his married daughter by his first wife. More significantly, he held half the reversion of the manor in common with his second wife, so this became her property at his death in 1580. The other half, held in his sole name, went to their daughter, Elizabeth Rokes, his principal heir. As she was not yet fifteen, the Court of Wards managed her inheritance.

Into the Rokes household and its convoluted arrangements soon after strode John Alford, a wealthy landowner from East Yorkshire, with a keen eye to familial advancement. First, he wed the widow. Then he contrived to get his stepdaughter, Elizabeth, married to his nephew William in 1586. This involved some dirty work, apparently, for his kinsman Francis Alford confessed to Lord Burghley, Master of the Court of Wards, that he feared imprisonment for his part in making the marriage contract. The Alfords thus secured Fawley, and together they also possessed the complete reversion of Filettes, with John controlling the widow's half and William the daughter's share. If they had any plan to unite them, however, it did

not come to fruition. Henry Alford, son of John, sold his inherited half of the freehold around 1614; the buyer was the leaseholder, Meller. William Alford of Fawley
Court (and also Meaux Abbey, Yorkshire) became in time an MP and a knight, but
his dynastic ambitions were ultimately thwarted. Elizabeth bore him two daughters
and died in 1608; his second wife bore him two more. Lacking a son, Sir William
could expect his property empire to be split between sons-in-law; hence, perhaps,
his readiness to sell off some acquisitions. In the short run this would mean further
change but, after a slew of lessees and lessors, proprietorship of the manor of Filettes
was actually about to settle down.

An Orthographical Coda

Legend supposes that Filettes Court was
'renamed Phyllis Court in honour of Phyllis,
the lovely daughter of Robert Rokes, who resided
there'. It is true that the letter 't' wavered and
then vanished from its ever-fluctuating spelling
between 1550 and 1650, but Rokes did not
occupy the manor, and his daughter's name was
sometimes written Felyce. The evolution looks
more like coincidence than cause and effect. For
convenience, this book will henceforth use the
modern form. Similar irregularities also affect
most personal names in the early history: Molyns,
Moleyns, Molines (with or without a preceding
'de'); Hales, Halys; Venner, Vennor, Venor, Fenner;
Byrd, Byrde, Birde, Bird; Smyth, Smythe, Smith;
Masham, Marsham, Massam; Swinnerton,
Swinerton, Swynnerton; Meller, Mellor, Miller;
Rokes, Rookes, Rooke; and, next up, Whitelocke,
Whitlocke, Whitlock (where the variants show how
to say it).

The Whitelocke Era
1622–1768

The Stuart period presents something of a paradox in the annals of Phyllis Court. On the one hand, these were exceptionally troubled years for the nation, with political and religious differences culminating in civil war and the removal by force of two monarchs in 1649 and 1688. These events made an immediate impact on Henley; the general history of England and the specific history of Phyllis Court never intersect more dramatically. On the other hand, the manor itself experienced greater stability in respect of ownership than it had known for quite some time. Of all the families associated with the property over seven centuries, the Whitelockes are the best remembered. They obtained Phyllis Court in stages, purchasing part of the reversion from William Alford for £1,410 in 1622, and then a further stake for £1,200 in 1632, before buying Sir John Meller's lease and share of the freehold in 1638, thus gaining vacant possession. These transactions were intermediate steps in a determined effort by two lawyers, James and Bulstrode Whitelocke, father and son, to establish a dynasty of county magnates. They also bought Fawley Court in 1616, Henley Park in 1638, Greenlands in 1651, and Henley Manor in 1659.

Sir James Whitelocke
James Whitelocke (1570–1632) was the youngest son of the youngest son of the squire of Beeches, a small manor near Wokingham. He came of gentry, therefore, but was not a landed proprietor by inheritance. His father was a London-based merchant, trading in France, Italy and Spain. James received a sound education at Merchant Taylors' School and merited a scholarship to St John's College, Oxford, where he read civil law and became a Fellow. Then he joined the Middle Temple, which called him to the bar in 1600. A good marriage two years later to Elizabeth Bulstrode helped the young barrister, since the Bulstrodes were a respected family in Buckinghamshire, and both her maternal uncles were leading lawyers. Whitelocke showed his appreciation of this kinship at the christening of his son. The vicar hesitated, preferring perhaps a more Biblical name, but a humorous godfather interjected: 'Bulstrode or Elizabeth, let them choose which they pleased.'

The early seventeenth century saw barristers emerge as the most prosperous professional group in the land. The expansion of commerce, the growth of a middle class, and a buoyant property market boosted demand for legal services, while administration of the law remained archaic and generally baffling to laymen. Whitelocke worked on the Oxfordshire circuit and pleaded cases at Westminster Hall while retained as Recorder of Woodstock. He represented this borough in the Parliaments of 1610, 1614 and 1621.

The importance of lawyer-politicians in the lead-up to the English Civil War has been much debated by historians. It is sometimes assumed, as a rough rule of thumb, that civil lawyers were more likely to be Royalist and common lawyers more often Parliamentarian. The civil law, rooted in Roman law, brought its practitioners closer to continental political thought, which included the divine right of kings. The common law, however, deriving from precedent, encouraged a belief in English exceptionalism. On this view, while Bourbons and Habsburgs might claim absolute power, English rulers should observe the (often rather arguable) conventions evolved over centuries of wrangling between Crown and Parliament. Unusually, Whitelocke studied both civil law (at Oxford) and common law (at the Middle Temple), and his ideas were informed by both traditions. He caused a stir in 1610 by raising in the House of Commons the matter of 'impositions' (tax rises unauthorised by Parliament). King James I had put up import duties – a breach of precedent, according to Whitelocke, who wanted the King to acknowledge the necessity of parliamentary approval:

Sir James Whitelocke portrayed in his judge's robes by an unknown artist. (National Portrait Gallery)

> The edict of a prince is not a law.... The sovereign power is agreed to be in the King: but in the King is a two-fold power; the one in parliament, as he is assisted with the consent of the whole state; the other out of parliament, as he is sole and singular, guided merely by his own will.... The power of the king in parliament is greater than his power out of parliament, and doth rule and control it.

Later Parliamentarians would give this speech wide publicity. At the time, James I brushed it aside: 'You cannot clip the wings of greatness.'

The barrister then became embroiled in the fierce rivalry between Lord Ellesmere, the Lord Chancellor, and Sir Edward Coke, the Lord Chief Justice. In 1613, Ellesmere took exaggerated exception to his questioning the legitimacy of the judicial functions of the Earl Marshal. Whitelocke was called before the Privy Council and sentenced to imprisonment at His Majesty's pleasure for 'a great affront to the regal power'. He spent four weeks in the Fleet Prison before the King pardoned him. Undaunted, in the next Parliament, he returned to the issue of impositions, while warning against fighting 'a duel with the King'.

On the other great controversy of his time, Whitelocke avoided taking a public stance. England had plainly not been Roman Catholic since the death of Mary I, but the precise degree to which it ought to be Protestant was hotly contested. In private life, he inclined to a moderate Puritanism, but he owed many of his best clients to the patronage of William Laud, a leader of the high-church party (and later Archbishop of Canterbury). Whitelocke followed a wary middle course. At Fawley, the absence of an altar rail satisfied the Puritans, while the presence of an organ appeased Churchmen.

Aspiring to a gentry lifestyle, Whitelocke borrowed heavily in 1616 to purchase the Fawley Court estate for £9,000, and soon after he urgently needed promotion to keep him solvent. Lobbying was required to win a judgeship. Whitelocke did not really approve of the ascendancy which George Villiers, Marquess (later Duke) of Buckingham, exercised over King James I and hence over royal appointments. He ingratiated himself with Buckingham, all the same, and received his reward in 1620, when he became Chief Justice of Chester and also a knight. The salary enabled him to begin the acquisition of Phyllis Court.

In 1624, Sir James Whitelocke was appointed a Justice of the King's Bench, one of the top common law courts. He did not find it a comfortable position. Charles I, who came to the throne a year later, was exploiting royal revenue-raising expedients from the start, and this generated test cases. Whitelocke's motto had always been 'Without fear or favour', but the sovereign was no respecter of judicial independence. Judges delivering unwelcome verdicts could see their pay fall into arrears. The Five Knights' Case of 1627 concerned a group of prominent men who found themselves imprisoned without charge after declining to 'lend' money to the Crown. When they petitioned the Court of King's Bench, Whitelocke joined other Justices in upholding the King's right to deprive subjects of their liberty without explicit reason. Eliot's Case of 1629 arose from the detention of a politician who denounced illegal taxation. Whitelocke rejected claims of parliamentary privilege, for 'No outrageous speeches were ever used against a great minister of state in Parliament which have not been punished.' It becomes understandable why Charles I praised Whitelocke as 'a stout, wise, and learned judge' – and why an attempt was later made in Parliament to impeach him.

In truth, Sir James Whitelocke cannot be labelled Royalist or Parliamentarian. Anxious to maintain the law, he saw the ancient constitution of England as a natural order upheld by the power of the King with the consent and counsel of Parliament. The gulf between this ideal and reality was widening alarmingly, however, for neither side manifested the willingness to achieve workable compromises. The judge did not live to see the cataclysm, but died on 22 June 1632,

The tomb of Sir James and Lady Whitelocke at Fawley.

Bulstrode Whitelocke by an unknown artist, c.1634. (National Portrait Gallery)

fortified by the notion that worldly prosperity indicated God's favour. An effigy in alabaster tops his marble tomb in St Mary's Church at Fawley.

Bulstrode Whitelocke

Judge Whitelocke's high hopes for his family rested on his one surviving son, born on 5 August 1605. Bulstrode Whitelocke did not let him down. For a start, he guaranteed that the Whitelocke posterity would be numerous by fathering seventeen children, nine of them boys. Remarkably, all survived infancy. He was twice widowed, however. His first wife, Rebecca Bennet, suffered grave psychological problems and died young in June 1634 in 'the highest extremity and raging' after refusing to eat for twelve days. Five months later, he eloped with Frances Willoughby, daughter of a baron. They arranged to meet near Greenlands as if by chance; Whitelocke offered her a lift, she got into his carriage before anyone could stop her, and they rode hell-for-leather to the chapel at Fawley Court. When Lord Willoughby caught up with them that evening, he asked if the business was 'past recovery'. Frances answered that it was, *and* that they were married. It proved a successful match. Whitelocke wrote that 'his greatest pleasure was in the most affectionate and sweet conversation of his dear wife'. Her death in 1649 left him badly shaken. It was primarily to provide a stepmother for his infants that in 1650 he married Mary Wilson, a young widow, but this too developed into a happy and fecund marriage.

Bulstrode Whitelocke secured his posterity in another sense too. He is the most famous owner of Phyllis Court (since it ceased to be Crown land). His father gave him an education like his own (Merchant Taylors', St John's, Oxford, and the Middle Temple), and by 1648 he claimed the largest legal practice in England. His parliamentary career began in 1626, when he sat for Stafford. Later he was elected for Great Marlow in 1640 and Buckinghamshire in 1654 and 1656. High office under the Commonwealth gave him influence over government policy in the 1650s. Historians also know him from his books, above all *Memorials of the English Affairs*, an invaluable compendium of information on politics between 1625 and 1660, but so stodgily written that Carlyle called him 'Dry-as-dust Bulstrode'. This no longer seems apt since the appearance of *The Improbable Puritan* (1975), an extremely sympathetic biography by Ruth Spalding based on his diary-cum-memoirs. Whitelocke comes across as a man of intelligence and urbanity, as well as considerable self-regard.

It is testimony to the power of Restoration propaganda that latterly all 'Roundheads' have been envisaged as hatchet-faced killjoys in black and white. Whitelocke was a Puritan in several respects: he led household prayers twice daily, kept the Sabbath strictly and did not celebrate Christmas (excepting a midwinter feast for tenants). His belief in the right of more definite Protestants to worship as they pleased put him decidedly at odds with King Charles and Archbishop Laud. His lifestyle, however, was far from ascetic. He enjoyed good food, wine, and tobacco, and diverted himself with dancing, theatre, hunting, hawking, fishing and bowls (which was not then thought entirely innocent, as often accompanied

Whitelocke's Coranto

The first twenty-two bars of Mr *Whitelocke's Coranto.*

by betting). As a talented lutenist, he supervised the music for *The Triumph of Peace*, a masque staged at the Banqueting House in Whitehall in 1634. One of the dances was his own composition; today 'Mr Whitelocke's Coranto' may be heard on two compilation discs.

Like his father, Bulstrode Whitelocke took out extensive loans to finance land purchases. On gaining full ownership of Phyllis Court in 1638, he set about making it pay, as recorded in his memoirs (written in the third person):

> This year he received £800 for Timber which he cut in part of Phillis Court woods, and there he cut 6,000 loads of firewood and 4,000 loads in Fawley woods, in all 10,000 loads, the charge of making it and carrying it came to £1,004, the clear profit of it was above £3,000, which did help well towards the raising of the purchase money…. He sold off some parcels of Phillis Court lands, lying two or three miles from the house which raised near £1,000, and by these means, by the blessing of God, he contracted his debts into a narrow compass, and made the estate entire.

Fawley Court remained his residence, when business did not keep him in London. Locally, Whitelocke was Recorder of Abingdon, where his refusal to prosecute Puritans (for such crimes as failing to bow to the altar on entering a church) gave rise to some controversy. In Henley, he advised the Corporation and served as a trustee of the school founded in 1609. Given frequent disagreements over access to the river, it may be surmised that bargemen and merchants were unenthusiastic about having a lawyer as the town's chief riparian proprietor. After 1640, however, Whitelocke's attention increasingly focused on national disputes.

The Civil War

> It is strange to note how we have insensibly slid into this beginning of a Civil War, by one unexpected accident after another, as waves of the sea, which hath brought us thus far, and we scarce know how; but from paper combats, by Declarations, Remonstrances, Protestations, Votes, Messages, Answers and Replies we are now come to the question of raising Forces and naming a General and Officers of an Army…. The sum of the progress of Civil War is the rage of fire and sword; and, which is worse, of brutish men. What the issue of it will be no man alive can tell: probably few of us now here may live to see the end of it.

So declared Whitelocke in a speech to the House of Commons on 15 July 1642. Typically for a Puritan, he attributed the state of the nation to Catholic plots and the wrath of God:

> Surely, sir, our enemies of the Popish church have left no evil arts unessayed to bring us to our present posture, and will yet leave none attempted to make our breaches wider, well knowing that nothing will more advance their empire than our divisions. Our misery,

whom they account heretics, is their joy, our distractions will be their glory, and all evil arts and ways to bring calamities upon us, they will esteem meritorious. But, sir, I look upon another beginning to our Civil War. God blessed us with a long and flourishing peace, and we turned his grace into wantonness, and peace would not satisfy us without luxury, nor our plenty without debauchery; instead of sobriety and thankfulness for our mercies, we provoked the Giver of them by our sins and wickedness, to punish us, as we may fear, by a Civil War, to make us executioners of Divine vengeance upon ourselves.

In reality, the crisis sprang primarily from an escalation of the longstanding tensions between King and Parliament over taxation. Heedless of inflation, the legislature kept the executive chronically under-funded, and Charles I had raised non-parliamentary revenues by methods that his critics regarded as tyrannical. Simultaneously, he alienated Puritans by seeking to impose religious conformity according to high-church notions. When financial necessity forced the King to call a Parliament in 1640 after ruling for eleven years without one, the members refused to approve new taxes unless he accepted restrictions on his power. Then a rebellion broke out in Ireland. Charles wanted to raise an army to suppress it, but Parliament obstructed him, for fear that he would use the troops to crush political opponents in England.

On the issue of military control, Whitelocke voiced arguments like those of his father:

… this power of the Militia is neither in the King only, nor in the parliament only; and if the law hath placed it anywhere, it is both in the king and parliament, when they join together…. If the power of Militia should be in the king yet the power of money being in the parliament, they must both agree, or else keep the sword in the scabbard, which is the best place for it.

When MPs considered the Grand Remonstrance, a list of grievances intended to discredit the King, Whitelocke opposed it 'as somewhat roughly penned' – but he did not join Royalist protests after it narrowly passed. In fact, there was never really much doubt about which way he would go if forced to choose between Parliament and Crown. In 1636, his legal advice had encouraged John Hampden in refusing to pay ship money. Five years later, he rose to fame by taking part in the impeachment of Strafford, the King's chief minister. After this, only a dramatic U-turn could have parted him from Parliamentarian company, though changes of heart were by no means unknown. While urging the Commons to seek a peaceful settlement, Whitelocke judged it prudent to add:

Yet, sir, when I have said this, I am not for a tame resignation of our Religion, Lives and Liberties into the hands of our adversaries, who seek to devour us; nor do I think it inconsistent with your great wisdom to prepare for a just and necessary defence of them. It was truly observed… that, if our enemies find us provided to resist their attempts upon us, it will be the likeliest way to bring them to an accord with us.

Each side thought in 1642 that by enlisting troops it would intimidate the other into making the concessions required to avert war. It was a tragic miscalculation.

The first violence in Oxfordshire occurred on 16 August, when the Earl of Berkshire tried to recruit for the King at Watlington, and Whitelocke and Hampden set out with a body of men to stop him. They succeeded but, in the skirmish, Whitelocke suffered 'the blow of a pistol, which broke and beat out many of his teeth and loosened the rest, yet by the goodness of God, the bullet and stroke did him no further hurt, only it caused great pain in his teeth, and was a hindrance to his eating and to his speaking'. The next month, he nevertheless joined Viscount Saye and Sele in occupying Oxford for Parliament, and he hoped to be appointed governor of the city. Saye, wary of tying down his troops (and disliking Whitelocke as an 'upstart lawyer'), chose instead to withdraw – which seemed a mistake when the Royalists took over.

After the Battle of Edgehill, King Charles advanced on London, and Whitelocke 'thought it requisite in point of honour and example to put himself into some troop or company as a volunteer'. He was trailing a pike at Turnham Green on 13 November, when 24,000 Parliamentarians faced 13,000 Royalists. The latter prudently declined to give battle, so Whitelocke did not see action. He spent most of the war with Parliament in London. The King returned to Oxford, which became the Royalist capital, and ordered his forces to secure the towns to the south-east: Abingdon, Wallingford, Reading, and Henley.

Was the Thames Valley going to be the decisive cockpit of the war? No, as things turned out; the strategic battles occurred further north, and, though Oxfordshire and Berkshire were an active theatre, Henley actually saw rather less bloodshed than the next three towns up-river. But hindsight should not obscure the fact that its people had reason to fear the worst, and what they endured was bad enough. When Cavaliers swept into town in early November 1642, Prince Rupert had a man hanged for espionage only a stone's throw from Phyllis Court. ('Rupert's Elm', the tree that bore him, stood in Northfield End till its massive dead trunk was removed in 1995.) Royalist troops looted Fawley Court, much to Whitelocke's indignation, but at least they did not harm the five of his children lodging with the estate-manager.

On 21 January 1643, Roundheads occupied Henley as a stepping-stone to Reading. A nocturnal counter-attack by Cavaliers was repulsed at the 'Battle of Duck Street' (now Duke Street); anywhere between six and thirty-three men were killed in fifteen minutes. Townsfolk feared the ghastly 'camp fever' (probably typhus) brought by the soldiers. Burials in that year totalled 229, triple the pre-war average. Requisitioning and emergency taxation verged on extortion and, while the town itself did not again change hands, gunfire continued to be heard in its environs, for a band of Royalists held out at Greenlands. This riverside mansion two miles downstream (today the site of Henley Business School) had ordnance sufficient to impede navigation of the Thames between London and Reading. The Parliamentarians therefore resolved in 1644 to counter it, as Whitelocke recalled:

> 4th of March, by the direction of Major General Skippon, Phillis Court house was made a strong and regular fort, and the Thames brought into the grafts [i.e., ditches] round about it. Cannon, and a considerable garrison of about 300 foot and a troop of horse in it; and this was the rather done to watch the garrison of Greenlands which for a little fort was made very strong for the King, and between these garrisons stood Fawley Court, miserably torn and plundered by each of them.

Troops had been billeted at Phyllis Court already; now it came under full military control, and, even though Whitelocke apparently exaggerates the first phase of fortification, the garrison would have presented a busy appearance. A troop of horse comprised fifty or sixty ordinary troopers, plus a captain, a lieutenant, a cornet, a quartermaster, three corporals, a couple of trumpeters, a farrier and a saddler. Scouting parties rode out regularly to maintain a watch on the enemy and solicit 'contributions'. Their leather coats, helmets, and breastplates did not amount to a formal uniform, though some may have worn the orange-tawny sashes that came to identify Parliamentarians (as Royalists generally had red ones). Scores of horses grazed the meadows, where infantrymen with sixteen-foot pikes were periodically put through their paces, moving to the beat of a drum. Most garrison troops were woefully inexperienced, being drawn from the indigent jobless. Musketeers, a minority of the foot soldiers, carried heavy matchlocks that needed a rest for firing. Training in the cleaning, loading, and aiming of cannon also took place, and the guns may sometimes have been fired in earnest, for the Royalist fort lay within range of the heaviest artillery.

There were probably never more soldiers in Henley during the war than on the weekend of 18–19 May 1644, when the top Parliamentary generals, Essex and Waller, met there to plan the encirclement of Oxford; and the Phyllis Court garrison seems the most likely venue for their conference. Essex saw for himself the problem of Greenlands and set in train the series of events that ended with Major-General Richard Browne advancing from Northampton with his brigade to besiege it on 9 July. Three days later a grenade blew up the powder magazine in the house, and the Royalists surrendered. Parliament extended its hold on the river, yet Phyllis Court was not stood down – far from it.

Later in the year, with the enemy still defiant at Wallingford Castle and Oxford, Major-General Sir James Harrington wrote to the Earl of Northumberland from Henley to complain that 'this town is untenable, by reason of the hills near about it, even for a winter quarter'; his men felt neglected 'in a frontier garrison as yet unfortified'. However, he continued in a letter dated 4 December 1644, 'If it seem fit to you, I can, with little charge, fortify Mr Whitelocke's house at Henley's town end, which I believe will command both the town and river, and 300 men raised in the town will be able to keep it against a summer's siege of a royal army.' It was not till February that the Committee of Both Kingdoms (the body overseeing the conduct of the war) set up a sub-committee under Saye to consider the suggestion. By then, the soldiers in Henley were turning mutinous. 'If this garrison be not rid of some evil instruments, here will be no safe subsisting', reported Lieutenant-Colonel Mark Gryme. 'All that I can do is little enough to appease and prevent combustion, especially seeing their pay is so little, and private incendiaries many.' The resolutions of Parliament's top military planners are recorded in *The Calendar of State Papers*:

> 14 February 1645.
> The Committee of Both Kingdoms to Col. [Edward] Montague. We have considered the reasons offered for the fortifying of Mr Whitelocke's house called Phillis Court, and approve of its being carried on and perfected. You are to proceed therein and put it into a posture of defence and safety as expeditiously as you can.

> 21 February 1645.
> Warrant for 300 shovels and spades for fortifying Phillis Court, near Henley.

> 3 March 1645.
> Warrant for ten barrels of gunpowder, 1,000 bandoleers, and a ton of match, to be delivered to Capt. West, for the garrison of Henley.

> 17 March 1645.
> That Lt.Col. [Thomas] Bulstrode be appointed Governor of Phyllis Court fort and house, and of the garrison which this Committee will appoint for its defence.

> 17 April 1645.
> That the drakes now at Henley be left at Phillis Court for the defence of that place.

Hennay's 1786 sketch of a wall-painting of Phyllis Court at the time of the Civil War.

Minion drakes were small cannon. Thomas Bulstrode was a cousin of Bulstrode Whitelocke.

The only known historical picture specifically of old Phyllis Court shows it at this juncture. It is a large watercolour bearing the inscription:

> The north view of Phyllis Court House during the time of the Civil War under Oliver Cromwell; from original drawing found behind the wainscoting of that old Mansion, carefully taken off and transcribed to its Proprietor Strickland Freeman by his most obedient and very humble servant R. Hennay, Nov. 16th 1786.

When, why, and by whom the wall painting was done are a mystery. Its date is especially puzzling – assuming the copy to be a faithful one – for the men in the picture are dressed in the kind of hats and coats worn by soldiers at least half a century *after* the Civil War. If, as appears likely, the original sketch was not contemporary, it is impossible to say how far the illustration of the fortifications may be based on recollection, information, or supposition, though they certainly look authentic. Since masonry and brick walls could be breached by artillery, it was standard practice in the 1640s to construct earthen banks by stacking turves to a height of about five feet. Sharpened wooden stakes called storm-poles were then driven into the parapet to form a barrier to infantry (in addition to the moat in this case). Projecting bastions, with cannon commanding the drawbridge, are also typical of a Civil War fortress. The Committee of Both Kingdoms reinforced Phyllis Court in November 1645 by moving four pieces of larger ordnance from Reading (two demi-culverins and two sakers).

During the last fifteen months of the conflict, Whitelocke himself served two short spells as military governor of Henley, 'which he rather undertook because Phillis Court was his own house'. The first was in spring 1645, the second in summer 1646. By now, the war was going Parliament's way, but moderates feared the consequences of outright victory for either side. Whitelocke had been a member of the parliamentary delegation at three rounds of futile peace talks with King Charles. His desire for a negotiated settlement was outspoken:

> Whose goods, I pray, sir, are plundered? Whose houses are burnt? Whose limbs are cut off or shot off? Whose persons are thrown into loathsome dungeons? Whose blood stains the walls of our towns and defiles our land? Is it not all English? And is it not time for us, who are all Englishmen, to be weary of these discords and to use our utmost endeavours to put an end to them?… There is as much gallantry in furthering a good peace as in making a good charge in the head of your forces.

All the same, his diary suggests that playing a martial role was not absolutely disagreeable to him, especially when a legal colleague, Judge Weld, dropped by:

> He came to visit Whitelocke in his Garrison at Phillis Court, who caused all the guards to be doubled and a strong guard at the drawbridge…. The Judge seemed much taken

Cromwell's Wall

On the river-wall at Phyllis Court there may be seen a plaque that states:

> THIS WALL WAS BUILT BY
> CROMWELL
> FROM THE BRICKS OF THE
> OLD TUDOR HOUSE OF
> PHYLLIS COURT
> A.D. 1643

Roy Finlay probably put it up sometime around 1928, when a Club advertisement made the same claim and described the bricks as 'the remains of the old house which had been burned by the Royalists'. There was for decades an idea in circulation that the manor house had been badly damaged and rebuilt in 1648. Pevsner's architectural guide to Oxfordshire repeated it in 1974, but Whitelocke's diary proves that the house stayed intact and inhabitable, even if roughly treated. (It was Fawley Court that was sacked.) As for Cromwell, local lore asserts his presence at Henley at some point during the war,

when he is said to have slept at nearby Harpsden Court. This is quite plausible, and, judging by his documented movements, 22 April 1645 looks a safe bet, as he travelled from Reading to Watlington. However, on each possible occasion, he was passing through as a Lieutenant-General of Horse on campaign. The brick wall can probably not have formed part of the fortifications in any event, since it seems that the raised path it protects was created by Whitelocke at the time of their slighting: 'In a few days they threw in the breast-works on two sides, made two even mount-works, one being on the side next to the Thames, the other on the north.' Thus Parliamentarian troops were indeed involved in constructing the earthen bank that the wall supports, and it is easy to see how 'Parliamentarian troops' became 'Cromwell's men' became 'Cromwell'. As for the actual brickwork, another quotation from Whitelocke may be pertinent: '28 August 1648: He began the new brick wall at his garden at Phillis Court.'

with Whitelocke's entertainment, and his posture of a soldier though by profession he was a lawyer. Whitelocke told him that the profession of a lawyer did not disable any gentleman from serving his Country as a soldier if there was occasion, nor lessen his Courage, and after much discourse, the Judge taking his leave, Whitelocke offered him a Linstock [*i.e.*, a forked stick with a lighted taper] according to the custom of Garrisons to give fire to what great guns he pleased, but the Judge startled much at it, saying that he knew not what belonged to it.

Whitelocke was back in London on 13 August 1645 when the garrison mutinied against his successor, Colonel D'Oyley. The next Governor, Colonel Purbeck Temple, also faced indiscipline. Unpaid soldiers took to plundering, and Henley became so unruly that martial law was imposed in December. The troublemakers had departed by the time Whitelocke returned in June 1646. With the war in its closing stages, he helped prepare surrender terms for the Royalists at Oxford and

Wallingford and sought permission to dismantle or 'slight' the defences of Phyllis Court at the earliest opportunity. The welcome day arrived on 18 August 1646:

> A great many of the Country [i.e., county] came in to Whitelocke with mattocks and shovels and some with teams to help in slighting of Phillis Court Garrison, and Whitelocke set his soldiers to work in it and allowed them 6d. a day besides their wages, the Country paid their own men, he threw down the Breastworks & made handsome walks of them on two sides, digged down the Bulwarks, sent away the great Guns and ammunition, and got pay for his soldiers, whom he pleased, but the Country more, to see his readiness to slight Garrisons.

The drawbridge was dismantled and the moat filled in, with the possible exception of a single straight inlet that lies at a right-angle to the Thames to this day.

Whitelocke and the Commonwealth

Whitelocke made Phyllis Court his home between 1646 and 1649. Fawley Court was temporarily uninhabitable and, while he retained accommodation in the capital, he desired a retreat from the stormy atmosphere of Westminster. There the victors of the Civil War were falling out with each other drastically, yet Whitelocke's mix of constitutional and religious opinions did not dispose him to either faction. Most other political moderates were Presbyterians; most other Independents (or Congregationalists) were political radicals. He kept a low profile and divided his time between legal work in London and family life in Henley. A light two-horse chariot enabled him to commute twice a week in half a day, and once in a while he treated himself to a rather more leisurely journey:

> Whitelocke and his wife and children, and Mr Hall [of Harpsden Court] and his wife and their servants took three pairs of oars to go by water from London to Phillis Court, they dined at Hampton Court and came by eight at night to Windsor and next day they came to Phillis Court; this way by water is the most easy and pleasant but the most chargeable way of travel.

At a personal level, these were happy times. He hunted in his manorial woods and improved the garden, levelling lawns and laying new paths. However, on 13 July 1647, politics of the most dangerous kind sought him out even here. King Charles, then a prisoner of the army at Caversham, retained some freedom of movement under guard:

> News came to Whitelocke that next day the King intended to come to Bowls at Henley and to dine with Whitelocke at Phillis Court, but he, to avoid jealousy, went this evening towards London and left his house at the King's service, and thus he was quiet in no place, neither at London nor in the Country. When he came into the house [of Commons] they wondered to see him there, and told him they heard that the King was

to dine with him at his house in the Country that day, but they saw that he would not be there to entertain him.

The King hoped that Parliamentarian disunity would even now allow him to evade the consequences of defeat. Whitelocke dared not risk accusations of conspiring with him.

Meanwhile, the interference of the army in politics on the side of the Independents created the conditions for Whitelocke's advancement. In April 1648, he was elected one of three Lord Commissioners of the Great Seal used to authenticate state documents. This placed him at the peak of his profession, for the Lord Commissioners were the Roundhead equivalent of Lord Chancellor. It also made him a potential target when Royalists staged an uprising in the summer: 'Whitelocke being provided with a design of the Cavaliers to surprise Phillis Court, so provided to prevent it.' In December 1648, a *coup d'état* by army officers ('Pride's Purge') ended the parliamentary dominance of the Presbyterians and engineered a potentially republican majority. When appointed to the committee drawing up charges against the King, Whitelocke promptly left London for Henley, and he shunned the pseudo-judicial proceedings that culminated in the fall of an axe in Whitehall on 30 January 1649. The dreadful deed once done, however, he helped draft the declaration that justified the abolition of the monarchy. He also joined the Council of State, the executive body of the new republic. The military men who really ran the Commonwealth had few civilian allies of comparable ability.

A subsidiary appointment as Deputy Constable of Windsor Castle entitled Whitelocke to the use of Manor Lodge by Virginia Water. This now became his country home, with Fawley Court and Syon House also in reserve. The loss of his much-loved second wife may have added a further psychological motive for moving. Phyllis Court was henceforth let at least some of the time, the tenant in 1658–59 being Sir John Lawrence – probably the second baronet of Iver and Chelsea, a lawyer who died in 1664. (The other Sir John Lawrence of the era, Lord Mayor of London, did not get his knighthood till 1660.)

Whitelocke strongly disapproved in 1653 when Cromwell forcibly dissolved Parliament and substituted a nominated assembly of 'godly men' (which did not include Whitelocke). Asked to lead an embassy to Sweden, he perceived 'a handsome way to be rid of him' but also recognised the importance of the mission. England was at war with the Netherlands, whose ally Denmark had closed the Baltic Sea to English shipping. His task was to win over Sweden and circumvent the blockade. His wit and style charmed the unconventional Queen Christina, but the Swedes were cautious procrastinators, only signing the Treaty of Amity, Commerce, and Free Navigation after the Anglo-Dutch War had ended. The embassy lasted eight months.

Meanwhile, Cromwell made himself Lord Protector of the Commonwealth. Whitelocke again disapproved, yet he saw his way to signing the pledge of loyalty that allowed him to sit in the Protectorate Parliament. His personal relations with Cromwell were generally friendly, and the Lord Protector esteemed his advice, especially on foreign affairs. They disagreed in 1655, however, over plans to reform the High Court of Chancery. Making a stand in defence of the professional standards (or interests) of lawyers, Whitelocke chose to 'lose his place rather than wound his Conscience and betray the rights of his Country'. Within four weeks of surrendering the Great Seal, he returned to government as a Lord Commissioner of the Treasury. (One other legal reform, by the way, was the abolition of feudal dues: the rose rent at last became history.)

Whitelocke retained his seat in the Parliament elected in 1656 and served temporarily as its Speaker. About a third of the members were excluded for criticising the generals. He played a leading part in 1657 in drawing up the 'Humble Petition and Advice' that invited Cromwell to make himself king. The Lord Protector declined, but nominated Whitelocke to the new second parliamentary chamber. Despite eschewing the proffered title of Viscount Henley (because he doubted the right of anyone save a monarch to grant peerages), the lawyer did sit in 'the Other House' for the short time that it lasted. His own preferred style was Sir Bulstrode Whitelocke, on the strength of his admission to the Swedish Order of the Amaranth by Queen Christina.

When Cromwell died in September 1658, Whitelocke was a pall-bearer at his funeral. He firmly backed the succession of Richard Cromwell as Lord Protector, who reciprocated by re-appointing him Lord Commissioner of the Great Seal. However, the younger Cromwell lacked his father's authority over the army, and the generals deposed him after just eight months. A new Council of State then emerged as the nominal government of the Commonwealth and, in August 1659, Whitelocke became its titular head – Lord President of the Council – and hence arguably the national leader. If nobody remembers him as such, it is because any pretence of a constitution was by now in tatters. Power lay with the soldiers, and they were increasingly at odds.

Another coup in October 1659 closed down Parliament and replaced the Council of State with a Committee of Safety, dominated by the army, although Whitelocke consented to serve on it. With hindsight, this must count as the worst decision of his career; the Commonwealth was a sinking ship, and he missed his chance to abandon it. Rival factions of military men now squared up to fight each other. General Monck, the commander in Scotland, repudiated the Committee of Safety and threatened to march on London. Whitelocke, rightly perceiving a move to restore the monarchy, told his colleagues on 22 December 1659 that they faced a stark choice: they could either fight Monck to try and save the Commonwealth or else pre-empt him by opening talks with the exiled Charles Stuart themselves. His

A portrait of Whitelocke, probably from the studio of Peter Lely.

own preference is plain from his readiness to set sail for Holland to negotiate the best possible terms for a transfer of power. General Fleetwood, the commander in London, fatally hesitated and then recalled Parliament. Having proposed a deal with the Royalists (and had it effectively rejected), Whitelocke was now dangerously compromised. Thomas Scot, a leading republican, said that he ought to be hanged. On the night of 30 December 1659, Whitelocke left the Great Seal with his wife (to be given to the Speaker), disguised himself in a wig, and fled the city. He headed for Hertfordshire and hid in the home of William Willoughby, his Royalist brother-in-law. His political career was over.

After the Restoration in May 1660, Whitelocke wasted no time in applying to King Charles II for a pardon. He bore no direct responsibility for the beheading of Charles I, and he could claim that he had always urged moderation and respect for the law throughout the Interregnum. When he eventually secured an audience with the Sovereign, they conversed in a civilised way about books. His Majesty then reputedly bade him farewell in these words: 'Mr Whitelocke, go into the country; do not trouble yourself any more about state affairs, and take care of your wife – and your sixteen children.' According to family tradition, a huge payment of £50,000 helped to secure this outcome. If so, it was a bribe, not a fine. 'Our King hath conquered the hearts and affections of his people', wrote Whitelocke in November 1660. 'I am sure he hath mine.'

Aged fifty-five, Whitelocke set about rebuilding his legal practice. Unsurprisingly, most of his clients were other ex-Parliamentarians. He preferred not to stay at Henley and took Chilton Lodge as his rural seat, near Hungerford yet just within Wiltshire. Perhaps he found it humiliating to remain in a county where his political influence had recently been potent yet nowadays barely registered. Adjusting to a lower income proved difficult and led to family tensions. Mary had borne him seven children between 1651 and 1659; conflicts with his eldest sons led him to conclude that the love of children for their parents does not match that of parents for their children. He consoled himself with writing on politics, history, religion, and law. He died on 28 July 1675.

Whitelocke's Reputation

It is not the fate of politicians to be universally admired. Even among Parliamentarians, Whitelocke had fallen foul of Presbyterians, social radicals, and ideological republicans, and opinions of him voiced openly after the Restoration naturally exhibit Royalist bias. Edward Hyde, 1st Earl of Clarendon, had been a very close friend until 1642, when they opted for opposite sides. In his *History of the Rebellion*, he classed Whitelocke with a second lawyer, John Maynard, and wrote, 'though the two last did afterwards bow their knees to Baal, and so swerved from their allegiance, it was with less rancour and malice than other men: they never led but followed; and were rather carried away with the torrent, than swam with the stream'. Elsewhere he presented this crude reason for Whitelocke's loyalty to the Parliamentarians: 'All his estate was in their quarters, and he had a nature that could not bear or submit to be undone, though to his friends, who were commissioners for the king, he used his old openness, and professed his detestation of all the proceedings of his party, yet could not leave them.'

Whitelocke often led interlocutors to assume that he shared their views. As he himself put it, 'I love a civility to all'. This sometimes worked to his advantage, but it could easily be misinterpreted and afterwards lead to contempt on the part of plainer-speaking persons. For instance, he might concur that the Protectorate lacked legitimacy, but it did not follow that he would favour its overthrow or decline to serve the Lord Protector. Vice versa, when he agreed to serve the Lord Protector, it did not follow that he endorsed the legitimacy of the Protectorate. Was this sophistication or just slipperiness? In *The Rump; or The Mirror of the Late Time*, a Restoration comedy by John Tatham, a lawyer called 'Lockwhite' is given the line, 'I am for that cause brings me most profit, be it good or be it bad'.

Within a few decades of his death, however, his reputation was recovering. Support for limited monarchy and freedom of religion (for Protestants) commended him to the new Whig Party, which made these causes its own. Seen in a favourable light, Whitelocke and other moderate Roundheads had struggled to preserve the ancient constitution from the absolutism of the Stuarts. It was not their fault that the stubbornness of the King and extremists on their own side prevented a settlement. During the Interregnum, Whitelocke had done his duty by accepting office in distasteful governments to contain the influence of dictatorial soldiers and religious fanatics. Or did he merely lend an air of spurious legality to hated military juntas? Tyranny is preferable to anarchy, he argued. A moderate Royalist might have given the same reason for backing Charles I.

Quite what one makes of this complicated man will depend on personal judgments about the proper balance between principle and pragmatism. It may be well to reflect (with relief) that few of us living in England today have had to face the sort of moral dilemmas that confronted our counterparts in the 1640s. The river frontage at Phyllis Court is still called Cromwell's Wall; when walking above it, a tremendous mental effort is happily required to imagine the air polluted by the reek of explosives and disturbed by reverberating cannon-fire.

William Whitelocke and the 'Glorious Revolution'

Bulstrode Whitelocke bequeathed his three chief properties (Fawley Court, Phyllis Court, and Chilton Lodge) to the eldest surviving sons of his three successive marriages, James, William, and Samuel, respectively. Sir James Whitelocke (1631–1701) mortgaged the rents of Fawley Court and then sold the estate, so it was Phyllis Court that provided dynastic continuity in Henley. Indeed, William Whitelocke (1636–1717) would spend more time there than ever his parents had done – between legal terms and assizes, that is, for he followed the professional path of his forebears, being called to the bar in 1655. Paternal influence won him a place in Richard Cromwell's Parliament, but 1659 was not a good year for going into politics (except as a Royalist). Maybe it was a better one for matrimony, as William wed Mary Overbury, daughter of Sir Giles Overbury. Their marriage lasted fifty-two years and produced at least eight daughters and five sons, nine of them baptised in Henley. They actually moved into Phyllis Court in 1664 at Mary's suggestion. Her father-in-law agreed, because the house stood vacant. Family disputes ensued, however, when William sold some Phyllis Court timber without telling his father, and Bulstrode mortgaged some Phyllis Court land promised to his son. Both being lawyers, they struck a deal whereby William leased his patrimony prior to inheriting it (in 1675). The manors and lands of Henley, Phyllis Court, and Henley Park together yielded an annual income not in excess of £700.

After the hardships of the Civil War, the local economy had swiftly recovered. Writing in 1677, Richard Blome emphasised the prosperity of Henley-on-Thames:

> It… enjoyeth a considerable trade for malting; its Inhabitants (which for the most part are Bargemen or Watermen) gain a good livelihood by transporting of malt, wood, and other goods to London, and in return bring such commodities as they and the Inhabitants of the adjacent Towns have need of at easy rates: and its Market, which is on Thursdays, is very considerable for corn, especially barley, which is brought them for their great Malt trade, there being oft-times in one day sold about 300 Cart-load of Barley.

This is the Henley so winningly depicted, complete with malt-houses and wharves, by the Flemish artist Jan Siberechts. The north elevation of Phyllis Court is clearly discernible in his *Landscape with a View of Henley-on-Thames* (1692). In *Henley from the Wargrave Road* (1698), the house is also present, minuscule and obscured by trees. It seems apt that these evocations of 'Old England' should date from when the manor was owned by a long-time resident (or, at any rate, *semi*-resident) squire. As a barrister, Whitelocke focused on Chancery cases and appeals to the House of Lords in London.

Siberechts' landscapes celebrate the agriculture and commerce of a country at peace. The situation could easily have been otherwise, for serious political and religious antagonisms endured in England. The Civil War had resolved nothing about the constitutional relationship between King and Parliament, while the Restoration entrenched the Church of England to the detriment of the Puritans, now labelled dissenters or nonconformists. The accession in 1685 of King James II, a Catholic convert of authoritarian temperament, caused apprehension, especially among Whigs, the political group whose first *raison d'être* had been a campaign to bar him from the throne. Whitelocke was known to be one of their number. With his friend, Lord Lovelace of Ladye Place, Hurley, he had joined a London tavern

coterie of Whig extremists called the Green Ribbon Club. Most people presumed that the King's desire to repeal anti-Catholic laws signalled a grand design to re-impose 'Popery'. Moreover, his tactic of trying to unite nonconformists with Catholics in opposition to the Anglican monopoly on public life alienated even Tories who had upheld his hereditary right to the crown. In 1687, James ordered Lord Lieutenants to carry out a survey of opinion among county officials. Did they support his religious policies? Men who gave the incorrect answer found themselves dismissed, including Whitelocke, formerly a Justice of the Peace. Local dignitaries played a crucial role in the selection of parliamentary representatives; James II was scheming to pack the Commons with yes-men. Then, in June 1688, the Queen gave birth to a son, raising the prospect of a Catholic dynasty. Opponents of the King denounced the baby as an imposture and invited Prince William of Orange, Stadtholder of the Dutch Republic, to defend the rights of his English wife, Princess Mary, the Protestant previously heiress to the throne. William was himself a grandson of King Charles I, and the Protestant Dutch badly wanted England as an ally against Catholic France. His army of over fifteen thousand men landed unopposed at Torbay on 5 November 1688.

What followed has been called a 'bloodless revolution', as James II found it impossible to organise resistance. There were minor passages of arms, however, as

Landscape with a View of Henley-on-Thames by **Jan Siberechts (1692). (Private collection)**

the Whitelockes had reason to know. Lovelace, on his own initiative, rode forth with some seventy horsemen to join the Prince of Orange. They had the misfortune to encounter rare loyalty to the King on the part of the Gloucestershire militia. In the affray, a few Williamites were killed; among them, as noted in the Cirencester parish register, 'Bulstrode Whitelocke, Esq., died at the King's Head when my Lord Lovelace was taken prisoner'. It has generally been assumed (since Victorian times) that this Bulstrode was William Whitelocke's son. If so, he was pitiably young, having been baptised in 1675. The possibility cannot be excluded that the dead man was another Bulstrode Whitelocke, since William Whitelocke had a younger brother and nephews of the same name.

The invading army moved with deliberation, as William of Orange correctly foresaw that he might need to fight no more than a battle of nerves. Defections and desertions caused his father-in-law's forces to disintegrate. At Abingdon on 11 December, Prince William rejoiced to hear that King James had fled the country. Instead of advancing on Oxford, he now turned towards London, reaching Henley on Thursday 13 December. Trumpeting, drumming, and cheering marked the arrival of the polyglot horde in which marched not only Dutch, English, and Scottish troops, but also very possibly Swedes, Brandenburgers, Flemings, Finns, French Protestants, Greeks, and even Africans (for all these nationalities were present in the army as a whole, although it progressed in half a dozen columns, spread out between Marlow and Reading). To Henley came the expedition's headquarters, escorted by dragoons. Dusk may have fallen by the time the Prince appeared at Northfield End. Among those watching was Daniel Defoe, a eulogist of the 'Nation's Saviour'. Short and slight, with a beaky nose, Willem van Oranje made an unlikely popular hero, yet townsfolk expressed tremendous relief and approval. At Reading on Sunday, the Dutch advance guard had fought and won a small battle against Catholic Irish troops loyal to the King. Despite the outcome, hysterical panic swept the Thames Valley (and all England) about Papists on the rampage. The residents of Henley believed that the Prince was saving them from massacre (while later historians credit his agents with highly effective propaganda).

The Prince dined with the Earl of Pembroke, Viscount Weymouth, Lord Colepeper and the Bishops of Ely and St Asaph, who had brought a declaration from the House of Lords:

> We do unanimously resolve to apply Our Selves to His Highness the Prince of Orange, who with so great Kindness to these Kingdoms, so vast Expense, and so much hazard to his own Person, hath Undertaken, by endeavouring to Procure a Free Parliament, to rescue Us, with as little Effusion as possible of Christian Blood, from the imminent Dangers of Popery and Slavery.

William did not seem impressed by this. Despite their rhetoric, the Lords failed to offer directly what he wanted (which was power). More to his liking was the

Another Royal Visit?

Where did William of Orange spend the night? One of his companions, Henry Hyde, 2nd Earl of Clarendon, wrote these words in his diary: 'Dec. 13 Thursday. We went to Henley: the Prince came hither likewise tonight, and lay at Mr Whitlock's.' This appears to indicate unequivocally that Phyllis Court had the honour. Nevertheless, there persists a tradition that he slept up the road at Fawley Court, at this time held by William Freeman on a twenty-five-year lease from Sir James Whitelocke. Given the number of Dutch and English dignitaries in his retinue, it is likely that several gentlemen's houses had to be called into service. If we cannot say with certainty in which of them His Highness rested his head, one thing at least is clear: it was William Whitelocke of Phyllis Court who acted as his host.

King William III by Sir Godfrey Kneller.

address presented on behalf of the City of London, stating that the capital implored his protection and promised a hearty welcome. Then the Prince received word that the King's army had been disbanded. Far from being pleased, he realised the danger of having thousands of redundant soldiers on the loose and issued an order 'from his Court at Henley', telling commanders to recall the troops at once by beat of drum. William of Orange was habitually undemonstrative, but now his spirits were high. The flight of James could be depicted as virtual abdication; the throne stood empty and, on reflection, all English parties would probably ask him to mount it.

Great was William's consternation when news arrived in the middle of the night that the King had been captured off the Isle of Sheppey by Kentish fishermen. This re-opened the prospect of negotiations and compromise, since Tories were bound to shrink from deposing an anointed monarch still among them. As a result, the Prince of Orange left Henley for Windsor feeling less confident than twenty-four hours before. The solution, of course, was to intimidate the weak and isolated King while giving him fresh opportunities to escape abroad – which he did nine days later. William then assumed the administration of the country at the request of the House of Lords. Seven weeks on, the Convention Parliament invited William and

Mary to rule as joint sovereigns after rejecting Tory proposals for a regency. The Bill of Rights stipulated that no Catholic would in future be permitted to ascend to the throne and asserted that monarchs must observe the rule of law. The 'Glorious Revolution' certainly contributed to the strengthening of Parliamentary government (though exactly how much is still debated).

From Whig to Tory

The small part played by William Whitelocke did not go unrewarded. In 1689, he became first a knight, then a Deputy Lieutenant, then a King's Counsel and finally a Member of Parliament, sitting for Great Marlow, his father's old seat. Almost immediately, however, Sir William's views began to worry his erstwhile political comrades. It had seemed natural that the son of an eminent Cromwellian should resist James II, so Roger Morrice was amazed to perceive that Whitelocke had now 'turned absolute Tory'. The first sign of this came in 1690, when he voted against a Whig bill requiring office-holders to abjure the ex-King.

Sir William seemed psychologically disposed to opposition, backing 'the country' against 'the court'. His first legislative endeavour created a Commission of Public Accounts, which offered MPs a platform for criticising corruption. Then a plan to suspend the Habeas Corpus Act (to permit the internment of Jacobites) incurred his ire: 'If an angel came from Heaven that was a privy councillor, I would not trust my liberty with him one moment.' Year after year, he brought forward a bill to reform trials for treason, arguing that existing procedures left such room for political manipulation that the outcome could amount to judicial murder. The Treason Trials Act (1696) owed much to his campaigning; it granted statutory rights to defence counsel and the calling of witnesses.

By then, however, Whitelocke himself had left the House of Commons, not having stood for re-election in 1695. His former patron, Lovelace, had died in 1693, leaving large debts, and Sir William thus acquired Remenham Manor, Farm and Park in settlement of a mortgage. Henceforth, when looking across to Berkshire from Phyllis Court, he had the satisfaction of seeing the transpontine portion of his own estate. Meanwhile, on the political front, he suffered a setback. When Queen Mary II died in 1694, leaving William III to reign alone, scruples about his legitimacy resurfaced among Tories attached to the hereditary principle. The governing Whigs called on holders of public office to 'profess, testify, and declare, that his present Majesty, King William, is rightful and lawful King of these Realms'. Their aim in doing so was partisan; Whigs knew that Tories, while accepting William as de facto monarch, would jib at the word 'lawful'. Whitelocke did and was thereupon removed from the Oxfordshire lieutenancy and magistracy. Only after the advent of Queen Anne and a Tory ministry was he fully reinstated in 1702.

The next year witnessed Whitelocke's return to Parliament as second member for Oxford University, an idiosyncratic constituency with an electorate composed exclusively of doctors and Masters of Arts. With Oxford being the principal semi-nary of the Church of England, religious issues predominated. Now an ultra-Tory, Whitelocke devoted his energies to the militant defence of Anglican supremacy and urged stronger measures to exclude nonconformists from public life and the teaching profession. The pragmatic leaders of his party found this embarrassing but refrained from undermining him too much, lest the dons elect somebody even more extreme. Whigs meanwhile found plenty to mock in this pedantic lawyer, with his antiquated fashion sense and mannerisms. When every other gentleman wore buck-les on his shoes, and had done so for decades, Sir William still wore laces. Hence readers readily identified the target of this piece of raillery in *The Tatler* of 7 July 1709:

> Thou dear Will Shoestring! I profess myself in love with thee! How shall I speak of thee? How shall I address thee? How shall I draw thee? Thou dear outside! Will you be combing your wig, playing with your box, or picking your teeth? Or choosest thou rather to be speaking; to be speaking for thy only purpose in speaking, to shew your teeth? Rub them no longer, dear Shoestring: do not premeditate murder: do not for ever whiten. Oh! That for my quiet and his own they were rotten!

The nickname 'Shoestrings' stuck to him ever after; when taunted with it in the Commons, he replied, 'Sir, I remember when there were more shoe-strings and fewer coxcombs in this assembly.'

More recently it has been suggested that Sir William's old-fashioned cloth-ing might have been a coded political statement: he always wore styles that pre-dated 1688. With advancing age, his public utterances grew incautious. By 1713, the son of James II was living in exile in Lorraine while claiming to be 'King James III'. When a motion came before Parliament to seek his expulsion from the duchy, Whitelocke alone opposed it, saying, 'he remembered in Oliver Cromwell's time, when he obliged France to banish the person Charles Stuart, it hastened on his glorious restoration'. Queen Anne by now was ailing and had no surviving chil-dren; the Act of Settlement (1701) named Protestant cousins in Hanover as her heirs. During the War of the Spanish Succession, Britain subsidised a Hanoverian army led by Prince George, second in line to the throne. When his conduct seemed to place Hanoverian concerns ahead of those of his British paymasters, Whitelocke did not spare him:

> What did one deserve who used them so, while he only expected the crown, and what might they look for from such a prince when he was possessed of it! If he had any regard or love for Britain, it would appear as much now, when such occasions offered, as after-wards, and if he now preferred his German interest and dominions to the interest and honour of Britain, he'd do the same when he was king and had it more in his power to do them good offices at Britain's expense. He concluded that King William's extravagance to his Dutch favourites had cast him a fair copy, and lest he should come to the crown, which he hoped he should never do, it was necessary to check him in the bud.

To Whigs, this sounded not far short of treason. Amid uproar in the chamber, Sir William showed that he still had his wits about him. Refusing to retract, he explained that, 'as the Queen was younger in years, he hoped she would outlive that prince, and he would be so bold as to say that in comparison with her he did not value all the princes of Germany a farthing'. Three months later, Queen Anne lay dead, and 'that prince' was King George I.

An annotated list of MPs (prepared for the new sovereign) characterised Whitelocke as a 'recognised Jacobite', who was always well heard by the Commons, 'because he never fails to cause laughter'. Of eighty-odd Tory members with Jacobite sympathies, very few returned after the 1715 general election, although Oxford ('the home of lost causes') ensured that 'Old Shoestrings' would still be there a little longer. He was almost a lone voice now, warning that the fruits of Hanoverian Whiggery would be foreign wars and land tax rising to 6s. in the pound. He died at Phyllis Court on 21 November 1717 at the aged of eighty-one.

Whitelocke had the distinction of having traversed the political spectrum all the way from Cromwellian to Jacobite, a fact not lost on his critics. Earlier in 1717 a Whig polemic had appeared entitled *Considerations on the Present State of Great*

The Later Whitelockes

For three generations, Phyllis Court had been the property of notable men – a senior judge, an influential statesman, a widely known backbencher – but this close connection to public life did not extend beyond the first century of the Whitelocke Era. The Jacobitism of Sir William Whitelocke might in itself have been enough to blight the political prospects of his family in early Hanoverian Britain. In fact, it made little difference, for he outlived all his sons. Back in 1696, he had actually made over his Henley estates to the last surviving one, another Middle Temple lawyer called William, on the occasion of his marriage. The property then comprised Phyllis Court and Henley manors 'and 15 Messuages, 15 gardens, 1 Wharf, 400 acres of land, 100 acres of meadow, 300 acres of Pasture, 400 acres of Wood'. William Whitelocke, junior, fathered four

children, one or two of whom died in infancy, and himself expired in 1709, aged just thirty-six. The manors became the jointure of his widow, Anne, daughter of Edward Noel, secretary to the Excise Commissioners. She apparently remained in residence at Phyllis Court with her father-in-law.

Her only son, Bulstrode William Whitelocke, was admitted to the Middle Temple in 1713, but the Inns of Court no longer provided formal education, so Mrs Whitelocke sent him to Rugby School in 1717. After he came of age in 1722, Bulstrode barred the entail on the family estates, preparatory to selling them to his brother-in-law subject to his mother's life interest. Evidently not a believer in deferred gratification, the twenty-three-year-old left Henley in November 1724 with a little in excess of £8,600 – and disappeared from history.

Britain (and thought by some to be the work of Defoe). Its denunciation of high-church Toryism is cast in the form of a letter, ironically addressed to Whitelocke 'in remembrance of your early joining and promoting the late Revolution by the Prince of Orange. 'Tis true you seemed to be some time after disgusted… yet the Pains and Charges you were at to Entertain that Prince on his Journey to London ought never to be forgot.' Unwittingly, Phyllis Court Club has followed this injunction by only ever remembering Sir William Whitelocke in the context of the 1688 royal visit – till now.

Gislingham Cooper

The political revolution of 1688 is sometimes credited with causing a financial revolution in turn, as it led to a transfer of fiscal and monetary know-how from Amsterdam to London. William III financed his wars through bond flotation managed by the new Bank of England, joint stock companies proliferated, and the beginnings of centralised markets in debt and equity offered new ways to hold wealth. These developments built on the innovations of the preceding half-century. It had become the norm for aristocrats and gentry to keep some money in the safe of a trusted London goldsmith for use when they visited the city, thus reducing their exposure to the risk of highway robbery. The goldsmiths learnt to put these deposits to work by making loans, discounting bills, and issuing promissory notes. In effect, they became bankers, although still sole traders or partnerships and vulnerable to losses. Nearly a third of London banks disappeared after the 'South Sea Bubble' burst in 1720.

One of the survivors was Cooper's Bank, on the corner of Arundel Street in the Strand. Its proprietor, a widower called Gislingham Cooper, in 1721 married Ann, sister of young Bulstrode W. Whitelocke. Hence it was a banker who bought the right to inherit Phyllis Court and associated properties. His father, Robert Cooper, had been a working goldsmith, and his mark ('RC' in a dotted circle) can be found on salvers and candlesticks. Gislingham concentrated on the financial side of the business. The location of his premises (West End rather than City) suggests a clientele of landowners rather than merchants. He was probably a Tory catering for Tories. It was normal for Georgian banks to have as few as a hundred clients, linked by party affiliation, religious persuasion, and kinship.

At Henley, Cooper was seen as the squire, even though rents continued to be paid to his mother-in-law till 1751. The following year two unexpected accretions to the estate served to get his name into the newspapers. Properties owned by executed felons were forfeited to the lord of the manor. What made these cases sensational was the fact that the criminals were both genteel spinsters. Mary Blandy poisoned her father, the town clerk of Henley, because he opposed her marriage; Cooper gained two fields. Elizabeth Jefferies had her uncle shot dead; Cooper gained a malt-house.

Queen Christina of Sweden by Sébastien Bourdon. She gave a copy of this portrait to Bulstrode Whitelocke in 1653, and it hung at Phyllis Court for a century.

Despite his commercial background, Cooper won acceptance in local polite society and enjoyed showing guests the Whitelocke heirlooms. These included a portrait of Christina of Sweden (by Munnichoven, after Bourdon), given by the subject to Ambassador Whitelocke, and *The Royal Family at Theobalds*, an unusual painting (possibly by Mijtens) of Charles I entering a long gallery, accompanied by his wife, two earls, a dwarf, three dogs, and a parrot. The latter picture is now in the Royal Collection, whence it might originally have come, for the banker thought that his wife's great-grandfather acquired it when Parliament auctioned the late King's goods during the Commonwealth.

Gislingham Cooper died at Phyllis Court on 16 February 1768, predeceased by a number of his children, for he had nearly reached the age of eighty. His heir was the Reverend Dr Edward Cooper, a forty-year-old bachelor, Rector of Buckland St Mary in Somerset, and a Fellow of All Souls, Oxford. 'His picture', according to Emily Climenson, 'represents a rosy, round-faced divine, with a most amiable expression.' He did not propose to live at the manor house, whose occupants dispersed within months. His sister Ann married and left for Oxford. Their mother moved to Southcote outside Reading.

A Literary Connection

Edward Cooper is nowadays recalled exclusively as the uncle of his niece. In December 1768 he married Jane Leigh, whose father was the Rector of the nearby parish of Harpsden. The Leigh and Cooper families had long been friends, so Edward needed no introduction to his sister-in-law Cassandra and her husband, George Austen. Jane Austen was their daughter. In childhood, the novelist met her Cooper relatives fairly frequently and lived for half a year with Edward's sister, Mrs Ann Cawley, 'a stiff-mannered person' who kept a little school. It would nevertheless be vain to seek descriptions of Phyllis Court in her books, for, although her mother must have known the house, Jane Austen herself was not even born when the Coopers sold it on 1 October 1768. Together the manors of Phyllis Court and Henley, with Remenham and Henley Park, fetched £42,000.

The Freeman Era
1768–1853

The new owner of Phyllis Court was not a newcomer to the district. Sambrooke Freeman was the great-nephew of William Freeman, who had acquired Fawley Court back in 1679. The two properties thus came together again after nearly a century apart, but this time it could hardly be viewed as a union of equals. By now, Fawley put Phyllis in the shade, as it was going to carry on doing throughout the Freeman Era, almost to the point of total eclipse.

While the Whitelockes waned, the Freemans had prospered. The 1768 transaction ended the process by which one local dynasty supplanted another. Ironically, given its name, the Freeman family owed its upward trajectory to slave labour. The man who saw his chance and seized it was William Freeman, born in the West Indies about 1645. He founded sugar and indigo plantations on St Kitts, Nevis and Montserrat, and sold slaves on commission for the Royal Africa Company before migrating to London in 1675 to engage in Atlantic trade from the controlling corner of the triangle. Soon his wealth ran to a country estate, and Freeman became the first of many colonial merchants to break into landed society in the middle Thames Valley. He did so with a flourish. By 1688, the manor house of Fawley Court, as restored since the Civil War, had been replaced by a showpiece red-brick residence in classical style (although the traditional attribution to Wren is now discounted). 'Ambitious and enterprising' to the last, on his deathbed in 1707, Freeman voiced a wish to be buried in the Whitelocke vault at Fawley. His widow dutifully conveyed the request to Sir William Whitelocke, who replied (surely crushingly), 'I have not known that any Gentleman has ever desired to mingle with another family in his grave.' Predictably, the Freemans afterwards erected a grand mausoleum for themselves by the church. The estate passed to John Cook Freeman, an East India merchant.

The Freeman family mausoleum in the churchyard at Fawley.

Unlike his predecessors, Sambrooke Freeman, who inherited in 1752, was born to gentry. His maternal grandfather was a baronet. He studied at Oxford. He went on the Grand Tour. George Morton Pitt, a friend of his father from India, helped him into Parliament as member for Pontefract

68   PHYLLIS COURT: CLUB AND MANOR

(1754–61), and he later sat for Bridport (1768–74), but without cutting a significant figure in politics. At Fawley, he employed 'Capability' Brown to landscape the park and James Wyatt to design the classical folly from which Temple Island in the Thames takes its name. It may have been an additional inheritance from Jeremiah Freeman, a short-lived younger brother, which financed the expansion of his Henley domain.

The manor house of Phyllis Court found itself redundant, permanently so in the narrow sense that no lord of the manor would live there again. The property was let, and tenants feature less prominently than landlords in the historical record. It must be assumed that some came and went without leaving a clear enough trace to secure them a mention in this book. The picture is further complicated by instances of furnished sub-letting. Occupants from the period fall into two categories: aristocrats and gentry who rented Phyllis Court chiefly for a change of scene; and professionals and 'pseudo-gentry' (admissible in polite society but not themselves landowners) for whom it was a principal home.

Very likely a sub-lessee, the earliest recorded resident of the Freeman Era belongs in this second category. Charles Round was a middle-aged man who had earlier lived at Bisham. Parish registers and trade directories yield a few snippets. His daughter Jane left Phyllis Court on 30 June 1774 to marry Thomas Gleed, a mercer from Reading, who later served as mayor of that town. Thomas Round, his eldest son, practised as an attorney in Wokingham and Windsor. Round died at Henley in 1785, over a decade after leaving the house.

His sub-lessor, successor or predecessor – possibly all three – was a City merchant called Benjamin Adamson, whose effects were removed from Phyllis Court, 'his late residence', to be sold in April 1775. The younger son of a Norfolk squire, Adamson had been apprenticed in London and had risen high in the Worshipful Company of Fishmongers, though he declined election as a Sheriff of the City in 1753. He did serve (nominally) as one of the numerous governors of the Hospitals of Bridewell and Bethlem and latterly as High Sheriff of Wiltshire (1765), his second wife having brought him the manor of Oaksey. When he died in 1783, aged seventy-eight, the *Norfolk Chronicle* reckoned him 'a benefit to society, and a credit to religion and every virtue in life'.

Countess Grandison

For his next tenant, Freeman found the most aristocratic person ever to live at Phyllis Court (as a resident rather than a guest). This was the Rt. Hon. The Countess Grandison in her own right in the peerage of Ireland. Her earlier designations included the Hon. Elizabeth FitzGerald Villiers, Lady Elizabeth Villiers, Lady Elizabeth Mason, and Viscountess Grandison. To friends, she was Lady Betty. With her came her second husband, Lieutenant-General Sir Charles Montagu, Colonel of The Queen's (Second) Royal Regiment of Foot. Most of what is known of them personally derives from two of the foremost letter-writers of the age. Lady Grandison was related to Mary Delany, and one of Montagu's brothers was a friend of Horace Walpole.

The Villiers were a very extensive aristocratic clan, all owing their initial ennoblement to George Villiers (1592–1628), 1st Duke of Buckingham, who infatuated James I and secured a plethora of peerages for his family. The original Grandison viscountcy was one of them, in a roundabout way, granted in 1620 to the childless Sir Oliver St John, Lord Deputy of Ireland, with remainder to the issue of his niece – a sister-in-law of Villiers. This Irish branch of the dynasty did not greatly flourish until an advantageous marriage in 1677 enabled the 5th Viscount to inherit the vast FitzGerald estate in Waterford. This supported his promotion to an earldom, and the Countess who came to Henley in 1775 had succeeded to the family fortune in 1766, when her annual income topped £7,000. (Working families survived on £25 a year.) Phyllis Court served as her country home in England, supplanting Beaumont Lodge, Old Windsor. In London, she lived in Grosvenor Square, while her titular seat was Dromana House, near Cappoquin in the far south of Ireland. Like many members of the Anglo-Irish ascendancy, the Grandisons paid only occasional visits to the properties that funded them. County Waterford had a particular problem with 'Whiteboyism', violent nocturnal attacks on landlords and their agents by Catholic peasants objecting to tithes and rent rises.

At first sight, it seems odd that so wealthy a woman as Lady Grandison did not make a brilliant dynastic match. She twice married beneath her. The first time, in 1739, she was not yet an heiress. Her father wished to avoid a big dowry, so he wed her to Aland Mason, an untitled Waterford landowner. Death then depleted the Villiers ranks, and Lord Grandison found himself with no descendant in the male line to perpetuate his earldom. As a member of the Irish House of Lords, however, the Earl was worth propitiating, so the King created a new peerage for Lady Betty, who became Viscountess Grandison in 1746. Widowed in 1759, she re-entered the marriage market after an interval, this time endowed with both patent and purse – but also with a young son called George to whom her estate must pass. Her fortune could not be annexed. If George predeceased her, by Earl Grandison's will, Dromana would go to his cousin, none other than William Pitt (the Elder), 'for raising the glory of his country… to a pitch of greatness hitherto unknown'. None of this put off Charles Montagu, a mere esquire till his knighthood in 1771. His wife had meanwhile been advanced to Countess, so her son would in due course enjoy the same status as his grandfather.

A portrait of Lady Grandison (in the guise of a shepherdess) shows a dark-eyed brown-haired woman of unimposing appearance, and the dramatist Frederick Reynolds thought her 'only remarkable by the numerous pack of poodles she maintained, and by her formidable hospitality'. Mrs Delany conveys a different image in a letter of 1771: 'The Countess of Grandison, with her great hoop of beaten gold

Lady Villiers by Edward Cunningham ('Calze'). Previously Lady Gertrude Seymour-Conway, she became the daughter-in-law of Countess Grandison in 1772.

and jewels, made such a blaze in my little nest on her way to the drawing room [at Dublin Castle] as to amaze all beholders.' Walpole found her 'formal, proud, and weak', and preferred her husband, who was both a brave and dutiful soldier and 'as good, as temperate, as meek, as if he were a curate on preferment'.

Sir Charles may not have minded being outranked by his wife, but even he probably found his stepson exasperating. George Mason-Villiers, styled Lord Villiers, was a terribly spoilt child. This was understandable. He was born of his mother's sixth pregnancy, after her five earlier babies had died, and his own health repeatedly caused anxiety. 'Our young travelled cousin', wrote Mrs Delany in January 1772, 'is a poor *weak-looking* soul.' After Eton had come the Grand Tour, from which he had only lately returned, with a reputation for wildness and a determination to shine as a gentleman of fashion. The cliché that marriage steadies a man was not borne out in this instance:

There are still stories about the gay and reckless doings of the beautiful Lady Gertrude, 'the toast of the town', as she was called in Dublin. For instance, it is said that she used to sit up gambling all night till dawn broke, and that she then used to pelt the crowd who had gathered under the windows with the empty wine bottles, the contents of which she and her friends had disposed of during the night.

The extravagance of the Villiers couple excited comment even in their far from frugal age. 'They set out furiously in jewels and other expenses, beyond the Mason finances', wrote Mrs Delany, 'and more won't come till the mother's death.' In the meantime, there was only one solution: 'Lord Villiers, who has fashioned away all he has, is to remove with his wife to his mother's and live there.'

In common with many of their class, Sir Charles Montagu and Countess Grandison led peripatetic lives. They moved between London and Phyllis Court, Dublin and Dromana, with sojourns at Bath and Cheltenham. Turnpike roads and steel-sprung carriages made travel less arduous than ever before, and Henley was emerging as a favourite stopping-place for persons of quality en route to the capital. Lady Grandison naturally had the entrée to all the local great houses. General Conway of Park Place, Remenham, moved in the highest circles, and young Lady Villiers was actually his niece. The Freemans too had excellent connections now that the passage of time had obscured their roots in trade. Even so, it is easy to imagine that Lord Villiers found life a trifle slow at Phyllis Court. All the family were ardent card-players, with loo their game of choice, but few neighbours could afford to match their stakes. He therefore hit on a fresh diversion to enliven New Year 1777: 'dramatic representations performed by people of distinction' – amateur theatricals.

Villiers selected his cast from the local gentry. The most valuable recruits were Anthony and Elizabeth Hodges, whose father owned Bolney Court, a mile and a half to the south. Its coach-house appeared better suited for a theatre than anywhere at Phyllis Court itself. Green baize was purchased to drape the walls and upholster seats for three hundred people. Scenery came on hire from Brighton. Admission was by invitation only, though the dress rehearsal was opened to interested townsfolk. Ice and snow deterred some invitees from making the journey from London. Those who did brave the roads resolved to stay a few days, and in this way the event expanded into a 'Gala Week' for Henley. 'Never before was it so gay, or so much money spent there', recorded Caroline Powys, the sister-in-law of the Rector of Fawley. 'Hadley's, the inn where the balls are to be, is already so fully engaged that he has bespoke forty private beds in the town; the other great inn, too, entirely bespoke.'

Phyllis Court, Park Place and Fawley Court accommodated the most illustrious guests. Lady Grandison spoke of thirty people sitting down to dinner in her parlour every evening, 'And yet, Mr Powys, you shall judge if my larder will not hold out. I've three does, a warrant gone for a fourth, three brace of pheasants, eight hares, six brace whistling plovers, twelve couple woodcocks, ten brace partridges, a peafowl, two guinea fowl, snipe and lark without number.' There were also at Phyllis Court ten musicians ('the best hands from Italy') and no less than five London hairdressers. Powdered wigs were then (literally) at their height; Lady Villiers went to 'Bolney Theatre' on Monday 6 January 1777 wearing a headdress two-and-a-half feet tall (and she sat at the front).

The principal play was a comedy, *The Provoked Husband* by Vanbrugh and Cibber, with Villiers acting the part of Lord Townly. He must have liked this role, for he played it again at Dromana ten years later. Would it be assuming too much to see in this a private joke? After all, the theme of the play is a gadabout gambling wife. On the other hand, it was suavely said in Henley that the only fault in his rendition of Townly was an insufficiently angry expression when confronted with wifely misconduct – because Lady Villiers never gave him any opportunity to practise it.

The performance went well, judging by the review in the *General Evening Post*. Villiers was 'easy, animated, and graceful', emulating the finest acting of the day (which to modern eyes would probably appear a strange succession of exaggerated poses). Mr Hodges, in his very small role, struggled to keep a straight face, but 'Miss Hodges made an incomparable Lady Townly:- It is but justice to say that this lady performed her part in a style far superior to any thing we have ever seen in the Theatres.' While professional actors were akin to vagabonds, it is conceivable that genteel amateurs sometimes did outshine them in upper-class roles. Mrs Powys, just as taken with the leading lady, observed that she had 'every advantage of dress, a pink suit of clothes, elegantly trimmed with gauze and flowers, all Lady Villiers' diamonds, valued at £12,000; four large bows making a complete stomacher, two of the same for sleeve knots, superb necklace and earrings, her head almost covered with a girdle of jewels'.

The choice of after-piece was more adventurous: *Pygmalion* by Rousseau, performed in French. For this, Villiers hired the celebrated reciter, Antoine Le Texier, who demonstrated all the attitudes of tragic woe and unexpected rapture in a virtual monologue. Mrs Powys rated it 'really the finest scene imaginable'. Cast and audience then transferred to The Bell Inn at Henley (the buildings at Northfield End now called Rupert's Bell and Denmark House) for a sumptuous supper with dancing.

Friday brought a complete repeat of both double-bill and ball, yet it was after the curtain had fallen that the greatest drama of the night occurred: a highwayman struck on the Reading Road as everyone returned to The Bell. First he stopped Mr Goodenough and robbed him of fifty guineas. Then he tried another hired chaise, only to find the Italian fiddlers, whom he let pass without further ado. When news reached Villiers, he guessed that the jewellery worn in the play must be the intended object, for his wife's duenna was bringing it back to Phyllis Court in a third hired chaise. Six armed men were sent to escort the gems. After an interval of anxious excitement, duenna and diamonds arrived without mishap, and the sense of relief only heightened the revelry. Once again, Mrs Powys took note:

> The suppers were very elegant, provisions of every kind, wine, fruits, etc.... No servants but those of the Grandisons and Villiers; indeed they have such numbers no others could be wanted. Everything was sent from the house, and their own three cooks to dress it. Soups and game as usual hot, the rest cold. We hear [it] cost Lord Villiers £1,000.

Hopes were voiced that Gala Week would become an annual event, but not even the Villiers could sustain expenditure on this scale. Letters from their agents warned of grave disorder in the family finances, and it is doubtful that Lady Grandison paid many more visits to Henley. In August 1777, her husband died in London ('a warning', thought Walpole, 'to all men of his age who may be tempted to murder themselves by becoming the *bon ton* at sixty-three'). Lord and Lady Villiers went abroad, beyond the reach of creditors, and the Countess usually shared their residences. She died in May 1782 at Spa, now in Belgium.

Gala Week may be seen in retrospect as the glittering finale of old Phyllis Court. Its prestige was about to take another knock from which it appeared unlikely to recover.

Strickland Freeman

Strickland Freeman inherited the Fawley Estate, including Phyllis Court, from his uncle in 1782 at the age of twenty-eight. He was said to be 'rather below the middle-size in stature – light and active in figure, with manners polite and elegant', close to the contemporary ideal of a country gentleman. Normally resident at Fawley, as a landowner in three counties, he took an active part in the public life of at least two of them as a Justice of the Peace. Prior to the advent of county councils in 1888, magistrates ran county government as well as courts of first instance. Freeman also served as High Sheriff of Oxfordshire in 1795; that is to say, he was the judicial representative of the Sovereign with responsibility for law and order. His duties included maintaining loyalty to the Crown, a task not taken lightly when republican ideology was emanating from revolutionary France. Wartime shortages gave rise that year to a fear that food riots might erupt even in Henley. Freeman organised a Loyal Address to George III from the inhabitants of Oxfordshire, who were 'truly sensible of the Blessings this Nation enjoys under Your Majesty's Government and the Constitution by Law established'.

The King knew and personally approved of Freeman, partly on account of their common interest in agricultural improvement. Rather surprisingly, Freeman had received his education at the Warrington Academy, Lancashire, a notably progressive school, catering chiefly for the sons of religious dissenters. There he acquired at least a mildly scientific outlook, which he later brought to bear on his favourite topic. Above almost all else, Strickland Freeman was an enthusiast for horses, and not only in the sense of the turf. He routinely spent two hours a day grooming and exercising them:

> In youth he was a keen sportsman with the gun as well as hounds – a bold and expert horseman. But a severe injury at the back of the head from a bench in the riding house, by a restive horse falling backwards with him, ever afterwards incapacitated him from using the gun, and also precluded him for several years from his darling exercise.

In the interim, he studied equine anatomy, initially guided by his doctor. The outcome was *Observations on the Mechanism of the Horse's Foot, its natural spring explained, and a mode of shoeing recommended, by which the foot is defended from external injury with the least impediment to its spring.* This appeared in 1796, priced at one guinea. It insisted on the elasticity of the foot and the need to preserve the moisture of the horn. For a further three shillings, the purchaser could also take home an actual hoof, shod in the approved fashion as an illustration. Veterinary science in Britain was in its infancy, and the London (later Royal) Veterinary College, founded five years earlier, concentrated on the care of horses' feet to the near exclusion of everything else. It was a controversial issue. Continental experts alleged grave shortcomings in the techniques of British farriers and accused them of creating 'The Hell for Horses'. As a layman writing for laymen, Freeman met with a hostile reception from a veterinary profession as yet extremely unsure of itself. His book was subjected to a scathing attack in the *Critical Review*, and most of the copies

A silhouette of Strickland Freeman, with one of his beloved horses, from the *Sporting Magazine*, April 1832.

remained in the possession of the author. Then, in 1809, the veterinarian Bracy Clark announced his own 'discovery' of the elasticity of the equine foot. When Freeman's *Observations* were brought to his attention, Clark accused the older man of plagiarism and falsifying his date of publication. This dispute went on exciting horse-doctors for years. The verdict of posterity seems to be that Freeman, though an ineffective writer, presented an important anatomical truth for the first time in print, only nobody initially took much notice. His second foray into literature proved happier. *The Art of Horsemanship* (1806), dedicated to the Prince of Wales, recommended plain bits and kindly treatment. 'The more the art of horsemanship is understood', he wrote, 'the less the very name of rough rider should be made use of.'

Demolition

Whatever his achievements, Strickland Freeman is bound to appear in a negative light in a history of Phyllis Court. The reason for this is simple: he demolished it, or, at any rate, knocked down the greater part of the structure in 1787. His reasons for doing so can only be surmised. A later owner, Roderick Mackenzie, offered this explanation: 'Phillis Court, which now had become Freeman property, was pulled down; tradition says because one of its owners objected to having any house on his own estate bigger than Fawley, the one he lived in.' At a first hearing, the story sounds apocryphal, but its plausibility grows on reflection. House-proud Georgian landed gentry really did behave in such ways, and all the Freemans delighted in enhancing Fawley Court. Strickland himself had it coated in stucco (afterwards removed) and added Ionic columns. He also built the flint wall along the Fair Mile and the Palladian lodges on the Marlow Road. His expenditure on beautifying the estate ran into tens of thousands of pounds. George Woodward observed in 1796 that Fawley Court 'may justly be ranked among the national palaces'.

In comparison, the manor house of Phyllis Court may have appeared a rambling old barn of a place. Predominantly Tudor in aspect, it could not meet the exacting standards of eighteenth-century classicism. Damage during the Civil War had necessitated repairs, and the domestic arrangements of 140 years earlier were old enough to be entirely outmoded without yet being rare enough to excite historical interest. Freeman was not especially scrupulous in relation to the past. He upset antiquarians by ripping ornamental masonry out of Crosby Hall (once the home of Richard III) to re-use it as decoration for his dairy. Henley itself was undergoing an aesthetic transformation in this period, acquiring the distinctive architecture on which it still prides itself. Much of the town was rebuilt in the latest styles, and even less extravagant householders added a frontage of brick or stucco to their old timber-framed dwellings. The supreme example of modernisation was the five-arched bridge across the Thames completed in 1786. It provides as pleasing a focal point for the view to the south from the garden of Phyllis Court as the Temple

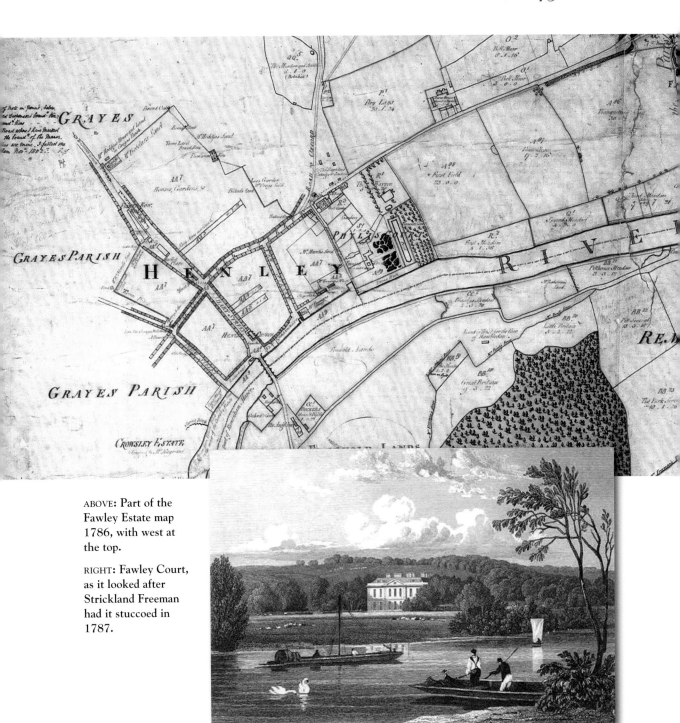

ABOVE: Part of the Fawley Estate map 1786, with west at the top.

RIGHT: Fawley Court, as it looked after Strickland Freeman had it stuccoed in 1787.

Island folly does for the northerly view. Georgian connoisseurs would have relished these vistas before turning to face a mansion that looked all the more offensive by dint of contrast.

Freeman had no specific use for Phyllis Court. His aunt preferred Henley Park as a dower house. If money counted for anything with him, it might have been difficult to find suitable tenants. People able to afford the rent of so large a residence would probably have expected modern conveniences. Some cosmetic efforts had been made to update the place, but its basic structure limited the scope for renovation. People of quality may also have desired a more secluded location. Freight traffic on the River Thames was nearing its height; wharves, warehouses, timberyards, and barge-builders stretched from the bridge to the boundary of the property. Phyllis Court was not quite in Arcadia.

First, in 1786, came the sale of the contents, presumably Grandison property, advertised in *Jackson's Oxford Journal*:

HENLEY-ON-THAMES

(At Phillis Court)

To be sold by auction by Benj. Moorehouse. On Tuesday the 6th June Instant, and Three following Days, – The Genuine neat HOUSEHOLD FURNITURE and Effects of a Person of Distinction, lately deceased; comprising a Variety of elegant and useful Furniture, fine seasoned Goose Feather Beds, Blankets, Quilts, and Counterpanes; fashionable Bedsteads, with Mahogany Pillars and Chintz, Cotton and other Furnitures; Pier and Dressing-Glasses; fine Mahogany Sofas, Chairs, Tables, Side-Boards, Bureaus, Book-Cases, and Chests of Drawers; Dressing-Tables; Floor and Bedside Carpets, and Window-Curtains; a Mahogany Billiard Table compleat; a Pleasure-Boat, with Awning, &c.; a large Iron Garden Roll, Cucumber and Melon Frames, and Lights; Hand-lights and Garden Tools; a Variety of Greenhouse Plants; a regular Assortment of Kitchen Furniture; Brewing and Dairy Utensils; seasoned Casks, and a Variety of other Articles, which may be viewed three Days previous to the Sale, which will begin each Day at Eleven o'Clock precisely.

Eight weeks later, shutters, oak-panelling, and 'several neat Marble and other Chimney Pieces' were offered for sale. The death knell sounded on 7 April 1787:

OLD BUILDING MATERIALS

Now pulling down, and selling by Hand in different Lots, – The REMAINS of that Old Mansion, PHILLIS COURT HOUSE, at Henley-upon-Thames: Comprising a Variety of old Timbers, in Roofings; framed Chamber and Ground naked Floorings, Partitions, &c., of various Dimensions; a large Outside Block Cornice and Facia; an Ionick and Truss Frontispiece, with their Doors, Fan Lights, and Stone Steps, compleat; a Pair of

Relics of Old Phyllis Court

Though the ancient manor house disappeared, isolated bits of it are presumably to be found in the fabric of surviving buildings in the district, if only it were possible to identify them. In one untypical case, it is. While demolition was under way, George Whitelocke, a great-grandson of Bulstrode Whitelocke resident in Ireland, visited Henley and obtained from Freeman the armorial painted glass from the windows of the dining-parlour. 'He with very great civility insisted on my taking it', recorded Whitelocke, 'and a picture of Queen Christina.' These heirlooms accordingly crossed the Irish Sea, but the glass returned in the twentieth century on the initiative of historian Ruth Spalding. In 1971–72, it was repaired and set up in the nave of Fawley Church (where the inscription, 'Glass originally from Fawley Court c.1654', assumes a transfer to Phyllis Court c.1680, though the windows have also been attributed to John Rowell, a craftsman who died as late as 1756).

One of the Whitelocke armorial windows in Fawley Church, probably removed from old Phyllis Court when it was demolished.

Circle-headed Folding Doors; several single, Transom, and Bow Window-Frames, with leaded Lights and Casements; a large Circle-headed Stair-Case Sash and Frame; the Best and Back Stairs, with their Railings, Wainscottings, and Wood Cornices; a Room of the best Bremen Paving, with Portland Dots and Borders; good Purbeck Pavement, with some channelled; old Bricks, &c., &c. The Whole immediately to be sold, and the Ground cleared with all convenient Speed. – Enquire of Wm. Shennan, Building-Surveyor, at Henley Wharf; where all Letters, Post-paid, will be duly attended to.

N.B. Near the above Premises are to be Lett, – Exceeding good Stables and Coach-Houses, with two large Yards, and every other Convenience, fit for any Gentleman or Coach-Master.

Some uncertainty surrounds what was actually left on site. Indeed, the following half-century constitutes a miniature dark age in Phyllis Court's history. The plot was not just a field, but contemporary descriptions dwell far more on the absence of the grand old mansion than on the less imposing presence of its remnants or successor. More informative than most is *The Henley Guide* (1826), which says of Phyllis Court, 'About forty years ago, it was pulled down, with the exception of a small portion which still remains. A fine terrace walk by the margin of the stream, the bowling green, fish pond, &c., attest its former magnificence; and, though in the formal style of antique gardening, are very picturesque.' A summer house is just visible in Peter de Wint's illustration of Henley (published in *Views on the Thames* in 1818). When this wooden structure was itself dismantled in 1830, a verse was found pencilled on one of its walls:

> Ah! much lov'd banks, my infancy's delight,
> How chang'd, how fall'n, ye meet my mournful sight,
> May this lone relic of the beauteous scene
> Long stand to shew what Phyllis Court has been.
>   S. Grandison 1794.

As an expression of the consciousness of transience, this has considerable poignancy. The authorship is puzzling, for Grandison was a title and not a surname. Could 'S. Grandison' be a misreading of 'G. Grandison', meaning George, 2nd Earl Grandison, formerly Lord Villiers? Perhaps, but he is not known to have come to Phyllis Court before he reached his twenties, which would make the reference to infancy an instance of poetic licence. But then, so too might be the suggestion that the garden pavilion was a 'lone relic' – unless it be accepted that the stables and coach-houses, spared destruction in 1787, had never really contributed to 'the beauteous scene'. Furthermore, an Oxfordshire history from as late as 1852 claims that 'the kitchen of the ancient mansion still remains' – and that cannot be all. The buildings surviving at Phyllis Court continued to house distinguished tenants. We know this from J.S. Burn, the Victorian local historian who, in this particular, was writing of times still just within living memory.

One possibility is that the 'small portion' still extant served as seasonal accommodation. The late eighteenth century witnessed a boom in domestic tourism relating to picturesque river scenery. It started with the Wye Valley on the Welsh border, but appreciation of the Thames also dramatically increased, especially where it met the wooded Chiltern Hills: 'A more beautifully marked country than this cannot easily be formed by the most romantic fancy, and nature has placed this British paradise within forty miles of the capital of our country.' People would take a house for the summer, attracted by opportunities for walking, boating and angling. Woodward noted the transformation: 'Travellers of former times observe that the inhabitants consisted of meal-men, malt-men, and barge-men; but thanks to the powerful influence of modern taste, over the mechanical notions of days of yore, Henley may now be ranked as a favourite resort of what is termed families of distinction!'

Lady Clive

Burn's *History of Henley-on-Thames* (1861) records that Lady Clive rented Phyllis Court 'about 1790'. Given that there were actually three Lady Clives then alive, can we assume that this Lady Clive was the famous one: Margaret, Dowager Baroness

Clive of Plassey, widow of Clive of India? Probably we can. The very fact that Burn did not specify tends to suggest as much, and the circumstantial evidence is supportive. Margaret Clive definitely knew the area for, from 1781 until at least 1788, she was tenant of Englefield House, near Reading, an Elizabethan mansion recently modernised (and also reduced, although not so drastically as Phyllis Court). It is tempting to think that she transferred from there to Henley. Complicating the picture is a newspaper report from September 1790 of her spending the greater part of that summer at Kelvedon Hall, near Ongar, but this may not signify much. Another paper, the *Public Advertiser*, had earlier observed that she was 'always fond of Change in her place of Habitation'. To Lady Clive, as to Lady Grandison, Phyllis Court would practically have been a holiday home. Her principal seat was Oakly Park in Shropshire. Of London she was less fond – it put her 'in a flurry', she said – and this may explain her taking a country house not so very far from her establishment in Argyll Street. She resembled Lady Grandison in her wealth, it may be noted, but not in her social life. Lady Clive's friends were professional people, minor gentry, intellectuals, and old India hands. Although eminently sociable, she hardly aspired to the role of grand hostess, so the remnant of Phyllis Court could have satisfied

Lady Clive by Nathaniel Dance. (National Trust Photo Library)

her requirements. The two other Lady Clives were her relatives by marriage, one of them her daughter-in-law. Henrietta Clive, wife of the 2nd Baron and daughter of the Earl of Powis, may have been in Henley for the Gala Week of 1777; her parents certainly were. In the 1790s, however, she was living in London and the Welsh Marches. That leaves Judith, widow of Sir Edward Clive, a Judge of the Court of Common Pleas. Not known to have had links to the Thames Valley, she died at her home in Wormbridge, Herefordshire, in 1796.

Margaret Clive, *née* Maskelyne, led an eventful life as wife of one the most controversial architects of British overseas expansion. Born in 1735, the child of a minor civil servant, she sailed for Madras at the age of seventeen in a party of young ladies of modest means, all seeking husbands among the staff of the British East India Company. One of her brothers was already there, and among his friends was Captain Robert Clive. Within a few months, they married. For her, it was a love match, and Clive made a faithful husband, despite his complex personality. This man displayed amazing energy when facing urgent challenges; at other times, he could sink into gloom. From his petite vivacious spouse he received unflagging support. She was with him in India, when he commanded the expedition to punish Siraj ud-Daulah, Nawab of Bengal, for the 'Black Hole of Calcutta'. First, Clive forced the Nawab to come to terms. Then he overthrew him after conspiring with his local rivals. Once installed as client-rulers, they gave Clive 'presents' worth £234,000. Back in England, he received a peerage.

Though widely acclaimed at first, the Clives were not fully accepted into London society. Many aristocrats deplored the sudden rise of newly rich adventurers, and antagonism came to a head in 1772 with the setting up of a parliamentary committee to investigate Clive's conduct. Accused of vastly enriching himself to the dishonour of his country, he memorably replied, 'I walked through vaults which were thrown open to me alone, piled on either hand with gold and jewels! My God, Mr Chairman, at this moment I stand astonished at my own moderation.' As the politicking grew vicious, he won some backing from General Conway MP of Park Place. This is a Henley association that Lady Clive would not have forgotten. She regarded her husband as 'one of the most virtuous of men'. He escaped formal censure, but the strain of proceedings may have affected his state of mind. In 1774, during a bout of abdominal agony (possibly caused by gallstones), he apparently took his own life. One version involves an overdose of opium, another has him thrusting a penknife into his throat – and Margaret finding the body. If it was indeed suicide, this very religious woman yet found some means of coping. She was only thirty-nine and lived on with outward serenity till 1817. Along with her son and three daughters, a wide range of interests, including astronomy and music, helped sustain her. Her other great love was cats. People who came to know Lady Clive usually testified to her charm.

Admiral Bowyer

What historians call 'the long eighteenth century', from the Glorious Revolution of 1688–89 to the Battle of Waterloo in 1815, is an epoch defined by conflict between Britain and France. Their recurrent wars altogether lasted for 64 years out of 127, and the British Empire ultimately won a preponderant position in international affairs that lasted for over a century. Sea power essentially decided the contest, and from this period date many legendary names in the annals of the Royal Navy, such as Anson, Rodney, Hood, Jervis and Nelson. Admiral Sir George Bowyer (1740–1800), tenant of Phyllis Court in the 1790s, does not rank with the immortals, yet he honourably exemplifies the solid professionalism that gave the Royal Navy its strength in depth, and this lesser-known sea dog did have his day – 1 June 1794, to be precise, though it very nearly killed him.

The third son of a Buckinghamshire bar-onet, George Bowyer went to sea aged eleven, as captain's servant on HMS *Glory*. The captain he served was Richard Howe, later Admiral Lord Howe, and this connection endured. His initial command came to grief when the *Swift* was captured in 1762, but the court martial fully exonerated him. As cap-tain of HMS *Albion*, he fought commendably in the American War of Independence. Then he spent six years in Parliament representing Queensborough, a rotten borough controlled by the Admiralty. His political activities were accordingly limited to supporting the

George Bowyer in a mezzotint by G. Every of a portrait by Reynolds.

Government and speaking on the Navy. Pitt reciprocated with his promotion to Rear-Admiral and a sea-command in 1793.

Thus Bowyer found himself one of half-a-dozen divisional admirals in the Channel Fleet under Howe. His flag flew in HMS *Barfleur*, an old 98-gun ship of the line, when they set out the following May to engage the French Atlantic Fleet on its emergence from Brest in order to protect a crucial grain convoy from America. The culmination of this expedition was the Battle of the Glorious First of June, so-called because it took place so far out to sea that no landmark could credibly lend it a conventional geographical name. On a Sunday morning, twenty-five British ships took on twenty-six French. Cuthbert Collingwood, flag captain of the *Barfleur*, wrote this account:

> Down we went under a crowd of sail, and in a manner that would have animated the coldest heart, and struck terror into the most intrepid enemy. The ship we were to engage was two ahead of the French Admiral, so that we had to go through his fire and that of two ships next to him, and received all their broadsides two or three times before we fired a gun. It was then near ten o'clock. I observed to the Admiral, that about that time our wives were going to church, but that I thought the peal we should ring about the Frenchmen's ears would outdo their parish bells. Lord Howe began his fire some time before we did; and he is not in the habit of firing soon. We got very near indeed, and then began such a fire as would have done you good to have heard…. In ten minutes the Admiral was wounded; I caught him in my arms before he fell.

A cannon-ball had struck Bowyer, requiring the amputation of one of his legs above the knee. It cannot therefore be said that he played a pre-eminent part in the battle, but his courage made a fine impression. The Admiral, reported Collingwood, 'was so raised up by the success of the day that he made his own misfortune of little consideration; and I believe he would have done himself material injury by his spirits if I had not at last shut him up and prohibited everybody but the surgeon and necessary attendants going near him'. In all, the British sank one French ship and captured six, victory giving a tremendous boost to national morale. Bowyer made a fair recovery. Reckoned a hero, he was awarded a baronetcy and a pension.

Sir George cannot have lived at Phyllis Court for long. His principal home was Warfield Grove, near Bracknell, and he spent his retirement at Radley Hall, near Abingdon, nowadays 'the mansion' of Radley College. That is where he is best remembered, for, although the boys have ceased to attribute bumps in the night to a peg-legged ghost, the school still flies a flag each first of June in his honour. Inhabitants of British Columbia may also occasionally spare him a thought on account of Bowyer Island in the Howe Sound, north of Vancouver.

Admiral Williams-Freeman

The next owner of Phyllis Court was also a naval officer and, at first glance, an even more distinguished one. William Peere Williams-Freeman rose to be Admiral of the Fleet, second only to the King in the hierarchy. For a true estimate of his importance, however, it is necessary to know that promotion through the flag ranks was simply a matter of seniority. Williams-Freeman reached the top in 1830, his eighty-ninth year, having entered the service straight from Eton in 1757 and languished on the reserve list since 1782. Longevity likewise won him the Fawley Estate in 1821, on the death of his childless cousin, Strickland Freeman. His surname, hitherto Williams, gained its double barrel to satisfy the terms of the will of William Freeman, the brother of his great-grandmother.

Williams had his one notable professional success as captain of HMS *Flora* in August 1780, when he captured a larger French frigate. A second bid for glory, nine months later, did not turn out so well. The *Flora*, along with HMS *Crescent*, attacked two Dutch ships off Ceuta. Williams overpowered one of them, the *Castor*, but half his crew was wounded in the process – and worse followed. On the voyage back to England, *Flora*, *Crescent* and their dearly won prize encountered a pair of French frigates. Williams judged that his damaged vessel could not stand further combat and therefore hastened away, while *Crescent* and *Castor* were lost to the enemy. Lord Mulgrave, who investigated for the

William Peere Williams, painted by George Romney c.1782. He acquired the additional surname of Freeman nearly forty years later. (Manchester Art Gallery)

Admiralty, brushed aside any imputation of cowardice, but rated the Captain deficient in abilities, a verdict which 'one would wish, both from his gallantry and connexions, not to appear publicly'. Williams stood no chance of obtaining a peacetime command and, even when war resumed, the offer of his services was declined. He put this down to his politics being too liberal for the Pitt administration – which may not have been complete nonsense. One of his friends was Major Cartwright, a leader of British Radicalism.

The Freeman inheritance came too late to make much difference to Williams-Freeman, who lived at Yew House, Hoddesdon. His son, also William Peere Williams-Freeman (1782–1830), moved into Fawley Court. For Henley, this was a lucky escape, as the Admiral had grown notoriously quarrelsome. The vicar at Hoddesdon vented his exasperation in his diary. 'Is it possible that a man so insufferably proud and rude can have anything truly good in him?' asked the Reverend William Jones. 'It is hardly to be expected that the most generous liquor can enter, while windy froth is issuing and blustering out of the neck of the worthless bottle!!' By coincidence, the tenant of Phyllis Court in 1823 was also called William Jones, but this cannot have been the cleric (who died in 1821). One possibility is William Jones (1762–1831), a retired maker of scientific instruments, but the commonness of the name has thwarted efforts at positive identification.

Reconstruction

When the Admiral died in 1832, his successor was his grandson, another William Peere Williams-Freeman, then a student at Oxford. This Williams-Freeman lived at Fawley Court, raised a large family, and happily filled the role of a country gentleman. He was High Sheriff of Oxfordshire in 1838 and a Deputy Lieutenant from 1846. His hobbies included hunting, shooting, fishing and sailing. More pertinently, he made two contributions to Phyllis Court that endure to the present. First, he redeveloped the property. Secondly, he joined other riparian landowners in supporting the foundation of an annual regatta. There is no clear connection between these decisions, despite their proximity in time. Indeed, very little is clear about the building of the new house. No records have been found to reveal how long it took or who designed it. The remnants of the old structure were swept away around 1837 and the replacement erected before June 1841, judging by its listing in the first detailed census. Only the nucleus of the current building, it was a plain stuccoed villa in what was then the modern style, vaguely Italianate, with a parapet roof and large sash windows, suitable for a well-off middle-class householder. The residents recorded in the census were Thomas Hews (aged thirty-nine), his wife Mary, two of their children, and a maidservant. Hews, originally from Essex, worked for Williams-Freeman as steward of the Fawley Estate. Perhaps he occupied the new house temporarily, pending a commercial let. His wife was a native of Henley, where they stayed for the rest of their lives, moving first to New Street and then

The First Regatta

Serious competitive rowing in Henley began with a one-off university boat race in 1829. Eight years later, St John's College, Cambridge took on Queen's College, Oxford over the same stretch of river. On both occasions, local tradesmen enjoyed the custom of wealthy spectators. Credit for the idea of making such contests a regular attraction goes to James Nash, but it was Williams-Freeman, lord of the manor, who formally proposed the motion at a meeting in the Town Hall on 26 March 1839:

> That from the lively interest which has been manifested at the various boat races which have taken place on the Henley reach during the last few years, and the great influx of visitors on such occasions, this meeting is of the opinion that the establishment of an annual regatta, under judicious and respectable management, would not only be productive of the most beneficial results to the town of Henley, but from its peculiar attractions would also be a source of amusement and gratification to the neighbourhood, and to the public in general.

He was chosen as one of six stewards to organise the event. Only seven crews competed on 14 June 1839 – but something of its potential was perceived by the *Reading Mercury*: 'If the most inauspicious weather had not darkened the horizon, with clouds, and rain, and storm, we should have had to record one of the most splendid aquatic galas... that has ever been assembled in any town in England.' By 1845, Williams-Freeman 'had very kindly given the use of Phyllis Court grounds for the accommodation of select visitors' at Regatta time. From this point the path of destiny becomes discernible – with hindsight.

to Hart Street. Hews set up as an auctioneer and estate agent, supplementing his income as secretary to the Henley Gas Light and Coke Company. He also served as a burgess and later alderman of the Corporation till his death in 1865. No other inhabitant of Phyllis Court in the nineteenth century engaged so fully in civic life.

By the 1840s, Phyllis Court was associated with both the new Henley Regatta and the Henley Horticultural Society, which staged shows of produce in its gardens. These continued even after the house itself was leased in 1845 to solicitor George Pritt. He sub-let Phyllis Court for some part of his tenure, and the actual resident in the early 1850s had no objection to displays of fruit and vegetables. He was John Wilson, lately resigned as principal of the Royal Agricultural College at Cirencester. The College, founded in 1845, was the first institution of its kind in the English-speaking world and it struggled in its earliest years. After a personality clash between Wilson and the chaplain caused ructions, the governing council proposed in 1851 to reduce the amount of science in the curriculum. As a scientist himself, Wilson predictably refused to co-operate. He passionately

'Oxford beating Cambridge at Henley, June 10, 1829' by William Havell. (River & Rowing Museum)

advocated the application of chemistry, geology, and natural history to farming in order to relieve it 'from the dark and misty atmosphere in which it has been so long enveloped'. Hence his sudden departure and need for a new home. With him to Phyllis Court came his wife, mother, and sister. The calling of agricultural scientist was still a novelty, but Wilson (not his critics) suited the progressive spirit of the age. In particular, the repeal of the Corn Laws in 1846 exposed British farming to competition, so new techniques were required to increase productivity. Wilson found employment in the agricultural section of the Great Exhibition, arranging trials for reaping machines, turnip-slicers and mechanical churns. He investigated 'fish guano', sugar beet, rapeseed oil as an industrial lubricant, and the potential for wine-making in Australia, along with many other innovations, and he did not ignore the claims of 'that least cared-for and worst-lodged animal on the farm – the poor Labourer'. In a period when religion and science were coming into conflict, his lectures made a point of acknowledging that, while human intellect adapted nature's gifts, 'it is *God* that giveth the increase'. In 1854, Wilson was appointed

John Wilson,
agricultural
scientist,
etched by
W.B. Hole.
(National
Portrait
Gallery)

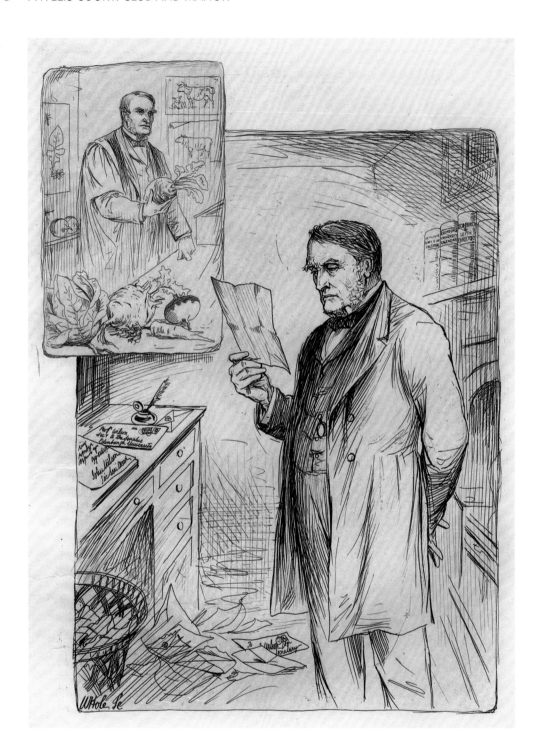

Professor of Agriculture at the University of Edinburgh. For Victorian farmers, his book *Our Farm Crops* (1860) served as a standard text. He may not have been an easy man: one obituarist noted 'a cold and distant manner', yet his teaching consolidated agriculture as a subject for academic study.

The Freeman Era was reaching its close. In 1848, Williams-Freeman had become an absentee landlord on moving to Scotland. He took legal steps to bar the entail and put the entire Fawley Estate of 3,100 acres up for sale. On 29 June 1853, it was auctioned in twenty-two lots. The sixth of these – 'A freehold residence, called Phyllis Court, near the town of Henley-on-Thames, with stabling, 8 acres, 3 roods, and 18 perches of land, also brick, stone, and part wood-built silk mill. Annual value £108 10s' – went for £3,000. (The mill was an outbuilding in Bell Lane, separately let, where cocoons of raw silk brought from London were distributed to outworkers for winding.) The auction realised £134,885, and Williams-Freeman bought the South Baddesley estate in the New Forest, where he lived for the last twenty years of his life. The transfer of the freehold did not bring any sudden change to Phyllis Court, which stayed a part of the same great estate, for its purchaser had also paid £90,000 for Fawley Court, the lordship of the manor, and the vast majority of the land.

5

The Mackenzie Era
1853–1905

Great Britain was the first industrial country. In 1850, its output comprised two-thirds of all the coal mined in the world, half of all the cotton woven, and half of all the iron smelted. True, the pits and mills and foundries were far from Henley, whose only significant industry remained small-scale brewing, but the momentous effects of the Industrial Revolution spread quickly, with railways as their transmission mechanism. Though Henley did not get a branch line till 1857, the impact of trains on its economy had already been dramatic. The Great Western Railway linked London to Twyford in 1839, Reading in 1840 and Bristol in 1841. For a town hitherto reliant on coaching and river traffic, this was disastrous in the short term. Henley found itself bypassed. In 1830, twenty-six stagecoaches had stopped there every day; by 1852 there was just one daily service to London. The number of barges fell too. The coming of the age of steam meant many local losers, with inns and shops forced to close. There were also, however, at least a couple of conspicuous gainers: the lessor and lessee of Phyllis Court both derived their fortunes from the railways.

Edward Mackenzie

Edward Mackenzie, owner of the freehold from 1853, was a very rich man. In addition to the Fawley Estate, he possessed Craigs and Newbie in Dumfriesshire and Auchenskeoch in Kircudbrightshire, and later acquired Thetford and Santon Downham in East Anglia. In 1880, the year of his death, only two grants of probate in the whole country were larger. It was all 'new money', moreover. His father had left Ross-shire in the Highlands as a young man to work on the Forth and Clyde Canal before becoming a minor contractor on canal works in England. Edward himself was born in Lancashire in 1811, during the digging of the Leeds and Liverpool Canal. His origins were thus fairly humble, yet to call him a self-made man would not be entirely accurate. The crucial creator of wealth in the family was his elder brother, William Mackenzie (1794–1851), a leading figure in civil engineering in the second quarter of the nineteenth century. After supervising bridges and canals as an assistant to Thomas Telford, in 1832 William won the contract to extend the new Liverpool and Manchester Railway by tunnelling from Edge Hill to Lime Street. Edward, aged twenty-one, joined his staff, and the brothers proceeded to collaborate on a succession of massive construction projects. William was the expert and something of an autocrat, but he relied on Edward as his eyes and ears when he could not be on site.

Between 1835 and 1840, the Mackenzies worked chiefly on the Grand Junction Railway, the North Union Railway, the Midland Counties Railway and the Glasgow, Paisley and Greenock Railway. Then William went into partnership with Thomas Brassey to bid for foreign contracts. In 1841, they took ten thousand British workmen across the Channel to begin the Paris & Rouen Railway. Edward and his first wife set up home in Mantes, where he oversaw operations and managed the finances. Half the capital for these early French railways originated in Britain. Four years later, Edward moved to Orléans to supervise track-laying. When revolution disrupted progress in 1848, there were contracts in England to occupy him, such as the Liverpool-Ormskirk line. This completed, he went back to France. Mackenzie & Brassey looked unstoppable – till William Mackenzie's health gave way. Although twice married, he had no children and left his enormous wealth to his brother in 1851

ABOVE: Edward Mackenzie, railway tycoon, who owned Fawley Court and Phyllis Court from 1853 to 1880. (National Portrait Gallery)

LEFT: A replica at Didcot Railway Centre of GWR *Fire Fly*, one of the first locomotives to run between London and Reading in 1840. (Chris Howells)

(despite doubting his ability to continue the business). Edward stayed abroad until the opening of the Orléans, Tours & Bordeaux Railway on 28 June 1853. The next day, he bought Fawley Court with semi-retirement in mind.

In some ways, Edward Mackenzie appears typically nouveau riche. He filled his picture gallery at a stroke by purchasing the eighty portrait studies for William Salter's then famous painting of *The Waterloo Banquet at Apsley House 1836*; today they are in the National Portrait Gallery. In 1863, he defrayed the entire cost of the British Orphan Asylum at Slough (about £14,000) out of the blue, just moments before the Prince of Wales arrived for the opening. The charity renamed it Mackenzie Park. 'My gift', he said, 'was unavoidably made in public.' In Henley, he served as a Steward of the Regatta and in 1862 was High Sheriff of Oxfordshire. Both offices pretty much went with the Fawley Estate. Although no longer a contractor, Mackenzie played a behind-the-scenes role in the rather dubious world of railway finance, making loans with security often in the form of railway shares. Transactions of this sort were the major factor in the financial crash of May 1866, when the bank of Overend Gurney failed. Mackenzie himself lost about £100,000 and later discovered that his French agent had defrauded him of £80,000 more. At least he could stand the losses. It seems unlikely that this international tycoon would have given much consideration to a leased villa bought for £3,000, even when it stood near his principal home. In the Mackenzie Era, Phyllis Court was a fragment of a fragment of a vast property empire.

George Pritt

The leaseholder from 1845 owed his prosperity to the railways only slightly less directly. George Pritt, originally from Liverpool, worked as a solicitor of a very specialised sort – a parliamentary agent. Often mistaken for party or election agents, parliamentary agents are non-partisan experts on legislative procedure who advise and represent the promoters and opponents of private bills. Private bills arise from the right of individuals and outside bodies to petition Parliament to enact proposals relating to specific people or localities. The number of such petitions had been growing throughout the eighteenth and early nineteenth centuries, reflecting demand for powers to enclose farmland, levy tolls and issue compulsory purchase orders for canal routes. Then came the heyday of railway construction and, with it, a torrent of private legislation. Parliamentary agents were never busier, as dozens of companies sought rights to build lines, while their rivals tried to block them, and all needed representation.

Pritt's career coincided almost exactly with the railway boom, and he was ideally placed to profit from it. By his own account, he first worked at the Palace of Westminster in 1825. His age was then fourteen, so it must be supposed that he served as office-boy to his father, the secretary of the Liverpool and Manchester Railway Company, then seeking approval for the first inter-city passenger railway in the world. The agent who handled this bill, Thomas Sherwood, accepted Pritt junior as his business partner seven years afterwards, and building on its pioneering experience, Sherwood & Co., later styled Pritt & Co. (or Burke, Pritt & Venables, or Pritt, Venables & Co.), grew into the leading agency for railway legislation. In the five parliamentary sessions between 1847 and 1851, for example, there were deposited 1,262 petitions for private legislation. Of these, Pritt & Co. promoted 354, of which 268 were railway bills. Thanks to Pritt's connections, the firm was especially dominant in north-west England, though its single most important client was the Great Western Railway. Municipal improvements constituted the other main type of work.

If the 'railway mania' of 1845–46 enabled George Pritt to lease Phyllis Court as his second home, the subsequent bursting of the speculative bubble may explain his sub-letting it so soon afterwards. Four railway companies had been promoting rival bills for a connection to Henley at the time he took the house. A rail link seemed imminent. Then the Tring, Reading & Basingstoke Railway, the South Midland & Southampton Railway, and the Midland Grand Junction Railway all dropped out and, by the time the Great Western's Act was passed in 1847, the sources of finance had temporarily dried up. In any case, Pritt's primary residence had to be in London: 109 Westbourne Terrace, followed by 10 Cleveland Gardens, both near Paddington station. As business recovered in the later 1850s, he could afford to keep Phyllis Court free for use during parliamentary recesses with his

To Let

Page four of *The Times* carried the following advertisement on 23 January 1861:

HENLEY-ON-THAMES. – To be LET, on LEASE for seven, 14, or 21 years, from Midsummer next the beautiful VILLA RESIDENCE and GROUNDS, called Phyllis Court, delightfully situate on the banks of the Thames, near Henley. The house, which is modern, is built on the site of the ancient manor house, on a lawn, sloping to the river, and surrounded by about nine acres of finely wooded, park-like land. It contains spacious drawing and dining rooms, breakfast room, entrance-hall, eight bed rooms, good servants' rooms, cellars and offices, and a conservatory adjoining the house; also excellent coach-house and stable. The grounds are beautifully laid out, terminating in a terrace walk on the bank of the river. The house is within half-a-mile of the Henley Railway Station, and the property altogether forms a compact and elegant villa residence, of a character seldom to be met with. For terms and further particulars, apply to Messrs. Cooper, solicitors, Henley-on-Thames.

In the interim, Dinah Johnson and her husband, a wire-worker, moved in from one of the Marlow Road lodges to act as caretakers.

expanding family of two boys and five surviving girls. His elder son spent most time in Henley, since he boarded at the grammar school in Northfield End. When the Twyford-Henley line finally opened on 1 June 1857, Pritt took part in the celebrations. He gave up the villa three years later, though, in favour of a house in the Lake District. Westmorland was the native county of his wife, and the couple retired there permanently in 1866. Both sons meanwhile followed in their father's footsteps as parliamentary agents. Nowadays the lineal successor of Pritt & Co. is a practice called Winkworth Sherwood.

Hugh Mair

Edward Mackenzie soon found his next tenant in the shape of thirty-five-year-old Hugh Mair, a fellow Scottish capitalist, born and brought up in England. Indeed, the 1860s might be viewed as the period of Scottish ascendancy on Henley Reach, as a third Scot, the Edinburgh banker Edward Marjoribanks, occupied Greenlands till 1868. Mair exemplified as clearly as Mackenzie or Pritt the social changes arising from the Industrial Revolution, though he belonged to the third generation to benefit. The rise of the Mair family in the late eighteenth century began, paradoxically, with a dramatic fall – from the steeple of Paisley church by a stonemason working on it. John Mair had missed his footing but clung to a projecting stone till mattresses were fetched to soften his landing. After this experience, he sought a safer occupation and entered the burgeoning textile industry in Glasgow. The newly mechanised cotton mills were providing plenty of inexpensive cloth, and Mair emerged as a pioneering purveyor of decorative sewed muslin, a substitute for lace. Women outworkers, previously made redundant by the spinning mule, found new employment on piece-rates, sewing what was initially marketed as 'Ayrshire needlework'. Mair organised production in Scotland, while his son, also John (1766–1848), arranged distribution in England from Friday Street in the City of London. Sewed muslin proved a great commercial success. Hugh Mair was born on 28 February 1826, according to the registers of St Andrew's Church, Holborn, though in later life he gave the date as 2 March 1827. (His parents appear to have been unmarried at the time, despite his being at least their fourth child.) Soon after, John Mair of London built a country house called Nightingales at Chalfont St Giles in Buckinghamshire, where Hugh grew up. He then joined his brothers in the family business.

In the 1850s, as a consequence of further mechanisation, sewed muslin grew so very cheap as to forfeit its fashionable appeal, but the Mairs had by then made their fortune and diversified. Hugh bought a collection of residential properties near Dartmouth and invested in shares and commodities, while his self-description evolved from merchant to landowner to gentleman. His wife from 1865 was Henrietta Mair (possibly a cousin, for she did not change her surname). Their only child was called Mary Cassandra.

Mair would retain the lease of Phyllis Court for over forty years. At the end of them, the *Henley Standard* could nevertheless observe that, although a staunch Churchman and Tory, 'he took comparatively no part in the public work of the district'. This was largely because he was usually elsewhere. As a rule, the Mairs came to Henley only for the spring and early summer. They then decamped to Scotland, leasing Rowardennan Lodge by Loch Lomond. Winter saw them at their London residence or else on the Riviera. Mair's only significant local activities centred on the Regatta, of which he was elected a Steward in 1879, having signalled his interest by joining the Oxford University Boat Club. His nephew, John Mair, had been a student rower. There was always a house-party at Phyllis Court at Regatta time, and it may have been for the sake of guests that Mair enlarged and modernised the property. 'Phillis Court is almost new, so much has been done to it', wrote Roderick Mackenzie in 1892. The domestic staff increased accordingly, from four in 1871, to six in 1881, to eight in 1901, including a yacht engineer. Very few of the servants were local.

The Rise of Henley Royal Regatta

The most distinctive development at Henley during Victorian times was the extraordinary rise of the Regatta. It was not the first English town to establish one: Durham, Newcastle, Ryde, Dartmouth, Tewkesbury and Chester all had claims to seniority, but Henley soon became the foremost. Geography explains why. The modern sport of amateur competitive rowing traces its roots to Eton College and Westminster School in the late 1700s. From there it transferred with the young men themselves to Oxford and Cambridge Universities. The leading sporting rivers were thus the Thames and the Cam, with a bias towards the former, and Henley Reach is the longest straight stretch of the non-tidal Thames, with sufficient width for two or even three contesting crews. In retrospect, the ease with which Henley Regatta won its pre-eminence creates an impression of inevitability. To the original events of 1839, the Grand Challenge Cup (for eights) and Town Challenge Cup (for local fours), there were added within a decade the Stewards' Challenge Cup (fours), the Diamond Challenge (single sculls), the Ladies' Challenge Plate (eights), the Silver Goblets (pairs), the Visitors' Challenge Cup (fours) and the Wyfold Challenge Cup (originally eights, later fours). For English racing oarsmen, the Henley course of 'about one mile and 550 yards' against the flow became the most celebrated length of river in the world. A subscription of £50 from Prince Albert in 1851 permitted this festival of rowing to style itself Henley Royal Regatta.

For the prosperity of the town, it mattered that the rowers (and their friends and relations) were overwhelmingly persons of wealth. The first Stewards issued their challenge to crews from Oxford, Cambridge, and London Universities, the schools of Eton and Westminster, Guards officers, and established gentlemen's clubs. Amateur rowing was plainly an upper-class sport. When the Regatta in

Regatta
spectators in
the grounds
of Phyllis
Court in
1888.

1879 adopted a definition of an amateur that barred from competition anyone who 'is or has been by trade or employment for wages, a mechanic, artisan, or labourer', this was actually seen as a liberal ruling, as it did not limit participation to public school and Varsity men. The restriction lasted till 1938. As for the spectators, holding races only on weekdays (before 1911) excluded attendance by most working people. The number of aquatic enthusiasts grew as more public schools introduced rowing as part of the cult of athleticism and team sports in Victorian education. In the words of R.C. Lehmann, it was 'a noble open-air exercise, fruitful in lessons of strength, courage, discipline, and endurance'. In addition, Henley benefited from the fact that social exclusivity can act as a magnet in itself. The Prince Consort never attended the Regatta, but the Prince of Wales did latterly, bringing with him an extensive party of royalty in 1887.

Another factor in the growth of the Regatta was the railway. The *Illustrated London News* reported in 1857 that the new branch line had 'brought together a larger number of spectators than has ever been witnessed on a previous occasion'. Trains also overcame the difficulty of transporting boats from far afield. The first foreigners were Americans in 1878; then came a German crew in 1880. Six years later, the Regatta had to be extended from two to three days to fit in all the heats. This in turn meant more visitors. The Great Western Railway built longer platforms at the station, doubled the line, and brought in additional rolling stock to cope with the annual surge in demand. In 1895, the total number of people attending was put at 34,000. The form of transport that had so damaged Henley at first now assisted its revival, as sporting fame and aristocratic patronage lent the town a certain lustre. Rail improvements also facilitated commuting to London, and the resident population grew markedly, necessitating a wave of house-building. Phyllis Court might have found itself boxed in by suburban terraces; that it was not is due to the survival of the Fawley Estate, whose owners were rich enough to pass up the opportunities for property development.

W. Dalziel Mackenzie

The children of Edward Mackenzie were the first upper-class generation of their family and perhaps the more conventional in consequence. Each of the four sons received a country estate on the death of the tycoon in 1880, but the bulk of the property naturally went to the eldest, William Dalziel Mackenzie. Born in Renfrewshire in 1840, he had spent his infancy in France and been patted on the head at the age of four by Queen Marie Amalie, consort of King Louis Philippe. His education was entrusted to Harrow and Magdalen College, Oxford. Although called to the bar, he never practised as a lawyer. Both his wives belonged to the Oxfordshire gentry. Mary Anna, the first, was a daughter of Henry Baskerville of Crowsley Park (and one of her sisters married another of the Mackenzie brothers). She died in 1900. His second wife, also Mary, was the widow of Sir Francis Stapleton of Greys Court.

While continuing the commercial interests of his father to the extent of serving on the boards of the London and North Western Railway and the Caledonian Banking Company, W. Dalziel Mackenzie concentrated on performing the duties of a magistrate in five counties and a landed proprietor in seven. Politics attracted him. At the General Election of 1874 he stood as a Conservative in the forlorn hope of Reading, and reduced the Liberal majority. In May 1884 he secured the candidacy for the safe Tory seat of Woodstock in succession to Lord Randolph Churchill. His speech at the selection meeting roundly denounced Gladstone for abandoning General Gordon and imperilling the British Empire, but Mackenzie did not have much luck. The Redistribution of Seats Act (1885) abolished the parliamentary borough of Woodstock, which joined the new Mid-Oxfordshire constituency, and Mackenzie had to stand aside for Lord Valentia (who lost).

After this setback, he assumed more the role of a grouse-shooting, deer-stalking, salmon-fishing Scottish laird, styling himself Mackenzie of Farr after buying four additional sporting estates in Inverness-shire and Ross-shire. Breeding and showing Highland cattle was one of his hobbies. In the *Empire Review* in November 1903, he lamented the plight of the British agrarian landowner after thirty years of mass importing of food from America, Australia and Argentina. It was time for urban compatriots 'to say whether they are satisfied to be almost entirely dependent on foreign supplies, a national danger in time of war, or whether it is not to their advantage to encourage home industries, and ensure certain prosperity'. The outcome of the 1906 general election – a large majority for the Liberals and their policy of Free Trade – provided him with an unwelcome answer.

Outside the game seasons, Dalziel Mackenzie was usually resident at Fawley Court. (It was he who removed the stucco from the building and, finding the

Fawley Court
as it has
looked since
its enlargement
by W. Dalziel
Mackenzie in
1884.

brickwork badly decayed, refaced it with the reddest of red bricks.) He proved
a very active Steward of the Regatta, serving on its Committee of Management
between 1881 and 1923. This must at least have made him conscious of Phyllis
Court each summer.

Phyllis Court in Regatta Week

From the earliest years of the Regatta, Phyllis Court often received a passing mention in race reports as a convenient landmark of the course. Such references
became more frequent after 1886, when the Stewards responded to longstanding
complaints that a slight bend in the river at Poplar Point gave an unfair advantage
in the final quarter mile to crews rowing on the Berkshire side. The course was
accordingly shifted a little way to the north, so races would henceforth finish at
Poplar Point. Since this is just opposite the southern boundary of Phyllis Court,
its grounds have ever since been one of the two best spots from which to view the
climax of each race. It tended not to be young oarsmen who gathered there, however; they stayed mostly on the opposite bank, while Mair played host to selected
local gentry – above all, family and friends of fellow Stewards. In particular, groups
including ladies found beneath its trees both welcome shade and shelter from hoi
polloi. *Bell's Life in London*, the top sporting newspaper, had noted back in 1856
that 'the fashion and beauty in Phillis Court… showed no falling off whatever
from former years', while *Baily's Monthly Magazine* in 1875 indicated why ladies
might value such a haven: 'Phillis Court again looked so charming as to make us

involuntarily break the commandment (we forget its number in the book) which warns us against coveting, and the meadows beyond contained bivouacking friends in a profusion that rendered perfect sobriety, even with the most virtuous intentions, practically impossible.' Each year from 1882 to 1903, the adjoining field was rented for half a week by the Isthmian Club of Piccadilly.

By the last decades of the century, the spectators had clearly become for many visitors an integral part of the spectacle. *The County Gentleman* considered the event in 1896:

> For pure gaiety, as well as brilliancy, grace and buoyant vigour, no scene on racecourse or cricket field or tennis lawn is comparable with the river and the river-banks on one of the regatta days. Take your place, as we were fortunate enough to take ours this week, in the charming enclosure of the Isthmian Club, and survey the Watteau-like groups upon the tree-shaded sward. Listen to the gay chatter and the rippling laughter, and look out upon the animated scene presented by the river surface. Or, leaving this pleasant coign of vantage for a while, make your way along the Oxon-Bucks bank after a preliminary peep at Phillis Court, with its joyous promenaders or its gay and graceful figures seated under the 'spreading chestnut trees'. The chartered pic-nickers will claim a passing glance, making merry under the elms by the old fish pond. But the chief 'objective' of your stroll will be the house-boats, which were never before so many, so luxuriously appointed, so brave with bunting, or so bright with flowers.

Henley Royal Regatta 1887.

The houseboats had indeed become a great talking point at Henley. The first to moor on the Reach was *The Ark*, a relatively modest craft, in the early 1870s. Over the next fifteen years, however, they grew ever more numerous and extravagantly palatial, often captivating bystanders with their profusion of ornament. Newspaper reports routinely remarked on the latest decor of such vessels as the *Rouge et Noir, The Fair Maid of Perth, Dolce Far Niente, Lazy Land* and *Rêve d'Or*. Best known of all was *The Golden Grasshopper*, owned and let out by journalist Raymond Radclyffe. Commercial enterprise lay behind the phenomenon of luxury houseboats; a good Regatta let in July could cover running expenses for the rest of the year. Not everyone was favourably impressed. In 1884, the House of Commons appointed a Select Committee on the preservation of the upper Thames for purposes of public recreation. W. Dalziel Mackenzie appeared before it to air the grievances of riparian owners:

> Henley Regatta takes place next Thursday and Friday, and the houseboats have been in position since the end of last week. There are at the present moment 23 extending from above Phyllis Court downward. These houseboats are higher than the bank. Phyllis Court has a beautiful terrace walk along the river, but during this fortnight the tenant of that place is debarred from the pleasant use of his grounds. Last year the houseboats remained just below Phyllis Court for four months. I happened to see an advertisement in *The Morning Post…* offering a houseboat for Henley Regatta. It says it is 70 feet long, makes up 10 or 12 beds, with detached kitchen, water laid on, and has been across the Channel; to all intents and purposes a house.

This houseboat controversy brought even Mair into the public eye. *The World* warned that if he succeeded in clearing the riverbank at Phyllis Court, all his neighbours would follow suit, and the Regatta might even move elsewhere. *Baily's Monthly* at once hurried to his defence: Henley of late had been so overwhelmed by vulgar ostentation that 'men really interested in rowing have often during the past decade longed for a revival of the quaint old days when steam-launches and house-boats were unknown'. In 1885, the Thames Preservation Act empowered the Thames Conservancy 'to make special regulations for the prevention of annoyance to any occupier of a riparian residence by reason of the loitering or delay of any houseboat or steam launch'. Soon such vessels had to be registered, and moorings along the course were allotted according to the amount subscribed by the boatowners to Regatta funds, with no sub-letting allowed. *The Standard* could report in 1890: 'Off Phyllis Court are some small boats, in order that Mr Mair and his friends may not be entirely shut in; while, in order that they may catch a glimpse of the racing, a space at the lower end of the grounds has been left free from craft of any kind.'

Spartan rowing-men carried on grumbling about the excessive prominence of the social side of the Regatta: 'It is nothing but a vast picnic, and an exhibition of

pretty gowns, pretty faces, and flirtation *ad lib.*' The very periodical that printed this complaint, namely *Hearth & Home*, lent it some justification with its own Henley coverage, such as the following from 1895: 'The Hon. Mrs French was in white spotted muslin, with pale blue ribbons, and she assisted in doing the honours of... Phyllis Court; Mrs Thompson wore pale green silk, strapped with black velvet; Miss Gore-Booth was in leaf-green crépon and large hat with roses; Mrs Hamilton looked pretty in cream muslin, with a profusion of lace.' The Hon. Mrs French was actually Mary Cassandra Mair, married into the Anglo-Irish aristocracy. Her wedding had taken place at St Mary's, Henley on 28 July 1885, with the Hon. Robert French in the uniform of an officer of the 1st Gloucestershire Regiment. He was the youngest son of the 3rd Baron de Freyne (who had so far defied sectarianism in County Roscommon as to marry a Roman Catholic). Did the couple possibly owe their engagement to a meeting on the riverbank one July? Henley Royal Regatta had become a recognised part of the 'social season', and hence a place for eligible young ladies to encounter eligible young gentlemen in an informal setting, where a chaperone might even be given the slip. *Judy*, a magazine akin to *Punch*, published 'A Henley Memory' in 1887:

'On a Houseboat at Henley: A Pleasant Interlude' by Arthur Hopkirk (1894). (River & Rowing Museum)

How sweet in skiff to lounge near Phyllis Court
    (The name hath quite the true Arcadian ring),
Sweet Phyllis courting, heeding scarce the sport,
    Though Henley racing is the real thing.
Sweet brown-eyed Phyllis with the classic brow,
    And full curved lip, clad all in filmy white,
Through which there gleams a purer tint, I vow,
    Than dazzled Paris's judicial sight.

And a good deal more in amatory vein. Maybe even Hugh Mair himself managed to turn these romantic associations to advantage. Widowed at the age of seventy in October 1896, he re-married fourteen months later. His second wife, Emma Winearls, was thirty-nine years his junior. Their union lasted four years. Mair died in March 1902, leaving £161,000, and Emma vacated Phyllis Court. In October 1903, she wed Major Alexis Doxat, VC (1867–1942), a hero of the Boer War.

During the occupancy of the Mairs, Phyllis Court had turned back into a mansion and, as such, it has ever since lent a subtle rotational symmetry to the riverfront at Henley. Standing on the left bank, about a quarter of a mile north of the bridge, it corresponds to Thamesfield, another long, low, stuccoed Victorian villa, on the right bank about a quarter of a mile south of the bridge. Thanks to proximity to the Regatta winning post, moreover, Phyllis Court had achieved a measure of fame. It nevertheless remained vacant for the next three-and-a-half years. Reports in 1902 of the Guards' Club of Windsor taking the lease proved unfounded, and the Fawley Estate may not have felt much urgency, seeing that it could make £500 or more by renting out the property for just one week of the year – to the Stewards of the Regatta, who used Phyllis Court as their chief enclosure between 1902 and 1905, passing on half the receipts. Its obvious popularity (and profitability) prompted calls that they seek to guarantee its future availability. The Stewards, a mix of local notables and retired rowers, shied away from long-term commitments, however; they had never invested in property at all before buying a boathouse in 1903. To lease Phyllis Court would have been a big step. The Stewards hesitated – and lost out to the Finlays.

Here the history of Phyllis Court reaches the turning point of 1906 depicted at the start of this book. Hitherto a private dwelling, it would henceforth be a clubhouse. Strictly speaking, the Mackenzie Era had not yet come to an end, for the family continued to own the freehold up until 1929, but to extend this chapter accordingly would privilege consistency at the cost of common sense. To almost all intents and purposes, the next thirty years are the Finlay Era.

6

Finlay's Club
1907–1918

The inaugural year of the Phyllis Court Club was definitely a success. Proof of this could be seen from the fact that, by the time it opened for its second season on 1 June 1907, the Clubhouse had doubled in size. Two new wings to the south and the west maintained the style of the early Victorian house, magnifying its presence without distorting its character. The addition of a further seven bays to the eastern elevation created a frontage whose length could not fail to attract the notice of passers-by on the river or the towpath opposite, and inside its impact was even more striking, for the ground floor comprised just one spacious room, then designated the Luncheon Court (now the Ballroom). Some two hundred people could dine there simultaneously off monogrammed plates ('P.C.C.') while seated on rush and cane chairs of ornately curlicued design. On one side, bounded by six Ionic columns, a conservatory offered utterly English views across the Thames to the wooded hills of Remenham, while potted Kentia palms and a punkah evoked the style of colonial clubs in Singapore or Bombay. The proprietor was very particular about dispersing food smells. When building his own home at Shiplake, on the theory that odours rise, he had gone so far as to have bedrooms downstairs and the kitchen and dining room above. Here he settled for a sliding

The Luncheon Court at Phyllis Court in 1907.

Original Phyllis Court Club crockery.

roof in the centre of the room and a very large ventilation shaft. The oaken floor was constructed with dancing in mind; the Luncheon Court could be cleared of its rattan tables, and a baby grand piano from Érard of Paris stood ready. The decor was white and pale pink, enhanced for balls by hanging baskets of chrysanthemums and Safrano roses, strands of smilax wound around the pillars, and rose-tinted shades on the gasoliers. 'It was the perfect harmony of colour, that, despite its simplicity, gave the room such a charming appearance.'

A large glazed partition of many small panes divided the Luncheon Court from the Grand Lounge, whose darker tones of green and golden brown provided a marked contrast. Here more cane furniture interspersed the easy chairs and chesterfields. The transformation of the Clubhouse had been effected by Waring & Gillow; building work as well as fitting out. Indeed, almost the only objects *not* from Waring & Gillow appear to have been seven stuffed animal heads and the paintings. These, lent by Laura Finlay, were largely contemporary rural landscapes of the conservative sort, for instance, Sutton Palmer's *Cattle Drinking*, Alfred de Breanski's *The Shrimper and the Sunset*, and an epic view of Mont Blanc by Joseph Jansen.

Accommodation upstairs now extended to a total of thirty bedrooms (including a couple of small ones for a maid, valet or chauffeur). These were divided between

The Club's entrance.

Phyllis Court Club. The Boat House

three separate corridors; one for married couples, another for single ladies, and the third for single gentlemen. While the riverside venues of Maidenhead had a collective reputation for illicit liaisons second only to Brighton, Phyllis Court enjoined propriety:

> Within limits, Members and Lady Guest-Members may introduce Guests of either sex to the Club by day, but they may only engage bedrooms in the Club for Guests of their own sex. Thus, a Member's Wife, or other lady relative, before she may *reside* in the Club, must gain election to Guest-Membership. She may then engage rooms for herself and other lady friends. Likewise, a Member may engage bedrooms in the Club for his male friends only.

An incident at the Club did feature once in divorce court reporting (in 1925); the ground was cruelty and the petition failed.

Members returning in 1907 also found changes outside. A handsome glass canopy had been erected over the entrance to shelter visitors alighting from motor cars. There were new courts for tennis and croquet and new greens for bowls and clock-golf. A local firm had converted the moat into a mooring basin and built a large timber boathouse at its western end. This had a balcony as well as a stock of dinghies, punts, and canoes. Bill Haines, the Club waterman, was ten times winner of the Thames punting championship (professional section).

To celebrate these improvements, the Club held a garden party that 'would have been an unqualified success but for the inclemency of the weather'. The bandsmen of the 1st West Yorkshire Regiment returned to inaugurate proceedings with

The County Ball

'At Henley, the Phyllis Court Club is becoming the fashionable centre of river life', stated a national Sunday newspaper, the *Observer*. It stayed open till December in order to host the South Oxfordshire County Ball, usually held at the Town Hall, with Deputy Lieutenants and magistrates aplenty among the guests. Also present was Lady Ottoline Morrell, whose fame as a literary hostess has outlived that of her husband as constituency member. The conservatory and two upstairs rooms offered diners the following menu:

Consommé en Tasse
Mayonnaise de Homard Norvégienne
Faisan en Cocotte Chasseur
Côte d'Agneau Bohémienne
Médaillons de Volaille Régence
Perdreau d'Écosse sur Canapé
Poulets de Surrey aux Cressons
Jambon d'York à la Gelée
Langue de Bœuf Epicure
Dindonneau Farcie Perigueux
Pâté de Gibier Lucullus
Salade Parisienne
Gelée aux Fruits
Mousse Tyrolienne
Charlotte Opera
Œufs Pôchés 2 a.m.
Dessert

The evening, 'a brilliant gathering' according to the *Henley Standard*, showed local gentry who had not yet joined the Club just what they were missing. Enlargement of the premises had permitted re-opening of the membership list (closed from July 1906 to June 1907), with the limit raised from 500 to 1,200. The subscription now stood at eight guineas.

the *Wellington March*, followed by the *William Tell Overture* and Brahms' *Hungarian Dance No.5*. They were under canvas, but the croquet teams led by Lady Clayton and Sir William Bruce (father of actor Nigel Bruce) doggedly persisted through driving rain with only the aid of umbrellas. Other entertainments, brought indoors, included fencing, a one-act play, and Japanese wrestling 'demonstrated by some of its most famous exponents'. Jujitsu had recently arrived in Britain, and Yukio Tani and Mitsuyo Maeda were making a living by staging displays.

The summer of 1907 continued wet and windy, putting a damper on Regatta Week, when few members cared to use the special 'Venetian Restaurant' that stretched for two hundred feet along decking at the water's edge. Compared with the open enclosures, however, Phyllis Court fared well, as 'phenomenally adverse weather' made people appreciate its advantages. On the Friday it welcomed the *Alliance Franco-Britannique, Littéraire, Scientifique et Artistique*, a group of intellectuals desirous of deepening the *Entente Cordiale* whose link to the Club was Sir John Murray, marine biologist and oceanographer.

Roy Finlay

It has sometimes been assumed that, when starting the Club, Roy Finlay must have been backed by a business consortium. Such was not the case. In the lead-up to its opening in 1906, he had spent about £2,000 of his inheritance from his grandfather on refurbishing Phyllis Court and received two loans of £300 each from Miss M.E. Finlay (his sister 'Mimi') and Mrs H.P. Savage (his aunt 'Floss'). At the end of the first season, after expenses had been paid, it was found possible to write off £2,500 towards the capital expenditure account of the Phyllis Court Club Company. A profit of £1,000 from the Regatta Week and £3,000-worth of subscriptions in January 1907 left the firm with £4,000 in hand. This was highly satisfactory, but not enough to fund the expansion of the Clubhouse. Finlay therefore sought to raise extra capital by offering £5,000 of debentures to members in units of £10. Their response to this was so favourable that he increased the total issue in January 1907 to £6,000. Debenture-holders would be paid annual interest on their investment of 5 per cent and receive vouchers for the admission of lady guests during the Regatta. Persons investing over £200 also became life-members. All the debentures soon sold. They would be redeemed by annual drawings of £500 each, beginning in 1911, so as to clear the debt by 1922.

Debentures being just a way of borrowing, ownership of the Phyllis Court Club Company remained incontestably with Finlay. Its stated capital was £3,000 in £1 ordinary shares, and he held the ones numbered 1 to 400 and 408 to 3,000. In other words, the company was a device to limit his liability, and the 'straw men' who owned the other seven shares were very likely 'straw women' (his mother, sisters, aunts, and nieces). Meetings, as recorded in the minutes, could take on a mildly surreal quality, as R. Gedye Finlay, Managing Director of the Phyllis Court Club Company Ltd, negotiated with R. Gedye Finlay, Honorary Secretary of the Phyllis Court Club, and R. Gedye Finlay, lessee of Phyllis Court. The only other person usually present was Freddie Norsworthy, who acted as unpaid company secretary while still market-gardening at Shiplake. The company never declared a dividend. Instead, Finlay drew a salary as Managing Director. This he set in 1907 at £300 per annum (plus board and lodging), with the intention of increasing it to £500 by 1911.

Looking back, it seems obvious that Finlay found his niche at Phyllis Court: a round peg in a round hole, so to speak. He had been born on 19 November 1881 at Woollahra, an eastern suburb of Sydney that took its name from an aboriginal word for 'camp', 'meeting place', or 'place for sitting down'. What could be more appropriate for the founder of a social club? It is notable, however, that his Australian origins did not lodge in the collective memory of Phyllis Court, although he can hardly be accused of concealing them. Every August in the early years he absented himself from Henley for a fortnight of military training as a lieutenant in the King's Colonials, Imperial Yeomanry, later renamed King Edward's Horse (The King's Oversea Dominions Regiment). Its distinctive khaki and scarlet uniform included a slouch hat (albeit one plumed with blackcock feathers in *bersaglieri* style), and the Australasian squadron wore a kangaroo cap-badge. No doubt many upper-class Britons treated colonials with condescension. Perhaps in reaction, wealthy Sydneysiders of the late nineteenth century were actually genteel almost to excess, eager to emulate the ways of the motherland, and second to none in their Imperial patriotism. Since leaving Australia at the age of fourteen, moreover, Finlay had lived in a cosmopolitan environment, thanks in part to polyglot paternal relatives. His education was undertaken by tutors of various nationalities and a school at Territet on the Swiss bank of Lake Geneva. Fashionable and fastidious, he played the piano, sang a passable tenor, smoked Turkish cigarettes, enjoyed theatregoing and participated keenly in skiing and rowing. To Henley he had taken an immediate liking, calling it 'a gem placed in as superb a setting as could be found anywhere in the world', and it pleased him to think that his work at Phyllis Court was adding a new facet to it. 'He was a lovable and witty person', recalled a friend, 'easy to get on with and an asset to any party'. Already well travelled, well read and, crucially, interested in people, he could draw on a wide range of associations in order to sustain conversation with new acquaintances.

For all his youth, however, Finlay was not so naïve as to suppose that easy manners and a gift for friendship were enough to ensure success (or even survival) as proprietor of a river club. His character, although superficially emollient, possessed a marked streak of determination – and he was going to need it. He had a sharp eye for detail, and no aspect of housekeeping was too menial to warrant his attention. This was a man who noted down recipes, thought hard and long about soft furnishings, and personally designed the patterns to be woven into the carpets. Gadgets held some appeal for him, as he always had to have 'the latest thing' and, despite abandoning commercial horticulture, he retained an interest in gardening. Mr Gatis, head gardener at the Club, received both close supervision and a generous budget. The priority outdoors was to eradicate the dense evergreens that had taken over in Mair's time, for Finlay wanted the bigger trees to be seen to best advantage. He also demanded a multitude of flowers, and within a few years the floral displays had become an attraction in themselves. Witness the admiration of this anonymous visitor:

> To me the old-world garden is one of the greatest charms at Phyllis Court. Roses were in profusion, and I have never seen such masses of delphiniums. Many of the trusses of blooms stood 6ft. high, and the colours were pale and light mauve, deep royal blue and purple, blue with white centres. In fact, save at a great flower-show, I have never seen such exquisite blooms.

Elaborate flower arrangements were also a feature of the interior. The proprietor had himself invented a device where 'by means of some green tin tubes the stalks of the roses and their foliage were so arranged that the effect of a magnificent standard rose with masses of foliage was achieved.'

Finlay loved Phyllis Court with an intensity that transcended purely commercial considerations. He never married and it was sometimes remarked that, apart from his mother, 'Phyllis' was the only woman in his life (though the men in his life were another story, one about which he had, perforce, to be highly discreet). The Club was his pride and joy, as well as his fortune and livelihood, so it is understandable that he felt concerned to guard his place in the seat of power, literally the leather-upholstered revolving chair in the Secretary's office. It is also understandable that the Founders' Committee should have expressed anxiety about this very young man taking so much upon himself. Finlay acknowledged that combining the duties of Managing Director and Honorary Secretary produced a heavy workload, but 'he

The 1908 Olympics

By 1908, the membership had nearly reached its limit, and Finlay had high hopes of a summer with not just one but two regattas: three weeks after the Royal Regatta, the rowing races of the Olympic Games (based in London) would take place on Henley Reach. Dating from 1896, the international Olympic movement was still in its formative stage; even the five-ring symbol had yet to be devised. Oarsmen from eight countries (Belgium, Canada, Germany, Great Britain, Hungary, Italy, the Netherlands and Norway) assembled to contest four events over four days, and Phyllis Court participated in the hospitality programme. First it presented a Grand Pastoral Concert ('pastoral' simply meaning open-air) with the Band of the Royal Irish Fusiliers and ballads from the young Australian baritone Peter Dawson. Then it gave a luncheon, one day before the races, with practically all the competitors attending. The Hon. Edward Stonor greeted them in English, French, German and Italian, and speeches followed from Count Brunetta D'Usseaux, Italian representative on the International Olympic Committee, and Lord Desborough, President of the British Olympic Association. The week proved a triumph in sporting terms, with Britain winning every event (and topping the overall medal table), but Society

Lord Desborough, President of the British Olympic Association and Vice-President of the Phyllis Court Club.

favoured Goodwood over a second round of Henley. 'The attendance at the Olympic Regatta could only be described as fair', lamented Finlay, 'and the money receipts were rather disappointing.' At least the Club could boast a valued Vice-President in the shape of Willie Grenfell, 1st Baron Desborough, all-round sportsman and head of the Thames Conservancy. He would later preside over the Marylebone Cricket Club and the Lawn Tennis Association.

preferred to fulfil the duties of Honorary Secretary as long as he could, as it saved the Company the extra expense of the salary and keep of a Secretary'. He had agreed in November 1906 to appoint a second director of the company. This was Captain Fitzroy Paget, over twice his age and the first cousin of a Committee member. Four months later, the company minutes recorded that the new director had ceased to act, having failed to take up his statutory share. Another seven months went by before Paget sent Finlay this one-sentence letter: 'Owing to want of time, and uncertain health, it would be as well to allow the subject of the directorship to lapse.' The company had in the meantime sought 'some suitable person who would give his services as Hon. Secretary in return for his keep'. Captain Charles E.M. Morrison, a friend of the Finlay family, worked at Phyllis Court on this basis during the 1907 season. Vernon Holt and St John Mildmay did so jointly the following year, before Morrison returned in 1909. The Committee was partially satisfied by these arrangements. No-one, after all, could dispute the popularity of the Club.

The final bill from Waring & Gillow came as an unpleasant shock in the autumn of 1908. Even after threats of legal action over unauthorised extras reduced it by £500, the total of the building and furnishing accounts amounted to £9,000. Finlay responded by offering members five hundred more debentures of £20 each at 5 per cent interest, repayable after twenty years. This second issue was not fully subscribed, but it raised £6,000 by May 1909, which sufficed (when added to profits) to clear all but £600 of the debt. It also financed construction of a large new garage, north-west of the Clubhouse; 'this, it is hoped, will get over the difficulties of the crowded drives in the height of the season'. Already the Club enforced a one-way system, with vehicles entering from the Marlow Road and exiting into New Street. Later in the year, work started on four new tournament-sized croquet courts, 'equal to any in the South of England', in addition to the existing two.

Another busy season had emphasised the need for more accommodation of all kinds. The rival attractions of the river and the turf came together neatly each June:

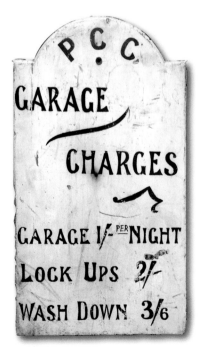

> Phyllis Court was all last week filled with the usual Ascot house party. Every room was taken by members and their guests, who went to the races during the day-time in motors and returned in the cool of the evening to dine and sleep at the Club. So popular has this become that the rooms are all booked up months ahead.

Military bands played every Sunday and many Saturdays throughout the summer. Members set up weekly archery meetings and tennis tournaments. As for the famous first week of July, Mrs Baillie-Saunders, writing in *The Star*, ended her survey of Regatta diversions with this ringing endorsement:

> So does one lay traps to keep bachelors during the whole time; these attractions plus those of the Phyllis Court Club, wherein there is surely nothing wanting to the heart of man: nothing unstudied or unprovided for. Here, should weather prove treacherous and rainy, as it is as likely as not to do, he can turn in to his billiards, his bridge, lively music, his gayest social life with the best of his 'set' ready to hand. His most Epicurean wishes will be forestalled. Nothing short of lunacy, or an entanglement, or a seat in the House of Commons would draw a man from such a Paradise.

Even so, in 1910, the Phyllis Court Club very nearly collapsed.

The Upheaval of 1910

The first significant skirmish between the Founders' Committee and Finlay had been fought in 1908 on territory universally familiar to clubmen in contention: the cost of meals. The Committee wanted prices cut; the proprietor feared damaging financial consequences. The Committee rigidly insisted; the proprietor gave way. The second dispute was specific to Henley. In Regatta Week, Finlay divided the grounds of Phyllis Court in two. The southern portion, including the Clubhouse, was reserved for members and their private guests, while the northern portion was open to anyone willing and able to pay £1 for a day-pass (a sum then equal to an unskilled labourer's weekly wage). Members complained of overcrowding, and the Committee demanded the exclusion of the general public from the entire site. Finlay firmly resisted this: the Visitors' Enclosure was highly profitable, and the Club prospectus had stated that the proprietor retained 'the right of throwing open the grounds' on race days. No meeting of minds proved possible, and relations deteriorated. Even when the catering made a loss of £674 in 1909, the Chairman, Sir Douglas Dawson, refused to retract. On the contrary, the Committee-men assumed a more active role by setting up a House Committee to meet weekly. It comprised five members of the Founders' Committee (Dawson himself, Churchill, Valentia, Stonor, and Egerton Green) plus Major-General Vesey Dawson (brother of Sir Douglas), Roderick Mackenzie, and Wilfred Rhodes. With civil understatement, Finlay noted 'that this would relieve him of much responsibility in ordinary matters of detail concerning the routine management of the household, but that he foresaw some difficulty in controlling the finances of the Company and at the same time acceding to the requests of the House Committee'. Solicitors were consulted.

Colonel Sir Douglas Dawson, Chairman of the Founders' Committee 1907–10.

In March 1910, an audit revealed unexpectedly large debts to caterers and suppliers. This was serious, as the Phyllis Court Club Company had used up its reserves to pay off Waring & Gillow, and a crisis of confidence developed. Tradesmen had learnt not to trust young river clubs. Finlay cut his own salary to £200, but plans for a third debenture issue met with a poor response. He attributed the problems to the fact 'that the policy of the Founders' Committee, whilst excellent in many ways, was disastrous in so far as the financial affairs of the Club were concerned', and he tried to win over the other people with a substantial material interest in its survival, the thirty-seven life-member debenture-holders. They elected a Finance Committee, chaired by Sir James Williamson, a former director of the Admiralty dockyards, but this new body disappointed Finlay by failing to stand up to the Founders' Committee at two emergency meetings at the Savoy Hotel in London. If their interest went unpaid, one lawyer advised, debenture-holders should appoint a receiver, seize Phyllis Court, and let it out during Regatta Week for their own exclusive benefit. Increasingly embattled, the proprietor perceived 'the presence in Henley of a certain set who were opposed to the presence of a Club at Phyllis Court, and who had not lost an opportunity of acting contrary to its interests upon occasion arising'. Precisely whom he meant is unclear, though it may be supposed that the Stewards of the Regatta (itself in financial difficulties) regretted his refusal to allow them any stake in the Visitors' Enclosure. For its part, the Founders' Committee held Finlay himself responsible for the declining credit of the Club, and resolutions passed on 28 April 1910 amounted to a palace coup. The outcome was announced in these terms:

> Drastic alterations have been made in the management of the Phyllis Court Club at Henley this season. The new secretary is Mr W. Onslow Secker, and the management has been entirely taken over by the committee. The catering has been placed in the hands of a prominent London club. The subscription has been altered to £5 5s with no entrance fee for the present, and ladies' badges are issued at £2 2s. Members of recognised London clubs will be admitted without a ballot. For Henley Regatta, it has been the practice in previous years to reserve a portion of the river frontage as a public enclosure. This will not be the case at this year's regatta…. In future, Phyllis Court will be sacred to the use of its own members only and to members' private guests. It will not be easy, therefore, for those who are not members of the Club to enjoy the beauties of 'Phyllis' unless they have friends at 'Court'.

Finlay, now sidelined, believed that closing the Visitors' Enclosure and reducing subscriptions would only make losses very much worse. The Founders' Committee imagined that these measures would prove the salvation of the Club by stimulating a dramatic increase in the membership. Time would tell, but Finlay himself could not be at Phyllis Court to witness the experiment. In June, he fell gravely ill with typhoid. His mother returned from Dinard to be at his bedside at the Hill View Nursing Home. Not till the autumn was he fit to address the affairs of the Club Company. He found them in disarray.

Income was £2,500 down on the previous year. The debt had climbed to £2,064, and there was 'a total absence of funds at the banks'. Finlay's sister Mimi (actually Mildred) had to lend the Company £300 to pay the rent. Almost every day brought exchanges of solicitors' letters. Finlay cannot have appreciated the intervention of Sir Frank Crisp, who proposed that he clear the debt by selling 95 per cent of his shares to members. To understand the scale of the deficit, it helps to bear in mind that £2,000 was enough to buy four semi-detached houses in 1910. On 13 October, Laura Finlay threw the business a life-line by offering to guarantee its £700 overdraft on condition 'that the present Secretary of the Club cease to hold office'. Finlay consulted the Finance Committee and then sacked Secker with immediate effect.

The Managing Director further stated that, prior to dismissing the Secretary, he was fully aware that such action on his part would probably result in the withdrawal of the Chairman of the Founders' Committee from the Club, owing to the fact that the Secretary had been introduced by him, and that… he had come to the conclusion that this could unfortunately not be avoided under all the circumstances, and that in the full knowledge of this he had still decided that there was no other alternative than to act as he had done. And Mr Finlay fully expected the resignation of the whole of the Founders' Committee should the Chairman resign.

This is what happened on 25 October and, of the nine founders, it appears that only the Hon. Edward Stonor subsequently returned to Phyllis Court. The Club, though in a parlous state, was back under Finlay's control, and he would combine the roles of Honorary Secretary and Managing Director for the next twenty-three years. Life-member debenture-holders agreed that its management should once again be undertaken by the Company, with a new Debenture Holders' Committee meeting twice a year (in lieu of the Finance Committee) to proffer advice and inspect the accounts. Finlay announced that a new General Committee would be elected, 'which, unlike the late Founders' Committee, would be composed entirely of paying Members… and would control, subject to the veto of the Company, the social affairs of the Club'. He also declared that he 'had several schemes in mind for increasing the membership of the Club in a manner consistent with the present exclusiveness'.

It is unlikely that Finlay ever worked harder to preserve the Phyllis Court Club than during 1911, even though lacking his full health and vigour until almost the middle of the year. Help with administration in the meantime came from Captain Percival Long Innes, late of the Royal Australian Artillery. This left Finlay free to concentrate on measures to tackle the debt. Two were obvious: a renegotiation of catering contracts and the reinstatement of the Visitors' Enclosure (later renamed the Junior Phyllis Court Enclosure). An additional £500 overdraft, guaranteed by his mother, kept the firm trading until the Regatta. He also persuaded some debenture-holders to accept interest payments in the form of vouchers to be exchanged at the Club, and this became a permanent arrangement. A longer-term danger had also to be faced: the impact on membership of the loss of the Founders' Committee, gentlemen of fashion who carried weight in Pall Mall and St James's. Finlay applied his social gifts to nurturing direct relations with London clubs and offered their members preferential terms. A form of country membership was created for people unlikely to visit frequently. Arrangements with Henley Golf Club (founded 1907) and Temple Golf Club (founded 1909) supplemented Phyllis Court's sports facilities.

Fortune now smiled on Finlay: the summer of 1911 was wonderfully sunny. Regatta attendance broke all records; for the first time, finals were rowed on a Saturday. Even on Thursday afternoon, Phyllis Court served two thousand teas, and profits for the week were almost triple those of the previous year. The General Committee could report that the Club 'had experienced its most satisfactory season since its foundation'. The deficit, which peaked at £3,015, was reduced to £1,392 entirely out of income, and confidence returned. Roy Finlay felt able to sail away on a two-month trip to visit his brother Alan, then stationed in Delhi with the Gordon Highlanders, though Phyllis Court was never far from his thoughts. He negotiated visiting membership schemes with several Indian service clubs.

'Social Tone'

The new Committee certainly proved better at running the Club – or letting Finlay run it – yet it could not match its predecessor in prestige. The Founders' Committee had boasted four peers, two sons of peers, and two grandsons of peers; the General Committee entirely lacked a lord. Its Chairman was Laurence Hancock, a stock-broker, of Ladye Place, Hurley. Captain the Hon. Charles Wentworth-Fitzwilliam, a younger son of the 6th Earl Fitzwilliam, held the post of Crown Equerry (in charge of the Royal Mews). The Hon. Lionel Walrond MP was heir to the new barony of Waleran. Sir John L. Langman was a first baronet, and Dudley Cory Wright the brother of a baronet. From the navy came Captain Edmond Hyde-Parker, Chief of Staff of the Portsmouth Command, and Lieutenant Hubert Gore-Langton, a nephew of the 4th Earl of Stowe. Lieutenant-Colonel John G. Adamson (a Deputy Lieutenant of County Leitrim) and Captain Hugh Grimes had retired from active service; Major Malcolm D. Graham would shortly become Assistant Military Secretary to the Commander-in-Chief in South Africa. F.M. Fisk was an American, head of the British office of Parke, Davis & Co., a pharmaceutical com-pany. Two other professional men completed the Committee: Alfred Michelson, a solicitor, and Morton Smale, a dentist, who chaired a section of the International Medical Congress held in London in 1913.

If, as looks likely from his press releases, Finlay kept a trophy list of titled people at Phyllis Court, it is probably because he felt the need. Some traditionally minded aristocrats disparaged residential clubs outside London, contending that persons of the highest social standing passed Saturday to Monday at the country houses of their family and friends, so only parvenus had to resort to commercial hospi-tality. 'Why are there no country clubs in England?' asked Ralph D. Blumenfeld in the American magazine *Town and Country* in September 1911. In the United States since the 1890s, country clubs had become recognised centres of élite social life, found on the outskirts of practically every prosperous town of any size, so Americans who crossed the Atlantic expected to find their equivalent. Blumenfeld answered his own question with an essay on the class-consciousness of the English:

> Of course you have to start your club with the usual layer of titled personalities in order to attract the smaller fry. Thus, no club sees the light unless it has at least three lords

and a couple of baronets on its list of directors, with usually an earl or a marquess for chairman. … But that is just where this country club idea fails in England. The class line prevents it. People will not go to such places because they either consider themselves too good to mix in social intercourse with others who may possibly own a shop in London, or else, owning a shop in London themselves, they may feel uncomfortable in the presence of their 'betters' or that there may be unkind remarks about their presumption in forcing themselves in.… Of course, Ranelagh is an ideal country club and so is Hurlingham, but they are exceedingly exclusive and no one sleeps there. Phyllis Court, on the Thames, approximates more closely to anything that is known in the United States, but the Thames is a negligible quantity owing to the weather. Sometimes, as in this year, the season goes on for five or six months; at others the rain kills it all. And even here at Phyllis Court, where they only admit people who are members of recognized first-class clubs in London, the eternal class line steps in. I have heard people say many times: 'Yes, Phyllis Court is very beautiful, but then the company is *so* mixed, isn't it?'

The suggestion that only those lacking a country home of their own would wish to join the Phyllis Court Club is demonstrably false. The membership included a fair proportion of the residents of riverside mansions on the Upper Thames, as well as of the fashionable set who rented one for Henley Week or the entire river season. The Regatta always gave Phyllis Court a special status among river clubs. Receiving Cliveden as a wedding present in 1906 had not discouraged Waldorf and Nancy Astor from becoming original members, though admittedly they were American. It is noticeable that some of the highest ranking users of the Club, such as the 12th Viscount Massereene, the 16th Lord Elphinstone and the 13th Earl of Kinnoull, were Irish or Scottish peers, whose ancestral seats were too distant from London for easy weekend entertaining. The 9th Duke of Manchester, a nephew of Lord Gosford, held a number of parties at the Club; a gambling addict, he had already gone bankrupt and later served time in Wormwood Scrubs. Newspaper paragraphs about Phyllis Court also mentioned the 7th Earl of Macclesfield and the 5th Viscount Exmouth, teenagers both. Any visits by three noble Vice-Presidents recruited in 1906 (the 6th Marquess of Anglesey, 14th Earl of Pembroke, and 9th Earl of Kintore) appear to have gone unreported.

The Hurlingham Club had enjoyed royal patronage almost from its birth. Phyllis Court had to wait. It disappointed all Henley that King Edward VII never once attended the Regatta after ascending the throne. His family seemed to lack real enthusiasm for sports involving neither horses nor dogs. The first royal visitor to the Phyllis Court Club was actually the Crown Prince of Serbia on 15 August 1907. He came as a guest of Sir Alfred Rollitt, a former Conservative MP turned Liberal, whose anti-German views made him keen to repair Anglo-Serbian relations as part of the imminent Anglo-Russian Entente. The pro-Russian King of Serbia had come to power in 1903 after conspirators butchered his pro-Austrian

The Club's first
royal visitor:
Crown Prince
George of
Serbia.

rival, and Britain deplored his failure to prosecute the murderers. Now this informal tour by his son, travelling as the
Count of Oreshatz, signified a reluctant rapprochement. The
Prince, incidentally, never became king. Forced to renounce
his right of succession after kicking a servant to death, he was
held in an asylum while his brother reigned, though he lived
out his later years quietly enough as Mr George Karageorgević
in communist Yugoslavia.

Three royal brothers brought to Phyllis Court by Sir Douglas
Dawson in 1908 and 1909 came closer to mainstream ideas of
good social standing. The Duke of Teck and Princes Francis
and Alexander of Teck were Serene Highnesses, related via
a morganatic marriage to the King of Württemberg, but they
were also British-born graduates of Sandhurst, and their sister
Mary was the Princess of Wales. The Duke, latterly Marquess
of Cambridge, served as military attaché in Vienna and secretary to General Sir Douglas Haig. Well-known in his day as
a fashionable clubman, Prince Francis is now remembered for
giving rise to a legal precedent after his early death in 1910,
when his will made such generous provision for a certain married lady that the
Palace intervened to seal it. All royal wills have since remained secret. Prince
Alexander, as Earl of Athlone, followed a career of public service, including terms
as Governor-General of South Africa and Canada. Prince Leopold of Battenberg,
a short-lived grandson of Queen Victoria, dined at Phyllis Court on 8 July 1911.

Finlay liked to keep the press informed of royal approval. Thus we know that
the Crown Prince of Serbia 'expressed his admiration for the Phyllis Court Club',
Prince Francis of Teck 'more than ever expressed his satisfaction at its advancement', and Prince Leopold of Battenberg 'was heard to remark that he had no idea
that Henley possessed such a beautiful Club'. Similar treatment was merited by
Ethel Roosevelt, eighteen-year-old daughter of the former President of the United
States, when she stayed the night at Phyllis Court on 1 June 1910. Her father
Theodore was to lecture at Oxford the following week. The American party 'was
greatly pleased by the Club'.

A few other royal connections could not be discussed out loud. The Marquise
d'Hautpoul de Seyre, an aunt of Lord Camoys, supported the Phyllis Court Club
for decades. As Julia Stonor, prior to marriage, she was reckoned a member of
'H.R.H.'s Virgin Band', that is, one of the several younger women with whom the
future Edward VII had brief affairs between his liaisons with Lily Langtry and Daisy
Warwick. She also maintained a lifelong platonic friendship with his son, King
George V, who had a considerable crush on her in his youth. Her husband, the
Marquis, was a French Legitimist, a director of the Ritz, and 'one of the finest

waltzers of the day'. The Hon. George Keppel belonged to the Club too. His wife Alice was King Edward's last mistress.

Running low on aristocrats, Finlay publicised politicians: 'Phyllis Court has become quite a rendezvous for Members of both sides of the House and every Sunday many well-known MPs are to be seen enjoying the cool of the Club's shaded lawns.' Even though the Founders' Committee had been over-whelmingly Conservative, it had not packed the Club with men of its own persuasion. True, Sir Robert Hermon-Hodge, the former (and future) Tory MP for South Oxfordshire, held honorary membership, while his Liberal successor, Philip Morrell, did not, but Hermon-Hodge (afterwards 1st Baron Wyfold) perhaps enjoyed a higher profile in hunting, racing, and rowing than in politics at the national level.

In fact, Phyllis Court's most prominent parliamentarians were at this time nearly all Liberals, with Alexander Murray and Rufus Isaacs topping the list. Murray, the Master of Elibank, combined natural bonhomie with a talent for intrigue and thus made a good Chief Whip. Isaacs, one of the foremost barristers of the era, joined the Cabinet as Attorney-General and would go on to become Viceroy of India and briefly Foreign Secretary, while rising higher in the peerage (as 1st Marquess of Reading) than any commoner since the 1st Duke of Wellington. Their guests were sometimes more famous than themselves. Murray entertained the Prime Minister, H.H. Asquith, at Phyllis Court in August 1911. Party antagonism was then extremely bitter because of the Parliament Act, and its fiercest Diehard opponent, Lord Halsbury, had himself paid a visit just a few days earlier; his heir, Viscount Tiverton, was a member. Isaacs brought his friend David Lloyd George to the Club on Sunday 23 July 1911. The Chancellor of the Exchequer was the talk of all Europe that weekend, having ventured beyond his depart-mental remit in a speech at the Mansion House on Friday night to intervene in the Moroccan Crisis, warning Germany not to delude itself that Britain wanted peace at any price. The conjunction of the three names – Isaacs, Lloyd George, and Murray – calls to mind the 'Marconi Scandal' of 1912–13, when their lack of candour about share transactions caused a political storm.

Cecil Harmsworth, Liberal MP for Luton, owned a house in Henley and had long frequented the Phyllis Court Club. A

Ethel Roosevelt, daughter of Theodore, visited in 1910.

Rufus Isaacs MP, later Marquess of Reading, the foremost politician among early members.

brother of the press barons Northcliffe and Rothermere, he served as Under-Secretary of State at the Home Office and then at the Foreign Office. Alexander Ure, 1st Baron Strathclyde, engaged in more partisan rhetoric than is usual for a Scottish law officer. Australian-born copper-importer Sir Charles Henry was another close friend of Lloyd George (while his wife was an even closer one). Less conspicuous at Westminster were Sir Charles Nicholson, Walter Waring and Sir Charles Day Rose, although the last, a Canadian banker given to faddish enthusiasms, may have achieved some kind of immortality, as his passion for driving around the Thames Valley at speed reputedly informed the character of Toad in Kenneth Grahame's *The Wind in the Willows* (1908).

Tory MPs among the early membership were all backbenchers. Old Sir Henry Kimber and young Viscount Helmsley addressed the House fairly often; the Hon. Arthur Stanley and the Hon. Lionel Walrond very seldom. Racehorses preoccupied Colonel Sir William Hall Walker (later 1st Baron Wavertree), founder of the National Stud.

Leading figures from the world of business had also joined the Club. The 1st Baron Joicey dominated the Durham coal industry, while the 1st Baron Knaresborough chaired the North Eastern Railway. Sir Hudson Kearley, 1st Baron Devonport, was an archetypal self-made man, whose entrepreneurial flair turned the International Stores into the largest grocery chain in the south of England. Sir Christopher Furness, 1st Baron Furness, was a shipping magnate from Hartlepool; his private yacht *Emerald* became the first turbine-powered vessel to cross the Atlantic in 1903. All four men had also been Liberal MPs. Sir Clifton Robinson, 'the Tramway King', ran public transport in numerous cities from London to Los Angeles. Sir Lincoln Tangye manufactured hydraulic systems in Birmingham. Financiers at Phyllis Court included Robert Fleming from Dundee, a pioneer of investment trusts (and the grandfather of novelist Ian Fleming), and Anthony J. Drexel II from Philadelphia, whose daughter was rated 'the catch of the season' when she wed Viscount Maidstone in 1910.

To re-burnish the reputation of Phyllis Court, in 1911 Finlay staged two grand functions to mark the Coronation. Guest lists were devised in consultation with the Hospitality Committee of the Festival of the Empire, a body co-ordinating activities for distinguished visitors from overseas. Publicity for the garden party on 17 June declared that the Dominion Prime Ministers had been invited. Laurier (Canada), Fisher (Australia), Botha (South Africa), Ward (New Zealand), and Morris (Newfoundland) were all in great demand, with invitations that very day to luncheon at the Constitutional Club and dinner with the Highland Society, so who actually attended the garden party is uncertain. 'The social function was of a private character', stated the subsequent press reports. Fortunately, Canada and Australia had plenty of provincial and state premiers to go round. The eight hundred guests that Saturday afternoon established a precedent for entertaining

Army and Navy

The number of army officers in the Club at first sight appears overwhelming. A proportion of them held commissions in the Yeomanry and had never fired a shot in anger, but the tally of professional soldiers is still impressive. Of the veterans, Major-General James Calder Stewart of the Bengal Army had taken part in the relief of Lucknow in 1857, and it would be hard to name a campaign thereafter in which no member had fought. Many gentlemen meeting in the Smoking Room or Billiard Room must have found a ready topic of conversation in shared experiences of battling the Ashanti, Zulu, Afghans, Boers, Egyptians, Sudanese or Burmese. Despite all these captains, majors, lieutenant-colonels, and colonels – or possibly even because of them – the very top brass were not much in evidence, though General Lord Methuen visited in 1907 and Field Marshal Lord Grenfell in 1909.

The Phyllis Court Club scored higher in admirals. The naval career of Sir John Hopkins lasted fifty years and saw him rise to Commander-in-Chief of the Mediterranean Fleet (1897–99). This same command was entrusted in 1912 to Sir Archibald Berkeley Milne, a favourite of the King since his time as captain of the royal yacht *Victoria and Albert*. His failure in 1914 to stop the enemy cruisers *Goeben* and *Breslau* reaching Constantinople (where they helped bring Turkey into the war on the German side) has reinforced perceptions of him as a 'spit and polish' peacetime admiral. Controversy also dogged Sir Albert Markham who, despite fame as a polar explorer, could never escape association with a disastrous incident in 1893, when his ship HMS *Camperdown* rammed HMS *Victoria*, which sank with the loss of 358 lives. The Royal Navy did not censure Markham, who had scrupulously carried out the misguided orders of his superior officer (who drowned), but many civilians doubted the merit of his unconditional obedience. Admiral Lord Charles Beresford, 'smart set' celebrity and sometime MP, came to the Club several times as a guest – but not after 1910.

the High Commissioners and Agents-General of the Dominions at the Club. Each year, usually on the weekend after Royal Ascot (when anyone who was anyone sought to be seen on the Upper Thames), influential folk connected with Canada, Australasia, or the Cape congregated at Phyllis Court. Soon visiting membership schemes had been agreed with thirty-five clubs in the colonies.

Twelve days after the garden party followed the 'Grand Ball in honour of the Visitors from His Majesty's Oversea Dominions'. The Great Western Railway ran a special train, leaving Paddington at 8.15 p.m. and returning at 2.30 a.m. Fortnum & Mason did the catering. Herr Stanislaus Wurm supervised the music. (These were the years when no ball was complete without *Gold and Silver* and *The Merry Widow Waltz*. Nearly all the dance orchestras hired by the Club for special events originated in central Europe: if not Herr Stanislaus Wurm's White Viennese Band, then Herr Moritz Wurm's Blue Viennese Band, the Wurms being brothers and rivals. Then again, there was Herr Viktor Vorzanger's Austrian Band or his Hungarian Band, with cimbalom, or Herr Julian Kandt's Austro-Hungarian Band.) Tickets were a guinea each, including champagne and supper, and Finlay had assembled ten titled patronesses. Two were duchesses, both American-born, the one of Manchester and the other of Marlborough; the latter, railroad heiress Consuelo Vanderbilt, brought a party from Blenheim Palace every day to Henley Regatta and took to using the Club. A third patroness was Lady Desborough of Taplow, only a baroness but recognised as one of the foremost hostesses of her day. 'The success of the ball is a most important matter', declared the *Henley Standard*, 'as there is a whisper that should the success prove complete the problem of the oft-suggested "Henley Ball" will be solved, and the function may be established as an annual one, taking place on the Thursday before the Royal Regatta each year.' This prophecy was fulfilled, although the ball later moved to the Saturday evening after the finals. Finlay announced that any profits (at least on this first occasion) would be donated to Regatta funds. Neither Coronation party directly enriched the Club, but that was not the point. Membership increased that year by approximately five hundred.

Consolidation

Phyllis Court was flourishing. The Regatta drew crowds of unprecedented size to Henley in 1912, due to the presence on the final day of King George V, Queen Mary, and Princess Mary. Arriving by train, they walked to Hobbs' Boathouse to board the royal barge, which liveried oarsmen rowed beneath the bridge to a

The Royal Barge at Henley in 1912.

special pavilion erected by the Stewards on the Berkshire bank of the river. Few had a clearer view of their Majesties than the members of the Phyllis Court Club opposite, though Finlay may have found it a trifle galling to see his estranged ex-Chairman, Dawson, over in the royal enclosure effecting introductions in his role as courtier, with Viscount Churchill at his side. The original impetus for the Royal visit had actually come from Finlay and Hancock, who approached the Stewards of the Regatta at the start of the year with two propositions: (1) that they invite the King, and (2) that they collectively accept honorary membership of the Club. The first had been pursued without further reference to Phyllis Court, and the second politely sidestepped. At least there were consolations: the crew from his native Sydney won the Grand Challenge Cup, and profits for the week were up 40 per cent. Nor can Finlay have felt nervous about tempting fate, given the set piece of that year's fireworks:

> This will represent the imaginary burning of the famous riverside club, Phyllis Court, the centre of fashion at the great aquatic festival. Thus the spectators in the actual building or its grounds may be, as it were, witnesses of their own destruction, and the most notable water festival in the world will end in fire.

Even before the debt was fully cleared (in December 1912), the Club had the confidence to embark on expansion, taking the opportunity to rent the neighbouring riverside residence to the south. This was Manor Garden, a large late-Victorian house with gables and red tiles. It added five single and nine double bedrooms to the Phyllis Court accommodation, and a new covered walkway linked it to the Clubhouse. A further advantage of this acquisition was the freedom it gave Finlay to erect a grandstand on the former boundary between the properties, directly in line with the Regatta winning post. A temporary structure having proved popular in 1912, he published plans the following March for a durable two-tier iron-framed grandstand capable of seating 550 people, to be 'erected only during the Regatta Week, so that the beauty of the river scenery will not be interfered with'. Members were invited to subscribe to a Regatta Improvement Fund to raise £3,500. Investments, to be repaid by an insurance policy maturing in 1926, would earn interest of 4 per cent and entitle them to privileges on a sliding scale. Persons subscribing £300 secured life membership and the use of a private box (for nine) in Henley Week for seven years; £50 secured a single seat. 'This year', remarked the rowing correspondent of the *Observer* in July 1913, 'a removable grandstand has been erected on the Phyllis Court side, and already some of the people who resent change have wondered, if it is removable, somebody doesn't remove it.' The building, topped by a blue-and-white awning, stood 114 feet long, 24 feet wide, and 24 feet high. Designed by D.F. Sainsbury, it actually stayed up all year, becoming in time a local landmark.

The proprietor did feel one anxiety about the Grandstand, for he asked Commercial Union to clarify the insurance: 'It is agreed and declared that the expression "Fire" appearing in this policy shall be deemed to include fire or explosion caused by Suffragettes.' An all-male sporting fixture might well have been a target, but, as things turned out, the only demonstration at the Regatta that summer was a punt full of ladies dressed in green, white, and violet (the alphabetical colour-code for 'Give Women Votes!'). In 1914, however, suffragette arsonists were blamed for burning down a church at Wargrave, not four miles away. Although the first woman to take a seat at Westminster had once been a member, it cannot be argued that the Phyllis Court Club was anywhere near the forefront of female emancipation (and neither was Lady Astor, prior to her election in 1919). Ladies were originally eligible as guest members only. Each had to be nominated by a gentleman member who was her husband, father, brother, son or nephew. In 1911, an additional category of 'Independent Guest-Member' came into being, partly to mitigate the harshness of a rule that excluded widows, but chiefly to boost recruitment. It thus became possible for a woman to join without being sponsored by a man, but the number of such members was limited to 150, and they were subject to annual re-election. Neither class of lady member had voting rights. Phyllis Court nevertheless remained the prime focus of fashion journalists at Regatta time. Fifty years later, when working on the film of *My Fair Lady* (set in 1913), art director Gene Allen found inspiration in photographs taken at the Club – and went on to win an Oscar.

Unlike the Grandstand and the Manor Garden annexe, a third initiative of this period failed to take off (literally). The Club proposed to stage 'a contest between different makes of hydro-aeroplanes' with Henley Reach as the runway. The Thames Conservancy would not allow it. New diversions instead included an

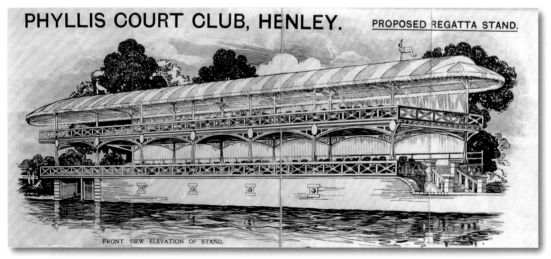

The Grandstand as built in 1913.

In the grounds
of Phyllis
Court, c.1913.
(River &
Rowing
Museum)

eighteen-hole putting-green, a string band playing every day, a performance by the English Folk Dance Society, and a number of small motor boats run by a firm called De La Poer Ltd (a subsidiary of the Phyllis Court Club Company). Finlay had noticed a high turnover of membership and concluded that the reason was a 'lack of attractions apart from the Regatta'. There would always be people who joined the Club, 'did' Henley for a year or two, and then moved on with curiosity satisfied, but surviving the crisis of 1910 had convinced the proprietor that the Club enjoyed a basis of support that was solid enough to justify a long-term commitment.

In contrast, the closest competitor of Phyllis Court had conceded defeat and vacated the field. This was the Grosvenor River Club, an offshoot of the Grosvenor Club of Piccadilly, which had opened its clubhouse in 1907 – a wooden bungalow on the Berkshire bank midway between Henley Bridge and Remenham Farm. It charged a lower subscription (four guineas) while advertising itself as 'the only club with riverside terraces and lawns shaded from sun and rain from which the Regatta races can be seen with comfort from start to finish'. Its President was the Dean of Hereford. Closure came after five years, and the premises were taken by the Remenham Club, 'a social combination of London oarsmen… managed purely by rowing men for rowing men', and therefore not a rival to Finlay's enterprise.

On 29 September 1913, he signed three new twenty-one-year leases for Phyllis Court (at an annual rent of £825), Manor Garden (£225), and New Street drive and the staff cottages (£101). He also decided that the Club would undertake its own catering, with the exception of Regatta Week, when Spiers & Pond would be engaged, a national chain whose other clients included the Gaiety Theatre and London Zoo. His annual salary, meanwhile, increased to £675. In 1914, for the first time, the Club opened fully for Easter, and the Regatta again went very well (except for the top English eights, all beaten by Americans, Canadians, and Germans). To Henley returned the social correspondent of the *Sydney Morning Herald*:

> I think I have mentioned before that the club was first initiated by the late Mr Finlay, a son-in-law of Mr Gedye, well-known in Sydney in the 'Eighties. I spent a week-end in Phyllis Court before it had been formally taken over, and admired then its old-world gardens and the magnificent lawns. In its way it is peerless. On his father's death in 1906, Mr Roy Finlay, then only 22 or 23 [actually 24], took on the responsibility of forming the club and making all the necessary arrangements for its government and finance. No light task for anyone with the history of river clubs behind him. Somehow the bent of Mr Finlay's mind seemed to suit the line of work he had embarked upon. He had studied glass-farming and gardening thoroughly, and this in conjunction with his artistic taste in furnishing and decorative work has led to the successful status of the club as it now stands. It is so beautiful a place that one might point to it as a show for strangers to visit.

The headline of the article read 'A Thames-side Paradise'. By the time it appeared in print, the British Empire was at war.

The First World War

Although he had stopped attending camp with King Edward's Horse, Lieutenant Finlay had placed his name on the Reserve of Officers. He therefore received orders on 5 August 1914 to hold himself in readiness. There was time for him to entrust the chequebook of the Club Company to Freddie Norsworthy, Morton Smale and Gerald Brocklebank before he was sent to reinforce the 6th Dragoon Guards. His comrades in King Edward's Horse were jealous when they heard of his despatch to the Western Front in November (as they had to stay for extra training). Finlay took command of a troop that had already seen action. His account of going to the trenches for the first time (near Bailleul) was later published in *The Times* as part of a series entitled 'Letters from the Front':

Lieutenant Roy Finlay in November 1914.

> Rather vague about what to take to the trenches; everybody advised differently. Took mackintosh, leather lining, and waterproof sheet. Got mounted 1.45, rode for about two hours, and then dismounted in a field to the right of the road. Pouring with rain all the time, field like a bog. … The men chatted in subdued voices amongst themselves, but I had not yet got to know them very well, so felt that my horse, which I had brought with me, was my only friend, sort of thing.

After trudging in silence through ruined villages in darkness, they met the French troops they had come to relieve. The *capitaine* told Finlay that the spot was '*fort dangereux*' and left after shaking his hand 'in a manner which indicated that we should never have the pleasure of doing so again on this earth'. Was it expected of a junior officer to sleep or keep awake?

> Nothing that I had ever been taught in all the courses I had been through bore in the slightest upon what we were doing; but this was explained, perhaps, by the fact that trench work was not the legitimate work of the cavalry, we only being in that position owing to the shortage of infantry troops at the time. Our duties seemed quite simple, however, and I felt that I would know what to do in case of attack. It was then 11 o'clock p.m. on the night of my birthday. What a birthday!

The regiment spent thirty-one days of the following year in trenches around Ypres. The rest of the time was passed in billets with a tedious routine of squadron parades, exercise and grooming. Cavalrymen were being held in reserve for the breakthrough that did not come. Finlay was posted to the regimental depot in Kent for part of 1915.

The Phyllis Court Club re-opened on 28 April. In the winter the grounds had been placed at the disposal of the Red Cross (which turned Henley Town Hall into a war hospital) and Lady Hambledon (who turned Wharf House into a hostel for Belgian refugees). The public mood inclined to austerity, as the likelihood of a long war grew apparent, and desperate hedonism had yet to grip the young. River clubs seemed a redundant frivolity. The previous season had been curtailed; subscription income was falling. The Club therefore waived its recent twenty-guinea entrance fee and made a series of press announcements:

Management at a Distance

Phyllis Court Club,
Henley

Aug.15th 1914

My dear Master,
Received your letter of the 12th & am glad to hear you are allright, we are enjoying lovely weather here & and have twenty people staying in.

I am still taking to rowing every evening, although they have cancelled all regattas throughout England. I cancelled that boat which we were going to have, also I have seen about papers you mentioned, & please Sir, may I have an order to Aprons and overalls for work in winter, for which I am longing to come.

And I do hope Sir that you won't get called abroad. Is there anything else that you want seen to or done.

I remain
Your obedient servant
Alfred E. Champion

Many a young officer preparing to face the greatest test of his life would have tossed aside such a letter, but not Roy Finlay. Through four-and-a-half years in the army, he kept abreast of events back at Phyllis Court and exerted the maximum degree of management possible at a distance. Conceding that 'the Club was, after all, entirely in the nature of a luxury', he saw that its decline was inevitable during a national emergency, and yet he remained insistent: 'the Club must be kept floating, the cessation of the Club meaning the end of it for all time'.

7 April 1915

Lady Relatives of Officers serving on the Active List will be admitted to Guest Membership free of entrance fee and at a special subscription of 3½ gns. per annum during the period of the War, subject to the usual conditions of election.

5 May 1915

Wounded officers in his Majesty's Forces and Allied Armies desiring to avail themselves of Honorary Membership of the Phyllis Court Club in accordance with the resolution passed by the General Committee on Saturday May 1st, are directed to communicate with the Secretary.

22 July 1915

Resolution, dated May 1st:- 'That Officers on the Active List stationed within a radius of 20 miles of Henley-on-Thames (which includes Aldershot and district) be entitled, subject to its Rules and Bye-Laws, to Honorary Membership (free of Subscription) of this Club for the year 1915.'

The wisdom of borrowing only from members now became evident. In June, the chairmen of the two Committees, Laurence Hancock and Sir James Williamson, appealed for loyalty while informing lenders that it would not be possible to pay interest on debentures or hold draws for redemption. 'In this way only can the ulti-mate salvage of the Club be hoped for.' Finlay reassured Williamson: 'Personally, I feel perfectly confident of being able to revive the Club when once this calamity is over, just as we were able to do so upon a previous occasion.' Races between public-school crews (Eton, Radley and Beaumont) were the nearest equivalent to a Regatta that summer, and the Club organised its own annual event for the neighbouring Royal Grammar School, presenting the Phyllis Cup to the boy who excelled in sculling, swimming, diving and life-saving.

Management grew rather makeshift. Norsworthy joined the army early in 1916. Mrs Noel Burke (the former Mimi Finlay) assumed the chairmanship of the Club Company. Captain E. Claremont, R.N., employed as Acting Secretary, proved unsatisfactory, and administration increasingly devolved on Miss P. Hunt, first engaged as a typist. The accounts meanwhile fell into confusion. Even the Committees stopped meeting. Finlay was therefore fortunate to secure Miss Helen Goff as his deputy in 1917. At the end of the war, he acknowledged how much the Club owed to her. She ran the establishment as a quiet country hotel. It helped that the Fawley Estate postponed collection of three-quarters of the rent.

By now, much of the British cavalry on the Western Front had been dis-mounted for regular service in the trenches, but Roy Finlay moved on from the dragoons. Early in 1917, he was appointed as a General Staff Officer, 3rd Grade (GSO3), with the temporary rank of captain, to the 1st Mounted Division. This was stationed in Norfolk in case of a German amphibious raid. He returned to

Admiral Jellicoe

One of many to find a temporary haven in Henley from the rigours of war was the First Sea Lord, Sir John Jellicoe, who stayed at Phyllis Court for a week in 1917 after a recurrence of neuritis. 'The doctors sent me away on Wednesday', he explained to David Beatty on 2 June. 'I am spending my time on the river and it is very delightful.' Later he lent his name to the Club as a Vice-President, and, of all the admirals associated with it, he remains the most controversial. The inconclusive Battle of Jutland had disappointed the public, and slowness in adopting the convoy system to protect merchant shipping from U-boats contributed to his dismissal. That said, Britain did retain mastery at sea.

Other senior naval members of the Club included Sir Martyn Jerram, who commanded the 2nd Battle Squadron at Jutland, and Sir Douglas Brownrigg, chief censor at the Admiralty. Military members were leading companies, battalions, regiments, and brigades on all fronts in numbers that would make selection invidious. The 18th Lord Sempill claimed to have been the first man from Kitchener's Army to land in France (by leaping ashore before the troopship had tied up at the dock).

Admiral Sir John Jellicoe.

France in April 1918, becoming first supplementary GSO3 with the 2nd Infantry Division, then a supplementary Brigade Major with the 99th Brigade. His role was to assist the commander, Edmund Ironside, with operations and intelligence. Miss Goff meanwhile posted weekly reports from Phyllis Court.

On 22 August 1917, the Club permitted a fête in its grounds in aid of the Henley Red Cross Hospital, to which the Marquise d'Hautpoul brought Princess Victoria, a sister of the King. The *Henley Standard* thought it 'well worth the humble shilling charged for admission in order to be allowed the privilege of sauntering uninterruptedly about the velvety lawns'. The garages were requisitioned that autumn by the Royal Flying Corps to store equipment for the Technical Officers' School of Instruction recently opened in Henley at the Royal Hotel and the Imperial Hotel. This restricted the supply of superior accommodation in the town just when German air-raids on London increased demand for it. The result for Phyllis Court was a return to profitability in 1918. Miss A.E. Stout gave a lantern-slide lecture on German atrocities to raise funds for the French War Emergency Committee,

The War Office postcard that informed Mrs Finlay in 1918 that her elder son had been injured.

and the Club hosted an entertainment for wounded soldiers on 9 August 1918; some came by boat from Maidenhead. 'On arrival all were served out with tobacco and cigarettes wherewith to enjoy themselves.' The steward prepared 'a sumptuous repast', the Club orchestra played, and members organised party games for the fitter men.

The following month, on 14 September, Finlay himself became a wounded soldier, poisoned by the explosion of a gas-shell that also burnt his thighs. He was then attached to the 11th Essex Regiment at Saint-Quentin by the Hindenburg Line. Ten days later, the Phyllis Court Club Company held a meeting at Lady Cooper's Hospital, Hursley Park, Winchester. The Managing Director 'had not quite yet recovered his sight', but at least he felt able to put his salary back up from £275 to £475 (and award a £50 bonus to Miss Goff). Doctors predicted two months' incapacity. On leaving hospital, Finlay went to his mother's home in Bournemouth. The minutes of the next Company meeting, held there, begin with an excusable digression:

> It was recorded with relief and satisfaction that on the 11th inst. an Armistice had been signed between Germany and the Allies, Germany having under compulsion agreed to all the conditions laid down by the Allies, and that this Armistice followed like unconditional surrenders of the other Enemy Powers:- Austria, Bulgaria, and Turkey, so that a complete cessation of hostilities had been effected with the Allies the overwhelming conquerors.

Granted leave, Finlay returned to Phyllis Court in December. Though the 6th Reserve Cavalry Regiment still had a claim on him, he could barely wait for demobilisation, 'having important work requiring my immediate attention'.

7

The Long Weekend
1919–1937

> With the return of normal conditions, society is returning to its old haunts, and never will there have been such a season on the river as the coming one if the present indications are fulfilled. With the revival of Henley Regatta, backed as it is by Royal interest and the promise of exceptionally fine sport, it is not surprising that our beautiful Thames has again come into its own, and that Phyllis Court, Henley, the headquarters of social life on the river, is faced with the very busiest season with which it has yet to contend. Lucky will those be who succeed in getting in before the entrance fee, suspended during the war as in the case of most of the leading clubs, is again brought into force, which we learn will be very shortly.

So declared an advertising feature published in *The Tatler* in April 1919 under the heading, 'Higher Life on the Higher Reaches'. Roy Finlay had feared that the coming of peace might actually harm the Club in the short run, due to the resumption of foreign travel. Doubts had also been raised as to the feasibility of a Regatta, with so many rowers still in khaki and out of practice. The Stewards decided to go ahead with a modified contest, the 'Henley Peace Regatta', with different events in order to avoid unfair advantages and false comparisons.

The first Club dance of the post-war era 'went with a "go" from start to finish' on 17 May. Phyllis Court had been thriving in the final summers before the cataclysm and, far from being forgotten five years later, it benefited from the nostalgia that now attached to the Henley Royal Regatta (and indeed attaches to it still, for though founded in the 1830s and continuing to flourish in the 2010s, it remains in some strange way 'Edwardian' in popular perception). *The Sketch* greeted the re-opening of the Club in verse ('Once more there's quite a decent sort of lunch prepared at Phyllis Court'). More impressively, 3,500 miles away, when British troops in the Third Afghan War set up an outpost ringed by trees beside the Kabul River, their officers borrowed the name for it.

By July 1919, the Club had four hundred new members. The jolly editorialist of *The Tatler* remarked:

> Leadin' out-door show of the week, of course, Henley, that's so bunged up with entries it's lastin' from Wednesday to Saturday. My bird's-eye view of this jazz will be taken, need I say, from Phyllis Court lawns, with *occasional* only plunges into the serried ranks of the vasty crowd on the river! Very matey, you know, these aquatic festivals of old

England, 'specially in these war – I mean peace – days, when everything's bung to the brim with the war profiteer, his wife, his son, and his daughters.

It was perhaps to meet such social concerns that the Club made explicit in its new rule book the basic prerequisites for admission. They warrant quotation in full:

Rule IV – The following shall, subject to the Rules governing Election, be eligible for Candidature to Ordinary Membership of the Club:-

A. Princes of the Blood Royal. Members, and their blood-relatives, of the Peerage, Privy Council, Baronetage, Knightage, Companionage, and Landed Gentry of Great Britain. Members of Parliament and of the Diplomatic Services.

B. Officers (Active List and Retired) of the Royal Navy and Regular Army (including the Special Reserve of or above the Substantive rank of Captain) being of not less than one year's service.

C. Graduates of the Universities of Oxford, Cambridge, and Trinity College, Dublin, and Public School men (such Public Schools to be approved for the purposes of this Rule by the General Committee).

D. Members of the following Clubs, which have, by arrangement, been placed upon a privilege list (with power to be varied from time to time): Army and Navy, Arthurs, Athenaeum, Bachelors, Bath, Beefsteak, Boodles, Brooks, Carlton, Cavalry, Conservative, Guards, Hurlingham, Marlborough, Naval and Military, Turf, Travellers, The Royal Yacht Squadron, United Service, Junior United Service, Wellington, Whites.

Records were kept of each member's qualifications; several had a full set, 'ABCD'. After the Under-Secretary of State for Air contacted Vice-President Lord Desborough, the Club rectified the omission of Royal Air Force officers from Category B. Finlay operated a scheme whereby the officers' mess of a regiment, battalion, naval ship, or RAF station could take out a group subscription. Further Clubs were added to the privilege list over the next ten years: Alexandra, Badminton, Bucks, City Carlton, Constitutional, East India United Service, Devonshire, Junior Carlton, New University, Oxford and Cambridge, Portland, Public Schools and Alpine, Princes, Reform, Royal Motor Yacht, Royal Air Force, Royal Societies, Roehampton, St James, Union, United Universities, and Windham.

In addition, Rule IVa stipulated that no person should be elected who was not a British subject by birth and descent. Maybe this reflected embarrassment about such pre-war members as Count Paul Metternich, the German Ambassador in London (1903–12), and the 4th Prince Gebhard Blücher. The contradiction between barring foreigners and admitting diplomats apparently passed unnoticed, and the nationality criterion does not seem to have been rigorously enforced. The Club rejected direct applications for membership; approaches had to be made through an existing member or a Category D club. As a further safeguard, all new members were subject to annual ballot by the General Committee for the first three years.

The election of a new General Committee in 1919 itself marked a step towards revival. Its Chairman for the next dozen years was Commander Sir Trevor Dawson, who had left the navy after specialising in gunnery in order to work in the armaments industry. As managing director of Vickers Limited from 1906, he played a major part in national defence, taking a particular interest in the development of submarines and airships. Dawson was tall, clean-shaven, and ebullient (and unrelated to Sir Douglas Dawson). 'An adept in all the arcane influences of the international arms trade', and perhaps too controversial for a peerage, he became 1st Baronet of Edgwarebury in 1920. Sir Vincent Caillard, the financial director of Vickers, subsequently joined him on the Committee, which did have three barons. Lord Camoys had been an honorary member from the first. Lord Tredegar (later 1st Viscount) owned large coalfields in Wales. Lord Hawke had captained Yorkshire County Cricket Club for the twenty-eight years to 1910. ('Pray God, no professional shall ever captain England', he memorably declared). Dudley Cory Wright, Lieutenant-Colonel Graham, Commander Gore-Langton, Captain Grimes, and Captain Michelson were re-elected, having served before the war, while five soldiers took places for the first time: two Brigadier-Generals, Colin Ballard and Edward Hoare Nairne, Colonel William Murray-Threipland, Lieutenant-Colonel Charles Boyle, and Major the Hon. John Lyttelton. Ballard had led the 14th Brigade on the Western Front and would soon preside over the Allied Police Commission in occupied Constantinople. Hoare Nairne, of the Royal Artillery, had commanded the 3rd Canadian Division at the Battle of Mont Sorrel in 1916. Lyttelton, later 9th Viscount Cobham, had been a Tory MP. So too had Sir John Jackson, although more significant as a civil engineer, constructing docks at Dover, Singapore, and Simonstown. Sir George Younger, later 1st Viscount Younger, was Chairman of the Conservative Party from 1916 to 1923, helping steer it in and out of the Lloyd George coalition. Well known in his own field, Sir Robert Abbot Hadfield discovered manganese steel and manufactured armour-piercing shells. Henry Hughes-Onslow and Major Douglas Roberts were both concerned with the law, the former as a Master of the Supreme Court of Judicature and the latter as Chief Constable of Oxfordshire. Sir Peter McBride was Agent-General of the State of Victoria.

A satisfactory summer gave Finlay the confidence to renew the leases for a fresh term of twenty-one years and, after naming W.A. Ingram as Acting Honorary Secretary, he felt able to absent himself for eight months from October. Taking advantage of provisions favouring ex-service students, he completed a short course at Trinity Hall, Cambridge (whose admissions register records his date of birth as 1890 instead of 1881). Thereafter a crested cigarette-case disclosed his sporting loyalties: 'Row Hall!' As a rule, the proprietor lived at his Club in the season, but he kept his home in Shiplake after leasing out the glass-houses. His sister Laura remained next door with her children, Jacintha, Prosper and Guinevere, who often came to Phyllis Court to play games or earn some pocket money. Their father,

Finlay's family
on the upper
tier of the
Grandstand in
1921: Mimi
Burke, Laura
Norsworthy,
Laura Finlay
and Jack
Rendle-Mervill.

Robert Buddicom, had emigrated to Australia, so their mother could divorce him in 1919 and marry Roy's friend Freddie Norsworthy. Finlay also rented a flat in London and spent part of each winter on the Côte d'Azur. Members were reminded to travel with their Phyllis Court badges to secure preferential terms at the Riviera Palace Hotel and the International Sporting Club in Monte Carlo. The Buddicom children had once suspected 'Uncle Dudie' of being the man in the song who broke the bank there. He gave them a roulette-wheel, remarking that no nursery was complete without one!

Rowing and Dancing

In these years, if Henley Week turned out sunny, everyone automatically hailed a return to pre-war glories. The Royal Regatta attracted exceptional levels of interest in July 1920: 'The Phyllis Court Club is already full and has been obliged to annex bedroom accommodation in the town, and a whole colony of tents has been erected in the club grounds for the same purpose.' High expectations on this occasion were triumphantly fulfilled; only the absence of houseboats saddened some traditionalists. People noticed that the Phyllis Court Grandstand, generously adorned with geraniums, itself resembled a houseboat on land. Such was demand in the Luncheon Court that members were fined one guinea if they failed to finish their meal within forty-five minutes. Lighter refreshment could be taken on the Tea Terrace (deckchairs under sun-umbrellas) or the Indian Verandah (cane chairs under canvas). Among rowing enthusiasts, spirits stayed buoyant even in 1922:

> Fierce cries of baby coxes mingled with the band's pert *Whose Baby Are You?* Quartets of… Indian colonels, parsons, stockbrokers, and aged dons delighted the lawns of Phyllis Court with song and dance. The steady downpour did no more than colour the harlequinade of punts with a sombre black of umbrellas and green of tarpaulin.

After three inches of rain fell during the 1927 Regatta, however, the Club invested in a thousand feet of red-and-white striped awning, which proved its worth two years later:

> When our correspondent visited Phyllis Court on Saturday, the last day of the Regatta, he found that nobody was in the least disturbed by the inclemency of the weather. Thronged with people though the Enclosure was, there was a dry seat for everybody under ample cover and only a few had even troubled to don their mackintoshes.… At last the weather during the Regatta may be delegated to a secondary place.

Finlay had to bear in mind that his Club now faced competition for the specific custom of élite Regatta spectators, namely, the Stewards' Enclosure over the river. There had always existed an enclosure for Stewards and their guests (and indeed Phyllis Court had once been its location), but 1919 witnessed the formation of an associated club whose members, elected by the Committee of Management of the Regatta, paid a subscription for the privilege of admission. This aided Regatta finances, and its official status attracted patrons who wished to demonstrate their commitment to rowing. It followed that perceptions of the Phyllis Court Club as social rather than sporting gained extra force by comparison. Even so, Phyllis Court had as a member one of the all-time Henley heroes: between 1885 and 1907, Guy Nickalls rowed seventy-nine Royal Regatta races and won sixty-seven.

A new golden age of British rowing caught the attention of the wider public. The Grand Challenge Cup would not go abroad till 1936. Cook's Tours included tickets for the Junior Phyllis Court Enclosure in their 'Six World-Famous Events' package, and growing numbers of American crews brought growing numbers of American spectators. Primarily for them, the Club produced *How to See Henley*, a booklet explaining 'the most English of all English Social Functions':

Guy Nickalls, legendary rower and member of the Club.

The sight is a very beautiful one. A 'Rhapsody in Colour', the River and the Enclosures on either bank are packed with the multi-hues of be-blazered youth, intermingled with the delicate chiffons and muslins of their feminine counterpart, the whole resembling a gigantic garden, set in the sylvan glory of an English scene…. On the last night of the Regatta (always a Saturday) a large Gala Ball is held at Phyllis Court to which everybody socially eligible, including the Crews, go, and in connection with which a special Restaurant train *de luxe* (at ordinary fares) is run at 2 a.m…. This is the only great Social Ball of the year at which it is correct to wear river flannels.

Vogue did not report rowing, but it knew a good ball when it saw one. 'As you come up the long drive you will be greeted by a vista of lamps in the trees as if the stars had come down coloured from heaven', it enthused. Beyond the brilliance of the crowded ballroom lay the magic of the moonlit river and the romance of the scented rose garden. 'Phyllis Court has that enchanting freshness and fluttering colour for which the English girl, entering the world of supper-parties and infinite invitation, is famous.'

When Finlay announced in 1919 that 'Dancing is to be a feature of the Club's diversions this year', he might equally have said 'this decade', so eagerly did it embrace the 1920s dance craze. A rhyming ABC of Henley, published in 1926, included the execrable couplet:

> P is for Phyllis Court, where Terpsichore
> May grant her attractions when racing is o'er.

Watching the Henley Royal Regatta in July 1923.

This was actually an understatement. The dance music hardly stopped in Regatta Week; as the *Daily Express* observed, 'There will be dances at Phyllis Court after

lunch, dances between races, dances after tea, dances after dinner, and a great gala ball on Saturday night.' All these foxtrots, quicksteps and charlestons, with the occasional slow waltz for variety, took place in a large 'pavilion marquee' that stayed up from May to September. Finlay had reservations about the new brass-heavy dance bands and believed in shielding diners from them. 'Saxophone droning was a craze amongst the second-class restaurants and Palais de Danse after the war', he opined in 1932. 'It was a nightmare from America… and never was popular amongst educated people.' *Valencia* and *Tiptoe through the Tulips* were presumably more often heard at Phyllis Court than the 'hotter' forms of jazz. In the first years of peace, the Club employed the Waldorf Orchestra led by Kneale Kelley, who later won radio fame on *In Town Tonight*. Then it formed its own ensemble for the normal Friday and Saturday dances, while hiring a big-name band for the Ascot and Henley Balls. In 1926, this was Jack Hylton's Salon Orchestra and, in 1929, the Savoy Orpheans (or at least one of the successor bands claiming the title). Newman's Hunt Ball Band and Jack Palmer's Monte Carlo Orchestra were regular bookings.

The Phyllis Court Club had held its first fancy dress party on 30 August 1919. Costumes were 'screamingly hilarious'. Finlay and Helen Goff played it safe as Pierrot and Britannia but, amidst Arabs, pirates, and Georgians could be found at least two embodiments of President Wilson's Fourteen Points. The idea of an amateur band performing alternately with the professional one was tried only once (in 1922). The fancy dress ball coincided with the annual Club Rag Regatta in August. This event largely consisted of competitive activities that carried a risk of falling into the river. The Honorary Secretary himself excelled at blindfold punting, while Prosper Buddicom organised the mop-fights in canoes. By the mid-1930s, some members were routinely sunbathing and swimming. Greater informality showed itself in nomenclature as well. Younger people now spoke of 'Phyllis Court Club' (without 'the'), and abbreviation went further. 'The Court' encouraged tennis-related puns, while many members followed Finlay's example and simply referred to 'Phyllis'.

Refurbishment

The practical priorities of the proprietor in the early 1920s were electrification and new kitchens. To finance these, he again borrowed from members. Although the Club Company remained indebted to the holders of first and second debentures, high inflation during the war had halved this burden in real terms, so fresh loans were not imprudent. Issues of bonds, paying 6 per cent interest and redeemable in 1936, raised £1,600 in 1921 and £600 in 1922 from a total of ten subscribers. This sufficed to install a generator and wire much of the ground floor, while what is now the Thames Room became 'the last word in luxurious cocktail lounges equipped by De La Poer'. There members could purchase the Club's own brands of champagne and cigarettes.

Electric light, new radiators, and the discovery that 260 members lived within ten miles of Henley prompted the Club to try staying open through the winter of 1923–24, but bridge and table-tennis tournaments, an Armistice dinner, and a Christmas gala failed to generate a viable level of trade. Meanwhile, the costs of the renovation programme caused concern, exacerbated by an uncertain political situation. Finlay cancelled plans to offer £17,000-worth of prize bonds in December 1923, when Baldwin called a snap general election and lost. The emergence of the first Labour Government triggered alarm in some quarters, and investor confidence at Phyllis Court took a downward turn. A third issue of 6 per cent bonds in 1924 raised only £220. To pay contractors, the Club asked members for a voluntary extra subscription 'to probably the best equipped Country Club in the Country'. A second urgent notice reported that the response could 'not yet be described as "general".' The membership was told 'That the sum required imperatively and immediately is £3,000. That this represents an average of £3 3s. per member. That in order to raise this sum it will be necessary for *every Member* to subscribe on an average £3 3s.' Names of subscribers would be added to a list on the noticeboard in the hall. It did not lengthen as quickly as hoped so, in March 1924, a different approach was adopted:

> The committee of the Phyllis Court Club have decided to create 200 vacancies for membership and a like number for lady guest-membership. The recently completed extension of the club building has made this expansion possible. An effort is now being made to acquire a suitable clubhouse in London in the neighbourhood of Piccadilly.

This proposal for a second clubhouse in the capital certainly broke new ground, it being much more common for a London club to set up a river-club subsidiary. Despite plenty of discussion in 1924–25, no metropolitan premises ever materialised. In Henley, however, it was true that the new service wing to the south-west of the Clubhouse freed up rooms for conversion into additional members' quarters. The twenty-guinea entrance fee was waived for six months, and Finlay sent a circular to all members of the London clubs listed in Rule IV, offering a reduced subscription to prompt applicants.

The 1924 recruitment drive succeeded. Within two months, the Honorary Secretary could publish a list of forty-six titled candidates. Moreover, in June, a rumour swept the town which he took great pleasure in confirming: the Prince of Wales (later Edward VIII) had 'graciously accepted the dutiful request of the Chairman and Committee to become Patron of the Phyllis Court Club'. The anomaly of an organisation with Vice-Presidents yet no President had finally been rectified. Quite how this was achieved remains mysterious. The Prince had held honorary life membership of the Leander Club in Henley since taking tea there in 1914, but he came to the Royal Regatta only once (in 1921). His closest link to Phyllis Court may have been the Earl of Medina, whose brother, Lord Louis

Mountbatten, was one of his best friends. Medina regularly used the Club in the immediate post-war period, sometimes bringing his father, the 1st Marquess of Milford Haven (who, as Admiral Prince Louis of Battenberg, had served as First Sea Lord). The Prince of Wales' American dentist, Victor Smith, belonged too.

As of January 1925, the Club had 1,150 gentleman members and 602 lady guest members. During the preceding twelve months, 150 resignations and deaths had been more than offset by 768 new elections. This 54 per cent increase in membership boosted subscription income by about £5,000, so enhancement of the Clubhouse could continue. 'Phyllis Court has never looked better than it did today', observed the *Evening News* in 1924. 'It has been repainted a dazzling white; and the lawns were thick, not only with flowers, but with beautiful women.'

'The Social Crowd'

The Phyllis Court Club was riding high in the social stakes, with the *Daily Mail* calling it 'the most exclusive river-side club in the world'. No one could query the noble credentials of the Duchess of Northumberland (who became Mistress of the Robes in 1937). The Marquess of Douro succeeded as 5th Duke of Wellington in 1934. The 5th Earl of Onslow was Under-Secretary of State for War. As democracy and agricultural depression undermined the landed classes, so aristocratic prejudice softened, and joining a country club ceased to be infra dig. An article in the *Illustrated London News* (composed in conjunction with Finlay) tactfully hinted at the savings:

> The phenomenal rush that has occurred in recent years, among the wealthier classes, to join one or other of our all too few recognised country clubs, was explained some years ago by a contemporary London journal as follows: 'High rents, the scarcity of houses, and the servant difficulty have all contributed to turn the attention of those who must have their sojourn in the country to the advantages of the country club, which means not only freedom from worry and care but the advantages of pleasant society, well kept tennis courts, golf links, first class catering and dance music, and all the things that go to make a visit to the country enjoyable.'

The membership at Phyllis Court included the 6th Earl of Ilchester, 9th Viscount Torrington, 4th Baron Chesham, 5th Baron Castlemaine, 3rd Baron Tollemache, and Countess Poulett, youthful widow of the 7th Earl. Viscount Curzon, later 5th Earl Howe, was a racing-driver, winner of the 24 Hours of Le Mans. The 5th Earl of Ducie farmed in Queensland and the 4th Baron Egerton in Kenya, while the 2nd Earl of Dudley had served as Governor-General of Australia. The 2nd Baron Roundway was a commander of the Yeomen of the Guard. A touch of disapproval marked the 6th Marquess of Donegall, gossip-columnist for the *Sunday Despatch*. Viscounts Deerhurst, Dunsford, and Tarbat were all heirs to earldoms. Lord Charles Kennedy became 5th Marquess of Ailsa.

Lady Diana Cooper, a Vice-President of Phyllis Court Club.

Finlay enlisted a few of these as Vice-Presidents (Ilchester, Howe, and Leigh) and wooed other celebrities. When free Regatta tickets were first sent to Margot Asquith (Countess of Oxford and Asquith) a secretary returned them, saying that the Prime Minister's widow hated Regattas. Finlay replied, 'Attending a Regatta from here is not in any way like the ordinary Regatta.' By 1934, the Countess was a Vice-President of the Club, as was Society beauty Lady Diana Cooper, a name with greater appeal for the younger generation. The Hon. Sir Harry Stonor, another Vice-President, was renowned as the finest shot in England.

Titled members were also numerous because the honours system had changed to recognise a larger number of more diverse individuals. Attendance lists in the newspapers prompt the thought that it would have been hard to throw a stone into Phyllis Court without hitting at least an industrial baronet. Several of these businessmen had temporarily entered government service during the Great War to help manage the growth of economic regulation. Accountant Sir 'Sammie' Hardman Lever had applied costing systems to munitions factories and taken a major role in Anglo-American financial relations, serving as Financial Secretary to the Treasury, though not a politician. At the Ministry of Munitions, Sir Percy Girouard had been Director-General (until he fell out with Lloyd George), Sir Charles Stewart Wilson had been Assistant Secretary, Sir Ernest Moir had been Controller of Inventions, Sir W. Charles Wright had been Controller of Iron and Steel, and Sir Gilbert Garnsey had been Controller of Accounts. At the Board of Trade, Sir Evan D. Jones had been Petrol Controller. Sir Thomas G. Jones was Director of Ships' Stores at the Ministry of Food. Sir Francis Towle and Sir Alexander Prince ran the Army and Navy Canteen Board, while war pensions were the province of Sir Stephen Demetriadi. Sir John Wormald headed the Civil Industries Committee, deciding appeals against the allocation of strategic commodities. Supreme in this category, however, stood Andrew Weir, 1st Baron Inverforth, the Scottish shipping magnate, who first oversaw procurement of all equipment for the army other than munitions and then liquidated the assets of the state war industries after 1918. He was sometimes called 'the man who saved Britain millions'.

Phyllis Court also collected big shots in shipping, with Sir Thomas Royden of Cunard, Sir Herbert Cayzer of Union Castle, Sir William Currie of P&O, Sir Alec Black, Sir William Nelson, Sir Samuel Instone, Sir John Latta, Sir Robert Rankin and Sir James Mills. The 1st Viscount Furness followed his father into the Club; better remembered today is his American wife, Thelma, precursor of Wallis Simpson in the affections of the Prince of Wales (circa 1930). Dundee ship-owner and Liberal MP Sir Charles Coupar Barrie, 1st Baron Abertay, sat on the General

Committee. Another British staple, the textile industry, was embodied in its traditional aspect by the 1st Baron Ashton of Hyde, Manchester mill-owner and laissez-faire Liberal. Samuel Courtauld pioneered rayon (and later collected art). Present too were Sir James Hill (Bradford wool), Sir William Hicking (Nottingham lace) and Sir Ernest Martin (Huddersfield worsted). Sir Arthur Cory Wright, Sir Charles Seely and Sir John Barwick profited from coal. As for new industries, the Club contained Sir Herbert Austin, the motor-car manufacturer whose popular 'Baby Austin' went on sale in 1922, and Sir Arthur du Cros, founder of the Dunlop Rubber Company. Bernard Docker would succeed his father as managing director of the Birmingham Small Arms Company, a vast industrial combine. Sir Robert McLean switched from railway electrification to aircraft construction, in which Sir Henry White-Smith also thrived. Sherard Cowper-Coles devised the Sherardizing process for preventing rust. Chemicals were the professional interest of Robert Mond and Sir Edward Brotherton, while members active in the food industry included Sir Charles Lyle (sugar), Ronald Vestey (meat), Donald Van Den Bergh (margarine), Sir George Watson (dairy products), Sir William Cain (beer) and Sir Norman Vernon (flour). Lord Waring was the former boss of Waring & Gillow, whose promotion from baronet to baron (in the absence of any discernible public service) contributed to the 'sale of honours' scandal in 1922. Sir John T. Davies, private secretary of David Lloyd George while Prime Minister, belonged to the Club as well. From the City came accountants Sir Lacon Threlford and Sir Arthur Lowes Dickinson and bankers C.J. Hambro, Baron Bruno Schröder and Sir William Goschen. Harry Gordon Selfridge was son and heir of the synonymous department-store founder. Ernest Cook, grandson of Thomas Cook, left the travel business to campaign for the preservation of historic houses (a cause that also interested fellow-member Oliver Brett, 3rd Viscount Esher). Henry Wellcome, the American-born pharmaceutical entrepreneur, had introduced the selling of medicines in tablet form to Britain. Among physicians at Phyllis Court were Professor James McDonagh of the Royal College of Surgeons and Lieutenant-General Sir Charles Burtchaell, director of army medical services in France in 1918 and now an honorary surgeon to the King.

Britain in 1924 was a country where most men between twenty-five and fifty had some military background, so plenty of members qualified via Category B of Rule IV ('Officers, Active List and Retired'). Jacintha Buddicom observed that ex-soldiers relished the tranquillity of the Upper Thames. She also said that some people at the Club made her think of characters in a Dornford Yates story. The square-jawed heroes of the thrillers or the bantering toffs of the *Berry* books? Very likely both. Lieutenant-Commander Augustus Agar had been awarded the Victoria Cross for sinking the cruiser *Oleg* in 1919 during the Allied intervention in Russia. General Sir Archibald Hunter supervised the Aldershot training centre during the Great War, but his reputation rested on earlier exploits as 'Kitchener's right-hand man' in the Sudan and South Africa. (Notorious tactlessness may have cost him a fighting command in 1914; he had to be recalled as Governor of Gibraltar after describing the locals as dishonest and insanitary.) General Sir John Maxwell was the man sent to Dublin in 1916 with full powers to crush the Easter Rising (which he did with harsh efficiency and a fateful lack of political sensitivity).

Politician members now seemed less conspicuous. Sir Thomas Morison and Cecil Norton, 1st Baron Rathcreedan, were Liberal office-holders in the Lloyd George Coalition, the former as Lord Advocate and the latter as an aide to Inverforth at Munitions. The collapse of the Liberal Party thereafter left Conservatives with a clear majority among the Phyllis Court contingent of MPs. Sir Alexander Sprot entered Parliament at sixty-five by unseating Asquith in East Fife. Animal welfare was a prime concern for Sir Robert Vaughan Gower, chairman of the RSPCA. Sir Richard Cooper and Sir Alan Burgoyne had both temporarily defected to the radical right-wing National Party during the war. Links between the Tories and commerce were increasing: Robert Yerburgh, 1st Baron Alvingham, was the son of a brewer, Sir Alan Sykes owned a bleaching firm, and several of the businessmen already mentioned (Austin, Cayzer, Du Cros, Lyle, Royden) sat in the Commons for a time. Esmond Harmsworth, later 2nd Viscount Rothermere, signified far more as chairman of Associated Newspapers than as a parliamentarian. Extra-parliamentary work for the party in the provinces may account for the ennoblement of Sir William Mason, 1st Baron Blackford, and Sir Thomas Fermor-Hesketh, 1st Baron Hesketh, while Almeric Paget, 1st Baron Queenborough, merited his by creating the Military Massage Service, though he later presided over the National Union of Conservative and Unionist Associations. In 1922, the Tory MP for South Oxfordshire, Captain Reginald Terrell, hired the lawn of Manor Garden as a private Regatta enclosure, and among his guests was Stanley Baldwin, then President of the Board of Trade. At lunch in the Clubhouse, Baldwin found himself sharing a table with a young businesswoman called Edith Thompson, who was hanged six months later for murder. When Premier, he watched the Regatta finals nearly every year – always from the Stewards' Enclosure. Phyllis Court did have at least one Socialist, Henry Harben, financier of the *New Statesman*, who stood as a Labour parliamentary candidate in 1920 (after standing as a Conservative in 1900 and a Liberal in 1906).

Though now without a Cabinet Minister, the membership ran to several colonial governors, such as Sir Hesketh Bell (Uganda, Northern Nigeria, the Leeward Islands and Mauritius), Sir Eyre Hutson (British Honduras and Fiji) and Sir Harry Cordeaux (Uganda, St Helena and the Bahamas). Sir Joseph Byrne successively governed the Seychelles, Sierra Leone and Kenya between the wars, but attracted more notice as the first Roman Catholic to be Inspector-General of the Royal Irish Constabulary (controversially dismissed in 1920). As High Commissioner of Mesopotamia (1920–23), Sir Percy Cox ranks as one of the key creators of the state of Iraq. Sir Thomas Haycraft also experienced the strife accompanying British rule in the Middle East as Chief Justice of Palestine.

In 1923, having negotiated arrangements with 147 service clubs in India, Egypt, and the colonies, Finlay introduced a new class of overseas membership for 'Officers and Civil Servants wishing to make Phyllis Court their *pied à terre* whilst in England'; when abroad, they could pay a subscription of just one guinea. Officials of the Indian Civil Service belonging to the Club included Moses Gubbay, Financial Secretary to the Government of India, and Sir Geoffrey Clarke, 'mainstay of the Simla Amateur Dramatic Club'. Eastern trade was meanwhile represented by Sir Percy Newson of Calcutta, Sir Percival David of Bombay and Sir Arthur Binning of Rangoon. Sir Dorabji Tata created a steelmaking concern in India that has since grown into one of the world's largest companies. Dominion links remained strong. One member, Sir Francis Bell, was Prime Minister of New Zealand (albeit for only sixteen days in 1925).

Phyllis Court on a weekend afternoon remained the place to bump into a Lord Mayor of Adelaide, Attorney-General of Alberta or Justice of the Supreme Court of South Africa, a point underlined by the Overseas Garden Party held in conjunction with the Royal Empire Society in June 1929. The guest of honour, Lord Meston, an active Liberal peer and former Governor of the United Provinces of Agra and Oudh, told the company that theirs was a great Empire 'which had not been built up by might or by force but by common ideals'. Sophia Duleep Singh (still a member) might have questioned this, given the history of the Punjab, but the reigning Indian Princes in the Club knew better than to argue. The Rajah of Pudukkotai lived permanently in Europe; married to an Australian, he died in Cannes. Sir Bhawani Singh, Maharajah of Jhalawar, ruled a small state in Rajasthan. The Maharajah of Burdwan, the senior Hindu nobleman of Bengal, had established his credentials in 1908 by interposing himself between an assassin and the British Lieutenant-Governor. He represented India at the Imperial Conference of 1926.

Phyllis Court was not a club particularly associated with writers. In retrospect, Roy Finlay's most significant literary acquaintance was not a member at all, but Eric Blair, the boy who lived next door to him in Shiplake. Eric grew friendly with the Buddicom children, who brought him to the Club, though he 'didn't seem to enjoy it very much'. As an adult, Eric Blair wrote as George Orwell (and the inaugural meeting of the Orwell Society took place at Phyllis Court in 2011). The most successful author among the membership, a superstar in her day, could hardly have been more different. She was Marie Corelli, whose bombastic religious fantasies, such as *The Sorrows of Satan* (1895), enraged critics while fascinating readers by the million. There was also Justin Huntly McCarthy, historical novelist and Irish nationalist. His bestseller, *If I Were King* (1901), inspired the operetta *The Vagabond King*. Sir Max Pemberton, clubman, dandy, and author of *The Iron Pirate* (1893) among other tales of adventure, enjoyed honorary life membership. John L. Balderston, London

Two monocle-wearing actor members: Heather Thatcher (left) and George Arliss (right).

correspondent of *The New York World*, helped script the earliest sound films of *Dracula* and *Frankenstein*. The writer who most often referred to Phyllis Court in print must be Cecil Roberts; it crops up in a good half-dozen of his books. Resident at nearby Lower Assendon, he produced light novels and discursive non-fiction.

Turning to performers, Phyllis Court could boast Dame Nellie Melba, the Australian prima donna, then at the peak of her fame. Baroness de Bush had also sung soprano leads at Covent Garden as Pauline Joran, while the Countess of Dudley was actually Gertie Millar, much loved star of such musical comedies as *Our Miss Gibbs* and *The Quaker Girl*. More recently, blonde starlet Heather Thatcher made her name with 'harem dancing;' off-stage she wore a monocle, as did the Club's most illustrious thespian, George Arliss, the first British actor to win an Oscar (in 1929 for the title role in *Disraeli*). Ivor Novello, songwriter and all-round man of the theatre, occasionally visited as a guest of Roy Finlay.

By now, the reader will probably appreciate the brevity of the Henley reporter who settled for recording in 1927 that 'Phyllis Court was, as usual, the headquarters of the social crowd'. Club announcements routinely appeared on the front page of *The Times*.

The Staff

Detailed information about the staff of Phyllis Court is generally lacking. Plainly, it needed to be numerous, and the working day started early. Heating and cooking still relied on coal and the bedrooms had no plumbing, so cans of hot water had to be carried upstairs. A group photograph from 1920 shows Finlay surrounded by fifty-one employees, twenty-seven male and twenty-four female. About a quarter looks teenaged, and only two boatmen can be confidently assigned to their roles, thanks to white caps. An equivalent picture taken two years later has fifty-eight people. Inevitably, many of the waiters, porters, barmen, and maids were seasonal and transient. Changes of chef sometimes merited publicity: Monsieur Daubin came in 1919, and Monsieur Rinaldi in 1922, the latter from the Trocadero in Shaftesbury Avenue. Notices in *The Times* heralded the appointment of James 'Sunny Jim' Califano, former head waiter of the Savoy, as catering superintendent in 1926, but he soon departed to run his own hotel. There was nevertheless also a core of longer-term employees resident in the district. 'No more enjoyable gathering takes place locally at Christmas time than the annual party given to the staff of Phyllis Court Club and their friends', asserted the *Henley Standard*. Families working together at the Club included the Champions, Rathbones, and Jacksons. A staff sports day every August comprised contests on both land and water, such as dongola racing (where teams paddle punts), a tug-of-war and an egg-and-spoon race. Three cheers for Captain Finlay would bring proceedings to a close.

Mr Theobald became a fixture at the boathouse (which ran a longer season than the Clubhouse). He stayed at Phyllis Court from 1920 till 1957. Eighteen acres, with orchards, greenhouses and a vegetable garden, kept outdoor staff busy all year round. Sidney Astley, the head gardener, had a tied cottage in New Street; Leslie Neale, his assistant, lived in the Marlow Road lodge. For eighty years, the most celebrated horticultural feature of the Club was the rambler roses covering the river wall. These had been planted during the war, and Mrs Finlay made it her mission to train them to hang low over the water. The comments of the *Manchester Guardian* in 1924 were typical: 'The flowers along the wall of Phyllis Court trailed

The Club's staff in 1920, with Roy Finlay in the centre.

as richly as if this was some Italian lakeside. Behind, the great weeping trees swayed their branches in the wind, and in between the towers of green the shaven lawn looked as artificial as a theatre garden "set".' Much was also made of soft fruit: 'One of the glories of Phyllis Court is the crop of prize raspberries, from bushes originally planted by William III [!], which has always obligingly ripened for Henley Week.'

'Anyone for tennis?'

A lot of tennis was played at 'the Court' between the wars, so much that references to the Club in the national press far more often related to the racquet than the oar. This reflected the status of tennis as the great social sport of the English middle classes, suitable for both sexes and a wide range of ages. At every level, it remained an overwhelmingly amateur activity with no sharp division between serious expo-nents and casual weekend players. The Club had catered for the latter from the start, Lady Wavertree being a particular enthusiast. By 1914, there were six grass courts and three hard sand ones under construction. Weekly tournaments for members resumed in 1919, but higher aspirations were signalled by the composition of the new Sports Committee. Rowing was represented by three Stewards of the Regatta, most notably Don Burnell, who had helped power the Leander Club to four Grand Challenge victories (1898–1901) and later won an Olympic gold medal. More inno-vative, though, was the inclusion of three Wimbledon tennis finalists. Frank Riseley had been runner-up in the gentlemen's singles (1903–5), and M.J.G. Ritchie won the gentlemen's doubles in 1908 and 1910, while Dorothea Lambert Chambers, seven times ladies' champion, stood alone as the top woman player of the pre-war world.

Phyllis Court Club also engaged a Sports Secretary 'at a salary of £200 *per annum*, with Board and Lodging, but not wine'. The first decade saw a swift turn-over: T.P. Stokoe (1919), Major Eric Skelton (1920–21), Captain M.C.W. Cobby (1922), Captain W.B. Webster (1923), Captain R.B. Watts (1924), Captain Hugh Gosling (1925–26) and H. Jackson-Feilden (1927). A primary duty of the Sports Secretary was to organise week-long Open Hard Court Tennis Tournaments under the sanction of the Lawn Tennis Association (LTA). By April 1920, when the first took place, the Club possessed seven all-weather clay courts, five made 'by a Wimbledon firm according to a special prescription'. Entry to tournaments was 'restricted to members, those introduced by members, and members of recognised tennis clubs'. Gentlemen competed for the Phyllis Court Challenge Cup (value 50 guineas), and ladies for the Phyllis Court Challenge Bowl (value 30 guineas), and along with gentlemen's doubles and mixed doubles there were four correspond-ing handicap events. The winners of the inaugural singles were Captain H.L. Barclay, champion of Tasmania, and Doris Craddock, ranked eleventh in the world (by modern criteria). Mrs Craddock won five more times and joined the Sports Committee. Tennis competitors (like Regatta competitors) were given temporary membership of the Club and then offered discounted 'sports membership'.

The Phyllis Court tournaments became regular fixtures in the LTA calendar, held twice a year from 1921 till 1933 and thereafter annually in early September. Results were reported in the London daily papers alongside those from the Queen's Club, Roehampton, Surbiton and such resorts as Bexhill, Sidmouth and Frinton. The *Observer,* always friendly to the Club, praised its playing surfaces, idyllic surroundings, and general air of sociability:

> At few meetings do players find, as a 'background' to the courts, a tall trellis covered with rambler rose-bushes! Tall, but not tall enough to prevent many a viciously smashed ball finding a watery grave in the pool behind, where the ducks quack loud applause, and even the solitary moorhen scarcely stirs from her brooding, still proud perhaps of having been once exhibited to a gullible couple of Australian visitors as a cuckoo on its nest! A very pleasant country tournament indeed is Phyllis Court; those who know it come again and again.

This popularity brought its own problems. By the late 1920s, four hundred matches had to be completed on seven courts in the space of six days, so a few showers of rain and hard-fought contests could easily upset the schedule. The one recurrent complaint of tournament players at Henley was long waiting times.

Afternoon teas and dances each evening did not preclude earnest sporting endeavour, and the spring event drew champions practising for Wimbledon. Brian 'Babe' Norton from South Africa took second place there in 1921 after coming first at Phyllis Court, whose ladies' winner that year, Kitty McKane (Mrs Godfree), triumphed at Wimbledon in 1924 and 1926. The foremost British player of the century, Fred Perry, took part in autumn 1927, going out in the third round; he was only eighteen. Major Ritchie had won the Challenge Cup in 1924 aged fifty-three. The referee and handicapper F.R. Burrow performed the same functions for the All-England Tennis Club, whose secretary Major Dudley Larcombe was also a member of Phyllis Court. Henley had its own heroes too, such as W.H. Powell, the Cambridge Blue, and Violet Chamberlain (Mrs Owen), who dominated between 1927 and 1932. Victors in the gentlemen's game hailed from as far away as Japan (Yoshiro Ohta 1928), India (Athar-Ali Fyzee 1933) and China (Wai-Chuen Choy 1937, Jin Ho 1938). Ted Tinling, champion in 1935, later flourished as a tennis couturier. Outside tournament weeks, the All-India Davis Cup Team (chiefly composed of British army officers) used Phyllis Court several times as its practice facility in England. Ordinary members who lifted a racquet never lacked exemplars, and the Club furthered their ambitions: 'Professional tennis tuition may be arranged upon application to the Sports Secretary.'

An Eventful Year

Nineteen twenty-seven was memorable in the annals of Phyllis Court for quite a variety of reasons. For a start, Finlay experimented with more popular

The Lenglen Matches

Intensive advertising preceded the appearance at Phyllis Court in 1927 of a sporting celebrity of the first rank. Suzanne Lenglen from France was arguably the greatest woman tennis player ever. She won Wimbledon six times between 1919 and 1925. In an age, moreover, when most sportswomen were self-effacing, Mademoiselle Lenglen was an exuberant personality. Her balletic movements, her chiffon bandeau, her daring hemline (just below the knee), and even her taste for brandy-soaked sugar-lumps all attracted emulation, while a refusal to wear stays made her a symbol of female emancipation. People otherwise ignorant of tennis knew about Suzanne, whose first name sufficed. Having controversially abandoned the amateur game, she would make her professional debut in Britain with matches at Henley on the first and final evenings of the Regatta. Cochran booked German champion Dora Köring as her opponent, while Wimbledon runner-up Howard Kinsey joined coaches Karel Koželuh and Evelyn Dewhurst to fill out the programme. Finlay made known that the fees totalled almost a thousand pounds. Alas, heavy rain prevented play on 29 June (a risk insured against), yet even on Saturday attendance fell short of expectation. While *The Scotsman* rated Miss Lenglen magnificent, the *Henley Standard* sounded less impressed:

Tennis star Suzanne Lenglen.

> From the outset Suzanne played with her opponent, played her as a cat plays with a mouse. At the end, beaten 6-1, 6-2, Fräulein Köring was gasping for breath, while the Frenchwoman was still perfectly cool and fresh. But she did not arouse the enthusiasm and interest of the crowd in the same way as when she was an amateur. Even during

a burst of brilliant play, when Suzanne and Howard Kinsey defeated Karel Koželuh and Miss Dewhurst, only isolated groups in the crowd broke into applause. The absence of the real element of competition was doubtless the explanation.

It may have been unwise to hold the event on the day when fanatical followers of tennis were bound to be elsewhere – watching the finals at Wimbledon. Billboards on the river bank had upset the rowing fraternity. 'Phyllis Court is now a centre for dancing and tennis, and has forgotten its historic past', complained the *Quarterly Review*. Although the Lenglen matches raised the profile of the Club, its entertainments policy soon reverted to past practice.

entertainers. Professional singers from the Clifford Essex agency had long performed at the Club on Whit Sunday and Ascot Sunday. This year they were supplemented by fashionable exhibition dancers arranged by top impresario C.B. Cochran, beginning with Vanda and Vladimir from the Piccadilly Cabaret. The pièce de résistance was a show by Santos Casani and José Lennard, who had recently been made famous by a Pathé newsreel of them dancing the charleston on the roof of a moving taxi (a clip now beloved of documentary-makers seeking to evoke the 'Roaring Twenties').

Not all the press coverage that summer was sought. On 19 July, Phyllis Court fulfilled an unusually sombre function as the location of a coroner's court after the discovery in the river of the corpse of a member, seventy-two-year-old Colonel Arthur Lysaght, who had been in the habit of canoeing after dinner. He was judged to have fallen asleep and capsized.

Two weeks later, on 4 August, Captain John Harvey, the Social Secretary, was required to give evidence again – this time at Henley Police Court in a case reported (not very seriously) all across the English-speaking world. The prosecution opened with the words: 'It has often been said of young men that they are not likely to set the Thames on fire, but you have before you today a young man who actually accomplished it.' Gavin Henderson, aged twenty-five, later 2nd Baron Farringdon, had held his stag-night at Phyllis Court on 1 June; at around 11.30 p.m., the guests adjourned to the lawn. Harvey reported what happened next:

> I suddenly heard an exclamation of horror from one of the waiters, and looking up I saw a sheet of flame of really appalling dimensions. It hid the trees on the other side of the river. The grandstand was being prepared for the Regatta, and it had been recently painted and tarred. The fire was so terrifying that I rushed down to the riverside. I found that all the shrubs, rose-bushes, and creepers on the riverside were blazing with flames, and the flames were so high that they burned the trees which stand about a yard and a half from the riverside and only a yard or two from the grandstand.

The party-goers, 'somewhat excited', were meanwhile hurling garden furniture into the river to follow the contents of eight two-gallon cans of petrol. The fire soon burnt itself out, but the Thames Conservancy pressed charges. Henderson was acquitted after denying advance knowledge, although someone in the Club that evening had put up posters denouncing the use of Soviet petrol. (Britain had just broken off diplomatic relations with the USSR, and the *Daily Mail* supplied such posters as part of its campaign for a trade boycott.) His friends all refused to identify the culprit, rumoured to be Brian Howard, a poet notorious for outrageous antics. The incident was not at all typical of Phyllis Court, as 'Bright Young Things' preferred Murray's Club at Maidenhead (where cocaine was readily available).

The high-point of the 1927 season was the 'Coming of Age' Ball, held on 24 June to mark the Club's twenty-first anniversary. The grounds were lavishly illuminated, decorated boats processed up the river and guests dined for the first time ever in the lower tier of the Grandstand, which had been encased with plate-glass screens. Finlay invested the evening with a cosmopolitan atmosphere by inviting not only Commonwealth High Commissioners but also the heads of foreign diplomatic missions, so members attending received a reminder that orders and decorations should be worn. Antonio Chiaramonte Bordonaro, the Italian Ambassador, and Dr Raul Régis de Oliveira, the Brazilian Ambassador, both enjoyed social renown. Also present were Baron Frankenstein (the Austrian Minister), M.V.K. Rackauskas (the Lithuanian Chargé d'Affaires) and Aziz Ezzat Pasha (the hypochondriacal Egyptian Minister, never without a bottle of disinfectant). India was represented by Sir Atul Chatterjee and Australia by Sir Joseph Cook, the one-time miner who had served as Prime Minister in 1913–14. This time the local paper *was* impressed: 'We doubt whether a ball of such brilliance and attended by such a distinguished company has ever taken place in Henley.'

A year on, Finlay wrote, 'As is well-known, Phyllis Court has become the recognised country club of the Diplomatic Services in London, and the various Ambassadors, Ministers, and Chargés d'Affaires are frequently to be seen there. The Japanese Chargé d'Affaires has been staying at the Club for some weeks.' Sadao Saburi was indeed a regular visitor, for he loved to row. The gradual internationalisation of the Regatta led to more diplomats taking up their option of honorary membership, especially after the return of German crews in 1931 was imbued with political symbolism. Thus Konstantin von Neurath, Leopold von Hoesch and Joachim von Ribbentrop, successive German Ambassadors, all made the acquaintance of 'Phyllis'. (The first and third were later convicted of war crimes; the second was possibly murdered by the Gestapo.) Uruguayan and Argentine envoys also came to support rowing compatriots from the 'Legation Box'. The next Italian Ambassador, Dino Grandi, an ardent Fascist, escorted Princess Maria to the Club on 28 July 1935. They went to Medmenham in Finlay's launch before returning for tea and tennis. The youngest daughter of King Victor Emmanuel III expressed herself 'delighted with everything she saw.'

Grand Designs

Refurbishment progressed as funds allowed. River club finances would always fluctuate, if only in response to the vagaries of the climate. Finlay, however, repeatedly envisaged the comprehensive renovation and enlargement of Phyllis Court to make it indisputably 'the most luxurious and entertaining Club rendezvous outside London, and in every way comparable with the best of the great Country Clubs of America and the East'. The later 1920s was accordingly an era of grand designs only partially realised.

The financial groundwork for expansion began with a call on the goodwill of debenture-holders. By ignoring the reality of inflation, Finlay was able to argue that these members who had lent money to the Club Company before 1910 were now receiving an annual return equal to 50 per cent, when the value of their Regatta vouchers was taken into account. 'It will immediately be realised that such a rate of interest… constitutes an exceedingly heavy tax.' To remove this obstacle to future improvements, creditors were invited to exchange debentures for '1925 Bonds', which (instead of paying 5 per cent in cash) offered 10 per cent in the form of a wider range of vouchers and franking dockets. Nineteen investors complied.

Then came the main flotation of eight hundred £25 'Income Bonds' to fund a whole raft of new facilities. Redeemable in 1940, they would pay 5 per cent interest, and purchasers of ten bonds also secured life membership. Finlay explained that the Company had made a net profit in the last full year (1924) of £3,005, three times as much as it would need to service even a sell-out issue. In the event, 203 bonds were sold at the start of 1926, raising £5,075 for the Extensions Fund. A double-page spread in the *Illustrated London News* on 27 March showed architect J.J. Joass's vision of a greater Phyllis Court under the heading, 'A feature of American life becoming popular over here: A famous English country club.' The sketches accompanied a general article on the Americanisation of Europe.

Alas, the next season was a bad one. In October 1926, debenture- and bond-holders were 'given the opportunity of accepting interest in the form of special Vouchers of Admission for Guests', as the Club was unlikely to 'be in a position to resume payment of interest in addition to shouldering the financial burdens left by the War'. The following summer was even worse, necessitating a further appeal: 'Owing to the unprecedented wet weather which has persisted throughout the past Season, following upon the General Strike of last year, the Club has experienced two of the most difficult Seasons in its history, which has resulted in a serious drain upon its liquid funds.' Finlay again urged creditors to exchange their holdings for non-cash '1925 Bonds'.

The Club resorted to a membership campaign in 1928, it being explained that, 'Whereas in the case of a London Club a large membership may be detrimental to the comfort of the Members generally, in a Country Club, within limits, the reverse is the case.' As in 1924, all members of associated clubs were offered the chance to join 'on exceptionally favourable terms [£5 10s 6d] without the formality of a proposer and seconder'. The normal subscription was now ten guineas. Finlay drew attention to 'the run-out-of-town accessibility of Phyllis Court', thanks to the Brentford and Hounslow bypass, and praised 'the beautiful drive through Maidenhead Thicket'. The Club already had its own petrol pumps and chauffeurs' room. Total membership increased to almost 2,500, its highest level yet, encouraging the issue of a thousand new 'Development Bonds' at £25 each. The interest rate was 6 per cent, and the redemption date 1950. Twenty investors altogether purchased 149 of them, injecting a further £3,725 into the Company in March 1929.

The modernisation programme yielded visible results. The Lounge assumed its present form with the addition of fluted Ionic columns and the removal of the

The Entrance
Hall after
refurbishment
in 1928.

double fireplace in the middle (a relic of the Victorian private house, left without its adjoining walls when several rooms were combined in 1906–07). Walls and woodwork were repainted in lighter colours. Waring & Gillow supplied new seating and plain green carpets. The former kitchen and staff quarters (to the west) became a new Cocktail Lounge, Billiard Room, and American Bar, while the previous Cocktail Lounge (to the north) reverted to a Reading Room. The new main staircase was said to be modelled on that of Arlington House (which stood on the site of Buckingham Palace between 1675 and 1703). It was wider than its predecessor, but not radically different. *Vogue* described the interior as 'a dream of roses and soft lights and deep country comfort'. The Club also gained an electric laundry, a Crossley van and 'a new type of motor punt-launch specifically designed for Phyllis Court' with a 10.9 horsepower petrol engine capable of ten knots.

Shortage of capital prevented reconstruction on a grander scale. Finlay's plans envisaged adding two upper storeys with a mansard roof and cupola, attaching an 'elliptical annexe' to the southern end of the Restaurant, and building an entirely new eastern façade, eighteen feet nearer the Thames. Those who love Phyllis Court as it is will probably not pine for the work of J.J. Joass, whose architectural drawings suggest a city bank, yet opinions may well differ over the unbuilt squash courts, bowling alley, and bathing pool. Then there were the much discussed Grosvenor gates, purchased with seven lamp-posts by means of another small bond sale in 1927, when Grosvenor House in Park Lane was demolished to make way for the Grosvenor House Hotel. In his mind's eye, Finlay saw these huge examples of ornamental cast iron (designed by Thomas Cundy II in 1842) set into a stone screen beside the Marlow Road. As this would serve as the Club war memorial, it was 'hoped that the gates, when re-erected, will be opened by the Prince of Wales'. Unfortunately, the existing road frontage was too narrow, negotiations for an exchange of land dragged on for twenty-odd years, and ultimately the money ran out. The four gates, each weighing three tons, were sold in 1949.

The proprietor meanwhile made a very substantial investment early in 1929: he bought the freehold of Phyllis Court from the Fawley Estate by private agreement. W. Dalziel Mackenzie had died, and death duties needed to be paid. Finlay promptly granted a fifty-year lease of the Clubhouse, tennis courts, and southern lawns to his own company for £7,000, plus rental of £1,500 per year. In December, he noted that 'the past year had been one of the best years in the Club's history, though in view of the slump on Wall Street and the reflected depression in this country… no further structural alterations would be contemplated until the outlook improved.'

Royal Patronage

The first reigning sovereign to visit Phyllis Court Club was King Alfonso XIII of Spain on 30 June 1927. Though Spaniards had yet to compete at Henley, he enjoyed all sports involving speed. The following Regatta brought the young Princess Xenia Georgievna of Russia (or Mrs William B. Leeds), best known for (mistakenly) accepting Anna Anderson as Grand Duchess Anastasia. While the Prince of Wales had given the Club his seal of approval as patron, he did not lend himself to further publicity. Finlay could only reprint a photo of him passing by on the umpire's launch in 1921.

In May 1928, local businessmen met to consider why the Regatta no longer enriched Henley as much as once it did. Recognising that Phyllis Court Club 'brought the right sort of people to the town', they listened with interest to the views of its owner:

> To go straight to the point, there is only one thing that Henley requires and that Henley ought to have, and that is the patronage of Their Majesties the King and Queen. Henley represents the principal event of the sport of rowing, and the sport of rowing is essentially a British National sport. It is, moreover, the cleanest of all the sports and the one that is most free from any form of betting or professionalism. Yet of all the sports, rowing is the one of them that remains for some obscure reason, unrecognised and unpatronised by the Royal favour… With Henley under the Royal umbrage the whole river remains out of fashion and under a cloud. This has been the state of affairs for years, going from bad to worse, whilst by the mere presence of their Majesties at the great annual rowing festival of Henley the whole position might be reversed, and the river occupy the position it ought to occupy as the national pleasure resort of the whole of London and the South of England.

He recommended a petition to the King signed by every man, woman, and child in the town. The Duke of Kent attended the Regatta in 1928, and the Duke and Duchess of York in 1931.

Meanwhile, Phyllis Court made its own arrangements, which came to fruition in 1930. On 3 July, the Club entertained Lord Carnegie and his wife Princess Maud, a granddaughter of Edward VII. With them came King George II of Greece, who often seemed happier as an exile in London than ever he did in Athens. On 4 July, the honoured guests were Prince and Princess Arthur of Connaught, accompanied by King Manuel II of Portugal (resident in Twickenham since 1910), and the Maharajah of Tripura (who was 'piquantly interested in the sword dances executed by the pipers of the King's Own Scottish Borderers on the lawn'). Prince Arthur and the King of Greece both became Vice-Presidents of the Club, but it was clearly the former who grew attached to it. His sister and brother-in-law were in fact already members, Princess Patricia having renounced her title to marry the Hon. Alec Ramsay. In his late forties, Prince Arthur of Connaught, a first cousin of George V, had been quite prominent in the early years of the reign, when the King's children were too young to carry out public duties. He then served a term as Governor-General of South Africa. His wife was also British royalty, formerly Princess Alexandra, Duchess of Fife. A degree of pomp attended their Regatta appearances at Phyllis Court in 1932 and 1933. As the band played *God Save the King,* the Prince's personal standard was hoisted over the clubhouse, while Committeemen and their wives lined up in the Luncheon Court for introduction by the Chairman, who then led the couple past a bodyguard of Henley Boy Scouts to their places in the Royal Box, where foreign crews were presented between races.

This was not all. At 3.30 p.m. on Friday 1 July 1932, a 'picturesque little ceremony' took place on the lawn. Colonel John O'Sullevan, representing the Committee, handed the new replacement flag of Phyllis Court Club to Prince Arthur, who stated 'that it gave him great pleasure to have that opportunity of showing his appreciation of that beautiful Club and he wished it every success in the difficult times through which we were all passing'. He then passed the banner to Harold Burton of the Scouts, who ran it to the top of the pole. 'Everyone stood to attention and gave three cheers as the flag broke into the breeze.' Then, as now, it comprised a saxe-blue symmetric cross on a white ground with a red rose in the centre and 'P.C.C.' in gold in the upper hoist quarter. Also in attendance were the Crown Prince of Sweden, later King Gustav VI Adolf, whose first wife had been Princess Margaret of Connaught, their daughter Princess Ingrid, Lady Patricia Ramsay, the Imperial journalist Sir Harry Brittain and Paul Mellon, son of the banking millionaire who was then American Ambassador in London. Three years later, Princess Ingrid's new husband, the Crown Prince of Denmark, later Frederick IX, also paid a visit. Phyllis Court's 'own' royal personage, however, indubitably remained Prince Arthur, who sometimes looked into the Clubhouse informally outside Henley Week.

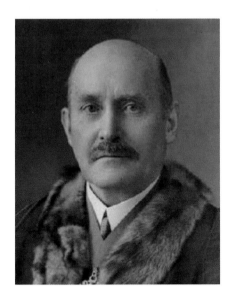 

Prince and Princess Arthur of Connaught, the Club's most regular royal visitors.

The Connaughts were among the many distinguished people first entertained at the Club by the Hon. Evan Morgan, later 2nd Viscount Tredegar, a Committee member with an extraordinary range of friends, whose flamboyant extravagance became legendary. On the one hand, he was a dilettante poet and painter, associating with Dylan Thomas, Augustus John and H.G. Wells. Aldous Huxley described him as 'the fairy prince of modern life'. On the other hand, Morgan mixed with royalty; Queen Mary called him her favourite bohemian. A convert to Catholicism, he served as a papal chamberlain. He was also – though this was not generally known – a practising occultist, rated as 'Adept of Adepts' by Aleister Crowley. Add in his unexplained connections with Ernst Röhm and Rudolf Hess, and Lord Tredegar must be considered one of Phyllis Court Club's more eccentric characters.

The Early Thirties
In 1931 there appeared in print a two-penny pamphlet with this title page:

A Brief Explanation, which
should be read by all.
THIS ECONOMIC
QUESTION
The Reason and the Remedy!
By ROY FINLAY
A Member of no Party, or
of any Party that puts
Country and Empire first.

The author's own line of business coloured his analysis:

> It will be obvious to any ordinary intelligence that the community, *any* community, is divided roughly into two sections – those who *spend money*, and those who *work for money*. We all spend money, but what I mean by those who 'spend money' in this sense, is, those who do not require to work for their living…. The spenders of a community are as much an economic necessity to a population as are its workers, and, man for man, infinitely more important to the community, as one spender may provide a livelihood for a multiple of workers, whereas one worker can only do the work of two hands.
>
> And yet, in their ignorance and their anxiety merely to 'catch votes,' it is against the very existence of our spenders that our recent Governments have, by legalised robbery, levied war, depleting their numbers as though they were a blight on the land and throwing them into the ranks of the already overcrowded mass of workers, there to compete for the very work which otherwise they themselves would have been providing. An interference with the essential laws of constructive progress…. Money, like water, can only exert power when in motion. So, *spend*, those of you who can, and keep the mill wheels turning.

The same message went out to Club members 'in face of the present phenomenal depression'. They should entertain as much as possible to protect Phyllis Court from disaster: 'The flag at all costs must be kept flying.' In May, Finlay thought about making an appeal to the Prince of Wales to visit, but the death of Sir Trevor Dawson intervened; Brigadier-General Hoare Nairne took over as Chairman. 'The general prospects of the country, and therefore of the Club also, continued to get worse instead of better', stated the Company minutes, and the weather was dreadful too, 'particularly at weekends'. By September, a decision had been made to reduce the level of overheads. 'Phyllis Court is, in a sense, a National Institution', declared the circular, 'and it is undoubtedly the wish of everybody that an earnest effort should be made to save the Club.' Each debenture-holder was offered a deal: he could have a quarter of his holding redeemed immediately in cash, if he would convert the remainder into 'Economy Bonds', receiving interest at 7.5 per cent for his life-time exclusively in vouchers. Over the next four months, the Company bought back £8,270 worth of debentures for a cash outlay of £2,067 10s. This operation was probably crucial to long-term survival. In 1932, the 'world-wide financial crisis was having a disastrous effect upon the membership of the Club, a great number of members having been forced to resign'.

Of course, amid the economic gloom, there were still those glorious days on the river when the charm of Henley waxed strong, and the Club jubilantly upheld its traditions in Regatta Week. Cecil Roberts captured the atmosphere in *Gone Rambling* (1935):

Finlay's Frustrations

Finlay became a regular writer of indignant open letters in the 1930s, chiefly to the *Daily Express*. One of his bugbears was the licensing laws introduced under the Defence of the Realm Act (1914) to regulate the sale of alcohol and not subsequently repealed. 'One does not fly to the South of France merely to avoid the English climate', he insisted, 'but principally to avoid D.O.R.A.' Another target was the entertainment tax levied since 1916:

> For the past few years we have had to hand the tax collector for entertainment tax alone as much as we have received ourselves from our principal meeting, and out of what is left to us we then have to find all the other rates and taxes and imposts. Result: staff reduced to less than half in order to continue in existence at all, and spending reduced to a cheese-paring minimum.

The catering contract, awarded to Gunter & Co. of Berkeley Square in 1928, was moved three years later to the 'Park Lane Catering Company, with the Club Steward, Mr Smart, in charge'. Repeated efforts to sell the lease of Manor Garden only succeeded in 1935 (when the Fawley Estate bought it back). Low revenues early and late in the season led to its contraction, till the Club was opening at the end of May and closing before mid-September. In 1932, Finlay cut his annual salary by 25 per cent (to £750). His frustration found release in diatribes against spineless politicians who were bleeding taxpayers white and reducing a once proud Empire to a timid Commonwealth. He pinned his hopes on Winston Churchill, then leading Diehard resistance to Indian nationalism. It frankly comes as something of a relief to discover that Finlay's only letter in *The Times* concerned a lesser grievance:

> The inevitable reply from caterers is 'Oh, the public only ask for strawberry or vanilla,' to which my obvious retort has always been, 'How do you expect otherwise when most of them in this country have never even heard of any other flavour?' How would the famous ice-cream bars of Italy and other Continental countries fare if they were only to serve 'strawberry or vanilla'?

The Honorary Secretary wished his members to experience 'a little epicurean excitement'.

All along the old river wall of Phyllis Court, covered with scarlet roses, lines of deck-chairs stand on either side of a canopied space, where the distinguished visitors, Royal if possible, and at least ambassadorial if not, will be roped in, and wrapped around with the local gentry.

I have just greeted ['Miss Arabella Mervyn-Morpeth and her brother Brigadier-General Poultenay Mervyn-Morpeth of Page's Bottom']. The latter has taken out of the press a Shantung silk suit whose lines were fashionable at the last Delhi Durbar. But the dear old Brigadier-General makes a striking if tropical note. This is the week of weeks, when he strings a monocle about his neck, and carries a rhinoceros-hide walking stick with a boar's tusk handle.

[Miss Arabella] is very neat, with her neck fenced round with lace and whale-bone. She knows everything about rowing, and answers at once what crew is paddling downstream, and what 'time' Jesus made in the Ladies' Plate. Her two cavaliers are stout gentlemen who wear absurdly small caps on large heads, and ties of the pinkness of an apoplectic baby. But hush! they are gods of the Leander Club, whose entrance is so narrow that only a slide in a varsity boat can carry one through.

I have just caught Sir John Lavery hidden away in a corner by a great elm busily paint-ing a summery picture of the terrace, dappled with sunshine, parasols, and frocks. Lunch is now ready, and my hospitable friend, Captain Finlay, has asked us to dine in his private sitting room. His hospitality being larger than his table, and twelve guests having grown to twenty-six, we will have to behave nicely and wait for the second sitting.

The Club bought Lavery's painting, as it had also *Cromwell's Wall, Phyllis Court* by Bertram Priestman, shown at the Royal Academy in 1929. The *Sydney Morning Herald* remarked in 1930 on the undiminished sartorial élan of members more modish than the fictional Mervyn-Morpeths:

If you go to Phyllis Court Club for the regatta, then it is almost an Ascot function, and you wear Ascot frocks. Lovely dresses were seen at the club this week…. Ankle-length dresses were the most popular, and they were worn with huge hats. There was a dis-tinctly international atmosphere about Henley this year, and Parisiennes and Germans and South Americans and Italians wandered about the lawns of Phyllis Court Club and made a delightful picture against their sylvan background. All the women seemed to patronise the long flowing skirt and the big picture hat.

Masculine attire incurred scrutiny too. An advertisement for trousers read: 'At the Carlton Bar at Cannes. On the lawn at Phyllis Court. In the "Gloucester" at Cowes. Wherever smart men relax – you'll find Daks.'

Without ceasing to be the guiding spirit of Phyllis Court, Finlay stepped down as Honorary Secretary and Managing Director on 1 January 1933 in favour of his twenty-six-year-old adopted son. Jack Rendle-Mervill had been Sports Secretary and Assistant Secretary since 1928 and a familiar face at the Club from boyhood. It was understood that his father, Jack Rendle, had been killed in the war at Merville in France after asking his friend and comrade, Finlay, to promise to look after his child in such an event (though attempts by Rendle-Mervill in later life to trace relatives proved unavailing). Educated at Radley College, while spending his sum-mers at Phyllis Court, Jackie (nicknamed 'Squeak') grew up a rowing enthusiast and coxed the Radley eight at the Regatta in 1923. He might not always have been able to match his mentor's easy manner with strangers – very few people could – but his loyalty to the Club would last a lifetime. To generations of members, his customary white blazer made him instantly recognisable even at a distance.

The social programme in the 1930s continued to revolve around three major events: the Ascot Ball, the Regatta and the tennis tournament. To these, Rendle-Mervill sought to add a fourth, a three-day motor-cruiser rally 'on the lines of the Monte Carlo rally for cars', with various prizes and dancing. The first took place on 17–19 July 1936. High winds disrupted the watermanship tests on Sunday and forced participants indoors, where Prince Arthur 'caused much amused discussion by asking, "When does a boat become a ship?"'

Finlay meanwhile pondered broader strategy. By 1934, 'the time appeared propitious to issue an invitation to suitable persons to augment the membership of the Club with a view to filling up the many vacancies created by the General Depression and, if the response should justify it, to continue the Development scheme'. He still wanted 'a Club on the "Grand Scale"' befitting 'the principal Sporting, Motoring and Social centre in the South of England'. His idea now was to finance new facilities by building a country club estate (as many American clubs had done). Near the drive and tennis courts, four terraces of 'Cloister Residences on the lines of the Colleges of Oxford and Cambridge' would be erected for renting out to members, who might also buy plots for detached houses, some to the north of the moat, others on newly acquired land across the Marlow Road. To compensate for the loss of space, he planned to lease College Green, Swiss Farm and the Deer Park from the Fawley Estate. These would enable the Club to create a golf course and also an athletics track and stadium 'with a view to establishing an international sports week'. Despite publicity, the scheme came to nothing, as the Fawley Estate backed out in June 1934.

Roy Finlay caricatured in the 1920s.

Eighteen months later, Finlay declared his readiness to sell Phyllis Court to its members: 'The ultimate destiny of all clubs that deserve a destiny is to become members' clubs, owned and conducted by their own members, and it is only right and proper that this should be so', he said. The buy-out would take over a year to finalise, but Hoare Nairne soon set the ball rolling. 'To people of this neighbourhood', observed the *Henley Standard*, 'who have known Phyllis Court under the suzerainty of Captain Roy Finlay ever since they can remember anything at all, the change will come rather as the passing of a milestone.'

8

The Members' Club
– Interrupted

1937–1957

At the age of thirty-one or so, Phyllis Court Club was re-born, although the gradualness of its reincarnation from proprietary club to members' club makes it hard to say which of the various dates in the process should really be seen as the birthday. The local press identified a meeting held at Claridge's in Mayfair on 7 April 1937 as the 'historic event in the annals of this world-famous Club' on account of a new Governing Council taking office under the chairmanship of Sir Gilbert Eliott, 10th Baronet of Stobs, 27th Chief of Clan Eliott, Laird of Redheugh, and stockbroker. For almost a year, he had led the Organising Group in charge of the legal and financial aspects of the transformation.

Phyllis Court, with contents and goodwill, had been valued in 1935 at £50,950. Had Roy Finlay cared only for money, he might have closed the Club and sold the land as building-plots. He preferred it to continue. While retaining one-and-a-half acres north of the mooring basin (an area known then as the Camping Field and now as the Paddock), he offered to sell everything else to the members for £31,100. A circular issued in June 1936 invited them to raise the necessary funds by purchasing Founder Debentures priced at £5 each. These would pay 4½ per cent interest, and an investment of £250 conferred life membership. The response was enthusiastic. By the spring, £19,115 had been subscribed. (Holders of older debentures and bonds were meanwhile invited to convert them into Founder Debentures at the rate of 60 per cent of face value, so the total issue came to £26,845.) To cover the shortfall, the Club took a mortgage of £13,155 from Finlay himself at 4 per cent interest. The deal reached completion on 29 June 1937, when four Council members formed the new board of the Phyllis Court Members' Club Company, and its shares were made over to trustees. 'It is our Club', declared Eliott. 'Let us all try to be as helpful as possible and pull together to make it a great success.'

The membership had already celebrated the advent of self-government at a garden party on 29 May. To this was invited a long list of people, chiefly (though not exclusively) from Henley and its hinterland, whom the Council hoped might join the Club. Among those sipping sherry on the lawn were Sir Charles Fawcett (historian of British India), Sir Hugh Stephenson (former Governor of Burma), Sir William Holdsworth (Professor of English Law at Oxford), and P.C. Wren (author of *Beau Geste*). Admiral Sir Hugh Sinclair was the serving head of MI6, not that many can have known it. And how did Arturo Toscanini rate the Band of the

4th Queen's Own Hussars? Also attending were Admiral Sir Barry Domvile, who would be interned in 1940 as a Nazi sympathiser, and Dr John Bodkin Adams, whose acquittal at the Old Bailey in 1957 did not end speculation that he might have been a serial killer. The absence of peers would have worried Finlay, but his successors did not trouble to feed titbits to Society correspondents. In any case, air travel meant that the smart set now preferred Le Touquet or Deauville on summer weekends to anywhere on the Thames. Evident since about 1930, the decline in media coverage of Phyllis Court Club accelerated. Eliot did enlist the 5th Earl of Minto, a distant kinsman, and Prince Arthur of Connaught was made Club President in September 1937, but when he died a year later, the office lapsed.

Power now resided with the Governing Council, simply called the Council from 1938. This initially comprised fourteen people, seven elected by the members (on the 'one man, one vote' principle), and seven by the debenture holders (according to their stake). Although Finlay had wondered whether the mortgage should also carry voting rights, he accepted the view of the Organising Group that to grant so much influence to one individual would be contrary to the ethos of a members' club. In practice, elections were not openly contested. Some Council representatives were Phyllis Court veterans, such as Edward Hoare Nairne, Alfred Michelson and Wilfred Rhodes. Charles Brownrigg and Captain George Hamilton had also belonged to the bygone General Committee, the former being the retired headmaster of Magdalen College School and the latter managing director of the Westminster Shipping Company. Others, like Eliott, had come to the fore as members of the Organising Group. Dr Percy Phillips had taught chemistry at Thomason College of Civil Engineering in Roorkee, India. George Beverley was an accountant from Surrey. Major Mark Kirby, formerly of the Royal Artillery, had been 'well known in Melbourne social, military, and business circles'. From industry came Major Samuel Thornley, manufacturer of varnishes, and W. Bruce Dick, blender of mineral oils. Sir William Alexander was a Conservative MP. As a director of Coutts, Alfred Dunphie had managed the finances of Queen Alexandra. G.S.M. Warlow lived at Plaish Hall in Shropshire. Almost right away, the Council sought to co-opt extra members. Lord Inverforth declined the invitation, as did Sir Arthur Evans, the archaeologist, but acceptances came from Sir Dennis Herbert, a Deputy Speaker of the House of Commons, and Sir Francis McClean, aviation pioneer and recent High Sheriff of Oxfordshire. They were soon joined by Lieutenant-Colonel Hugh Iltid Nicholl, a solicitor prominent in Freemasonry as Director of Ceremonies of the Grand Lodge of England.

The Secretary from May 1937 was Colonel Charles Pickering, ceremonial head of the Duke of Wellington's Regiment. A year later, during the Sudetenland crisis, he surrendered his Club salary of £400 and became Honorary Secretary in order to be free to work for the Home Office on civil defence. Day-to-day management of Phyllis Court fell to E.M. Osborn, Assistant Secretary.

The new Club, keen to be perceived as such, distinguished itself from the old by promising to open all year round; hence the increased emphasis on local recruitment. Of 159 members elected in 1937, two-thirds lived in Oxfordshire, Buckinghamshire, or Berkshire. This trend was intended to supplement (and certainly not to replace) traditional ties to the metropolis. It is striking that the Council still held most of its meetings in London, usually at the Great Eastern Hotel in Liverpool Street. In order to encourage membership growth, the standard subscription had been cut from ten guineas to six, and a family scheme admitted a wife for three guineas. The re-founding of the Club on a more democratic basis prompted debate about the position of women. Eliott proposed to grant them full membership, but his colleagues consented only to the creation of a Ladies' Advisory Committee (LAC). When Inez Petrie and Lilias Hoare Nairne were invited to report the LAC's views (on bedroom and bathroom refurbishment) to the Council in person, it was pointed out to them that 'this was a man's Club but admitted Ladies as Independent Guest Members and Lady Guest Members'.

Winter opening, many argued, required investment in indoor facilities. Eliott regarded a swimming pool as the priority. Henley had fallen behind Maidenhead, where the Brigade of Guards' Club, Showboat Club, and Hungaria River Club all possessed pools. Calls for one at Phyllis Court had been stimulated by Finlay's abortive development scheme, which included sketches of a 'Grecian Pool' boasting Ionic columns. 'I hope that it can be completed before the hot weather arrives', said the Chairman in April 1937, 'and that it will be made long enough and deep enough to attract the younger members.' Squash courts stood next on the list; the Hurlingham Club had built theirs in 1934. And what about making more of the Grandstand?

> It is of a sufficient size internally to be visualised as the Sports Deck of a large P&O liner, and for a reasonable expenditure it could be so fitted up as to provide every day in the year all the recognized Deck Sports together with other popular pastimes, such as Roller Skating, which will specially appeal to our younger members. It is also at a point or site farthest removed from that class of members who wish to be away from the noise which usually accompanies the efforts of youthful members; therefore it serves two useful purposes: the young members, who it is hoped will be attracted to the Club, will have a spot provided which caters for the exclusiveness of youth, and others who wish for quiet will not be interfered with, but left in peace.

More mundanely, Clubhouse bedrooms needed hot water and central heating. The Council allotted its Development Committee a budget of £4,000. In December, this figure was halved in view of disappointing accounts. Subscription income in 1937 totalled £3,653, the profit from Regatta Week was £54, and the Club had made a loss of £1,571. Worse was to come. When heating engineers took up the floorboards, they discovered extensive rot. Lifting the roof tiles disclosed even more serious problems. Repairs to the fabric of Phyllis Court cost nearly £3,500. Did it make sense to go on planning squash courts and a pool?

The Council grew unstable during 1938. First, the Chairman obtained a new power of suspensive veto; then he was obliged to relinquish it. His immediate response was to resign; then he withdrew his resignation. In July, a new rule limited any holder of the chairmanship to a maximum of two consecutive terms. In September, Sir Gilbert Eliott again resigned and this time withdrew from the Club. Hoare Nairne returned to the chair.

The Members' Club had been launched on a wave of excessive optimism. Now came the reaction, and a variety of factors deepened the gloom. A doubling in the fees for military bands led the Club to buy loudspeakers and gramophone records. The number of new members fell to 83 in 1938 and 55 in 1939. Fears were expressed that some of the ancient trees were getting dangerous, and five massive elms needed to be felled. When the Council finally admitted that there could be no swimming pool or squash courts in the near future, few people were surprised. Commander Robert Glen declared that the river was 'quite good enough for him, and he felt sure it would be for scores of other members'. The Annual General Meeting in 1939 opened with a warning: 'It would be impossible to carry on the Club as at present unless more support from the members was forthcoming.' The essential problem was simple: winter opening lost money.

Brigadier-General Edward Hoare Nairne walking with his wife Lilias at Eastbourne. His army nickname was 'The Long 'Un'.

At the start of May, a season of regular Saturday evening dances was announced; at the end of May, this notice appeared: 'It has been decided to discontinue the Saturday evening dances. As from June 3rd, a dance can always be arranged on application to the Secretary, provided a minimum of 50 people can be guaranteed.' The Council meanwhile thought about asking debenture-holders to accept just a token payment. Even the centenary Regatta took place in dismal weather, and superstitious people said that Harvard's victory in the Grand Challenge Cup looked ominous. They had previously won in 1914.

The Early War Years

On the day that Germany invaded Poland, an advertisement on page one of *The Times* read, 'Phyllis Court Club, Henley on Thames. Tranquil and sheltered, near the Chiltern Hills and the river. Some bedrooms still available for members.' They were

Blackouts and Binoculars

That there were many inconveniences at the Club during the early years of the War goes without saying. When Pickering left to take up his war work (which culminated in his appointment as Deputy Regional Commissioner for the North of England), his place as Honorary Secretary was filled by solicitor Guy Blaker. When Blaker enlisted in the army, W. Bruce Dick took over. More than once the Club was fined for infringement of the blackout; an air vent in the kitchen was the problem. In October 1940, the Council acknowledged 'the necessity as well as the duty of taking in a certain number of evacuees' and offered to make the Ballroom available to a school, preferably one for girls. There may have been relief when the Ministry of Works intervened with an alternative. Lord Derby, a well-known racing-man, launched an appeal in November on behalf of the Ministry of Supply for 125,000 pairs of binoculars for the armed forces: 'Put your binoculars now in the hands of the man who is waiting for them – you will never spot a better winner.' People were asked to label their binoculars 'Sale' or 'Gift' and take them to local opticians, who would forward them to regional depots. One of these was in Reading, whence suitable pairs came to Phyllis Court for cleaning and repair by technicians who took over the Ballroom and Reading Room. Workshop and Club contrived to co-exist, and the rental of £643 *per annum* seemed very fair. It was too good to last.

quickly filled by people escaping the anticipated aerial bombardment of London that did not materialise – yet. In 1939–41 (as in 1917–18), the Club largely functioned as a residential hotel. Persons introduced by a member could take up temporary membership (at one guinea per month for a minimum of three months) and then book accommodation. At the time of the Battle of Britain, debenture-holders agreed to waive their right to interest for a year. Ironically, it was most likely on account of the Blitz that takings were 'very satisfactory' in the second winter of the war. The Billiard Room served as an air-raid shelter, and fire-spotters underwent training. The siren in Henley sounded 260 times over the six years of the conflict, but bombs fell on the borough only once (in the Greys Road area, far from Phyllis Court).

The Air Ministry requisitioned Phyllis Court on 23 August 1941, giving the Club four days to vacate it. Hoare Nairne and Dick enlisted the help of a younger member, estate agent Paul Rosewarne, in removing the contents to a repository in Reading. The staff was given notice. The garden vegetables were sold. Phyllis Court Club practically ceased.

Annexe of RAF Medmenham

Phyllis Court had been taken over by the military before, of course, three centuries earlier, only this time its initial personnel was female, since the Air Ministry used it to accommodate Flight Officers and Section Officers of the Women's Auxiliary

Air Force. Among them was Joan Rice, who published her wartime diary in 2006 under the title *Sand in My Shoes*:

> 16 September 1941
> There was also the exodus of the WAAF officers from Marlow into our Mess at Henley, Phyllis Court, once a luxury tennis club now bare, barren and bleak, bereft of carpets and all of its comforts, and the walls boasting revolting antelope horns. However, I've got a room to myself, and, even if it's small and has a view of three grey walls, it does possess a radiator and one of the very few remaining carpets, with a large ink stain in the middle of it. Anyway, with time I expect the place will improve and the food is wizard and the gardens are lovely.

The fact that the Club had inadvertently left behind its hunting trophies may be indicative of the waning popularity of taxidermy. The animal heads became objects of mockery, and, during one rowdy party, some visiting RAF men ceremoniously launched a couple of them onto the Thames. Next morning, so the story goes, a fisherman near Temple Island had rather a shock. If the food was good at Phyllis Court, this was partly because the Air Ministry kept on three of the Club's staff to 'dig for victory' and supply the kitchens. Mollie Chadsey, another WAAF, still remembered the asparagus forty years later.

These young women in blue all worked shifts (twelve hours on, twenty-four off) at RAF Medmenham, previously known as Danesfield House, an even larger riverside mansion, less than four miles along the Marlow Road. In their jargon, they were PIs at the CIU – that is, photographic interpreters at the Central Interpretation Unit. This had moved from Wembley to Buckinghamshire in April 1941, after bombing forced the Photographic Reconnaissance Unit to transfer its special squadron of Spitfires (painted pale pink or turquoise) from RAF Heston to RAF Benson. The CIU scrutinised aerial photographs of enemy-occupied territory, looking first for signs of the movement of troops, ships and aircraft, and new fortifications, and then for developments in communications, industry and camouflage. The emblem of the unit was a sharp-eyed lynx. At this stage of the war, much attention centred on U-boat pens, the battle-cruisers *Scharnhorst* and *Gneisenau*, and newly discovered radar installations. The PIs sat on high stools at sloping desks, peering at pictures through stereoscopes and using dividers and slide rules to scale up dimensions. The work was highly skilled and intense; it also could get monotonous. Some WAAFs found happy recreation in tennis at Phyllis Court. After nine or ten months, however, the servicewomen were re-housed in a hutment at Rassler Wood, closer to their workplace.

Security at Phyllis Court increased markedly in the summer of 1942. The lodge turned into a guardhouse, and sentries, dogs and barbed wire gave the impression that something 'hush-hush' was afoot. A small group of American soldiers had taken up residence, but RAF men arrived from Medmenham by truck or bicycle at all hours. Rosewarne, who represented the vestigial Club in rent negotiations, found it hard to gain access to take measurements. When eventually admitted, he found officers holding up sheets to limit his field of vision.

These precautions were necessary because Phyllis Court housed V-Section of RAF Medmenham for a year in the middle of the war. V-Section created intricate scale models of targets for use in military briefings, ranging from a 1:104 model of a Horch 36 armoured car to a 1:5,000 model of the port of Bordeaux. In particular, the large topographical models (8 × 4 feet) achieved sensational levels of realism (albeit with the vertical scale exaggerated for enhanced visibility). First the land forms were replicated by building up layers of hardboard, smoothing the edges with an electric chisel and applying a mixture of plaster of Paris, wood-pulp and glue. Then came the tricky part: fitting the 'skin'. This was a 'mosaic' of re-scaled vertical aerial photographs, painstakingly stretched to fit the contours without distortion. The landscape was then painted in colour (which called for guesswork) before trees and buildings made from wood and linoleum were affixed. A coat of matt varnish finished the job.

Once the Bruneval Raid of February 1942 had convinced the top brass of the value of such visual aids, demand for them never abated. The workshop on the ground floor of Phyllis Court operated twenty-four hours a day, seven days a week, under the command of Flight Lieutenant Geoffrey Deeley, former head of the Regent Street Polytechnic Sculpture School. Most of the model-makers had been put into uniform only very recently. Among the British contingent were the artists S.R. Badmin, Alan Sorrell and Wilfred Fairclough, the sculptor Cecil Thomas, and the silversmith Leslie Durbin. Major Harrison Reed, previously lecturer in architecture at Cornell University, led their colleagues from the US Army Engineers who lived upstairs. British and Americans worked amicably side by side, though the latter did grumble about RAF food. Alas, the American model-maker at Phyllis Court who made most impact locally was Private John Waters, an ornamental plasterer. After acquiring an English girlfriend, he shot her dead in a draper's shop in Greys Road on 14 July 1943. 'I don't like her pushing me around', he explained. The death sentence was enacted.

During its sojourn in Henley, V-Section's output included models of Dieppe, the Vemork heavy-water plant, the fjords where the *Tirpitz* hid, the landing places for the Allied invasions of French North Africa and Sicily, and the Möhne, Sorpe, and Eder dams, preparatory to the Dambusters' Raid. A start was also made on modelling the beaches of Normandy. At the time, model-makers had to endure much teasing about playing with toys. Later, General Eisenhower credited them with making a real contribution to victory.

Phyllis Court reverted to a WAAF hostel in the latter half of 1943 (after V-Section moved to purpose-built workshops at Danesfield). The establishment of RAF Medmenham reached its numerical peak early the following year. After D-Day, many PIs were transferred to airfields in France, and Rosewarne heard rumours that the British Army wanted Phyllis Court for a transit camp. Having seen the rough treatment of army-occupied buildings, he did not like the sound of this. Fortunately, another of his commissions was to find properties for use by the US Eighth Air Force as rest and recuperation homes. The coincidence was perfect, and arrangements were agreed in August 1944. The Americans even reinstated the furniture of the Clubhouse.

USAAF Station 494

In December 1944, Phyllis Court turned into US Army Air Forces Station 494, run by detachments of the 93rd Station Complement Squadron Reinforcement Depot. With headquarters at RAF High Wycombe, the US Eighth Air Force carried out daylight strategic bombing of the Third Reich from over 120 airfields in eastern England. Its 200,000 men lived mainly in Nissen huts, and aircrew faced the peculiar nervous strain of frequently passing in and out of peril as they counted off the twenty-five combat missions required of them (supposing they survived). After the mid-point of their tour of duty or a particularly harrowing experience, individuals or crews might be ordered to spend seven days at a rest and recuperation home, called a 'flak farm' in service slang. Phyllis Court was the sixteenth and last of these to open in England; Pangbourne House, Moulsford Manor, and Bucklands Hotel in Wallingford were others in the neighbourhood. The rest home manual advised:

> If you want to make these men better fitted to win their own battles, surround them with as many as possible of the symbols (like civilian clothes or baseball) and qualities (like laughter) which take them back to their own homes, their own memories of America, even their own interpretations of democracy. Though it may sound fantastic to you, if they can live for a week as they once lived, with freedom to think and act as normal individuals, they can better face their unreal, chaotic, over-disciplined combat world.

The day began with a waiter bringing each guest a glass of tomato juice in bed. Breakfast was served between 9.30 and 10.30 a.m. – usually bacon and fresh eggs. Later there might be steak or ice cream on the menu; rationing did not apply. Men could opt for riding, cycling, golf, tennis, archery, billiards, bridge, skeet-shooting or idleness. They wore uniform only at dinner; rank meant little. Adding 'the feminine touch' were American Red Cross hostesses, schooled in 'good clean fun' and 'the girl next door approach'. They danced in the evenings to the latest hits, such as *People Will Say We're in Love* and *Mairzy Doats*. To a degree, Phyllis Court had reverted to its old ways, albeit with a different cast of characters. There were twenty-eight airmen in residence at any given time, and the holiday benefited most of them. A minority, however, given leisure to reflect on their

Officers of the USAAF at Phyllis Court in April 1945: seated, L to R, Captain Leo Morris, Lt. Colonel M. Selegee, Colonel Fra A. Rader, and Major R.J. McCarthy.

situation, left feeling more anxiety rather than less. In the US Eighth Air Force, relief on VE Day was tempered by the prospect of re-deployment to the Asian theatre. As things turned out, Hiroshima intervened before its combat missions could resume.

A Time for Decision

'To be or not to be' was the question for Phyllis Court Club at the close of the European War. The Club Company, of course, persisted as a legal entity, registered at the offices of its accountants, Gibson, Appleby & Co. of Aldwych House in the Strand. The Council had held a perfunctory meeting there in March 1943, but it did not address the existential issue till the following year. Hoare Nairne, still Chairman (as term limits had been suspended), believed that they had 'a moral obligation... to re-open the Club and to do their utmost to put it on a paying basis'. Some members had shown their loyalty by paying a voluntary subscription of a guinea. On the other hand, the Club's largest creditor, Roy Finlay, took a pessimistic view. Ever since the members took control, Phyllis Court had 'made nothing but financial losses all along the line', and nobody could possibly imagine that trading conditions after the war would be easier than before it. The 'spenders of the community' now faced basic income tax at 50 per cent and a top rate of 97½ per cent. Hoare Nairne conceded that it would be necessary to broaden the basis of membership and do away with the restrictive Rule IV. 'He also hoped that many respectable tradesmen and other residents in the locality would be encouraged to make frequent use of the Club and so help it along.' The Council resolved in March 1944 to re-open as soon as circumstances made it possible. This did not prevent rumours to the contrary.

Six months later, the Committee of Management of the Henley Royal Regatta sent a letter expressing interest in buying Phyllis Court after the war, if the price was such as to make it a viable proposition. Hoare Nairne replied that members were being consulted about the future of the Club, but 'My Council wish your Committee to know that, if a sale should eventually be contemplated, there is no person or body of people whom they would be so glad to see in possession of Phyllis Court as your Committee.' So far encouraged, the Stewards selected two of their number, Jack Beresford and 'Gully' Nickalls (Olympic medallists both), to investigate the potential of the property. Their report was enthusiastic. The Royal Regatta still lacked any permanent headquarters, whereas Phyllis Court offered all the spectator facilities that could be desired. It might even be possible to build a tunnel under the river. Accordingly, in February 1945, the Committee of Management resolved to negotiate for the purchase of Phyllis Court at a sum not exceeding £14,000. Who advised on price? The Club had already received a far higher offer from the East Anglian & Scottish Investment Trust, which aimed to turn the Clubhouse into a hotel. Aware of this, Finlay announced his intention of calling in the mortgage.

Thirty-one members attended a Special Meeting at Aldwych House on 29 May 1945. On the agenda stood the following motion:

2. To consider and if thought fit, authorise the sale or disposal on terms to be approved by the Council of the Club of either:-

    (a) all or any of the shares belonging to the Club in Phyllis Court Members Club Ltd., or

    (b) all or any of the freehold property, furniture and other property and assets belonging to that Company.

If this were rejected, Hoare Nairne explained, they would have to confront the need to pay or replace the mortgage and pay interest to the debenture-holders or persuade them to forego it. Henry Tapscott proposed the motion, but Sir William Alexander tabled an amendment: 'That the Club be carried on as a Club.' More importantly, he declared his willingness to take over the mortgage. Phyllis Court Club had found a saviour.

Who was Sir William Alexander? Born in Glasgow in 1874 and 'brought up in the hard school of trade' (in his own words), he joined the army in the First World War and rose to Brigadier-General as Director of Administration of the National Explosives Factories at the Ministry of Munitions. There he went on to serve as Controller of Aircraft Supply and Production and Director General of Purchases. His knighthood dated from 1920. Next the Government appointed him managing director of the ailing British Dyestuffs Corporation, which he saved from collapse by drastic rationalisation before merging it into ICI in 1926. By then, Alexander had entered Parliament. He represented the central division of his native city for twenty-two years but spoke in the chamber only eight times, usually to urge that party politics be set aside in favour of a commercial approach. His views carried more weight in industrial circles, where his interests extended from bleach manufacturing to iron and steel and plastics. A member of the Club's Council from 1937 to 1953, he latterly made Jersey his home.

Alexander's intervention determined the outcome of the Special Meeting: his amendment was passed and then carried as a substantive motion. Three other members volunteered to invest £1,000 each, and the mortgage of £13,155 was transferred in July to the joint names of Marlston Estates Ltd (for Alexander), Commander Glen, Major Thornley and Ernest Coward, who all waived their right to interest until the Club was in a position to pay. Glen, a chartered accountant, joined the Council in August and assumed the chairmanship. He was well placed to keep an eye on Phyllis Court, for he lived next door at Manor Garden.

The next pressing problem was debenture interest. None had been paid since 1939, but the Club had secured agreement on prolonging the waiver till 1945 and now requested a further extension. These decisions required the consent of the holders of at least three-quarters of the total debt of £26,845. The Council went further and appealed to debenture-holders either to give their debentures to the Club or to sell them for four shillings in the pound. This, wrote Glen, offered 'the opportunity of bringing back to life our celebrated Club for the benefit of *yourself* and future members'. The response was encouraging, with donations worth £6,160 at face value and a further £2,105 sold at the nominal figure. These surrendered debentures were registered in the name of trustees for the benefit of the Club.

Finlay objected to this arrangement, whereby the trustees would wield a sizeable block of votes in future polls of debenture-holders. In his view, the refusal to sell Phyllis Court had been a very precipitate decision taken in ignorance of the facts. He therefore called on the Club to think again at its Annual General Meeting in October. The East Anglian & Scottish Investment Trust now offered £40,000 for the property on the basis of its continuing as a Club. This would have cleared the entire debt. The members present nevertheless rejected the idea of selling and re-affirmed their wish to remain a members' club.

Post-War Revival

Phyllis Court was de-requisitioned on 26 October 1945. It had come through essentially unscathed, and the Air Ministry had even introduced mains electricity. Theobald and Edwards, the long-serving maintenance men, set about painting the Clubhouse exterior and clearing the remnants of RAF huts. Indoors, carpet-cleaning took place, and gas replaced coal as the fuel for cooking. The Council first appointed J.S. May as Secretary, but he died twelve days later. It fell instead to Major 'Dickie' Dunn to revitalise the Club, helped by his wife Lorna as house-keeper. They had previously run the Thermionic Club in Portland Place. On the basis of five-year-old records, 454 renewal notices were posted. The sub-scription now stood at £10 (when the average weekly wage for a man was about £6). Concessions remained in place for lady relatives, but women could hence-forth apply for full membership, as Phyllis Court Club had granted female suffrage in October 1945 (which happened to be the same month that France did). A warm sun shone on five hundred members and friends who came to the cocktail party marking the Club's re-opening on Wednesday 17 April 1946.

Attracting more local members was a priority, despite warnings from Pickering, the last pre-war Secretary, 'that little encouragement in that direction had been given in the past by residents in the neighbourhood'. Originally, the local mem-bership had largely derived from the mansions of the district, but the number of these in private residential use was falling fast. Greenlands had just become the Administrative Staff College, Thamesfield operated as a residential youth centre, Huntercombe Place was now a Borstal institution, and the Marian Fathers would soon establish a school for Polish boys at Fawley Court. The erstwhile landed gentry faced a painful transition, yet the decline of the country house might actu-ally boost the country club, as fewer people could entertain on a large scale at home.

Phyllis Court was once more 'a mass of roses' for the Royal Regatta of 1946 (attended by Princess Elizabeth). The *Observer* described the event as 'a monster pre-war garden-party in a piece of unchanged England'. It certainly raised spirits at the Club. The Council reported a very successful season and looked 'to the future with every confidence'. The tally of membership had reached 714 by the autumn, with 554 ordinary members, 120 life members, 28 overseas, and 12 honor-ary. Among the entrants were retired MP Sir Adam Maitland, *Punch* illustrator Lewis Baumer and Teri Zogu, known as Princess Teri, a niece of the exiled King of Albania (who had spent most of the war years in Buckinghamshire). By the spring, the Club felt able to reintroduce its ten-guinea entrance fee.

The politics of the Council nevertheless grew heated in 1946–47. It was pro-posed to seek assent to the non-payment of debenture interest for a further three years. This provoked Finlay to organise an 'Independent Committee of Debenture-Holders' to defend the rights of fellow investors, and a fierce contest ensued between rival slates of candidates for the Council seats reserved for debenture-holders' rep-resentatives. There was actually a market for these less than lucrative bonds while the two camps tried to increase their blocks of votes. The critics wished to end what they saw as a concentration of power in the hands of those who were simul-taneously members of the Council, trustees of the Club and holders of the Club's mortgage. After arguments over the validity of nominations and the interpretation of rules, the challengers succeeded in ousting the incumbents, and Henry Tapscott supplanted Robert Glen as Chairman in October 1946. The new Council set out to replace the existing appointed trustees with elected ones. Before this could be done, however, the trustees (Glen, Alexander and Coward) engineered a counter-stroke. Alexander purchased debentures with a face value of £5,310 and combined their votes with those attached to the £8,330 of debentures held in trust for the Club. This produced a clear majority, which was deployed in January 1947 to re-elect Glen, Coward and Kirby to the Council. This substantially restored the status quo ante, with Glen resuming the chairmanship. The defeated faction was outraged, but threats of legal action faded away after the Club repaid in full (at a cost of £3,200) the debentures held by Finlay, Rendle-Mervill and Phillips. (Thereafter Finlay ceased to be granted a free box in the Grandstand in Regatta Week, though he carried on letting the Club use his paddock in return for storing his boats.) The issue of debenture interest was subsequently handled differently. The Council did not seek a general waiver, but asked each holder individually to waive his own payment for the good of the Club. These appeals, along with the earlier donations and buy-backs, reduced the burden from £1,208 to about £300 per year.

The proportion of members taking an active interest in the governance of the Club in this period was small. Thirty-seven (including the Council) came to the Annual General Meeting in 1947. In contrast, attendance at weekly dinner-dances had held up very well during the winter, thanks to the lively entertainment arranged by Major Dunn. Though it was a staple of the Maidenhead river clubs, cabaret had hitherto been a rarity in Henley, so novelty sharpened the appeal of Erle Raymond ('The Man with the X-Ray Eyes'), Gaye and Nevard ('The Two Gay Girls from Mayfair'), Maurice Fogel ('The Mentalist') and numerous magicians and speciality dancers. Other bookings went to the novice comedians Bob Monkhouse and Jimmy Edwards and Brian Reece (on the brink of stardom in *The Adventures of PC 49*). Music normally came from the EXANA Band, so called because its performers were all ex-army, navy and air force. Dunn also devised a busy Christmas programme, comprising three dinner-dances, a children's party and a 'Teen-Age' Dance ('enjoyed not only by those for whom it was intended'). Topping the bill on New Year's Eve were the Beverley Sisters.

Another factor contributing to the popularity of these events might have been the menus. In 1947, the Secretary was fined £57 10s on six summonses of obtaining meat from Eire in contravention of the Food Rationing (General Provisions) Order. The Club reimbursed him. This incident highlights the difficulty of running such an establishment in an era of austerity. Mrs Dunn had to ask members for spare coupons in order to buy fabric for re-upholstery. When the Club wished to put running water into eighteen bedrooms, a licence was required from the Ministry of Works, which withheld it 'on grounds of National Economy'.

Phyllis Court Club believed itself to be doing well in the circumstances. Membership reached 1,055 in 1948, when the rowing and canoeing events of the

XIVth Olympiad took place at Henley. Eighty-six crews from twenty-six nations made a total of three hundred oarsmen. All were invited to a garden party at the Club on 8 August, though only a fraction of them actually attended; top international sportsmen increasingly displayed Spartan single-mindedness. Two British victories delighted spectators: Wilson and Laurie in the coxless pairs and Burnell and Bushell (both local rowers) in the double sculls. With profits of £947 from Olympic Week and £1,086 from the Royal Regatta, the Club nevertheless recorded an annual deficit. Indeed, after an initial surplus of £238 in 1946, it made nothing but losses. The Council explained that its classification as a licensed residential establishment under the Catering Wages Act (1943) had greatly increased staffing costs. Furthermore, the withdrawal from private motorists of the basic petrol ration in December 1947 (in order to improve the balance of payments) had prevented members outside the district coming so often to Phyllis Court. All clubs were struggling in the current economic climate.

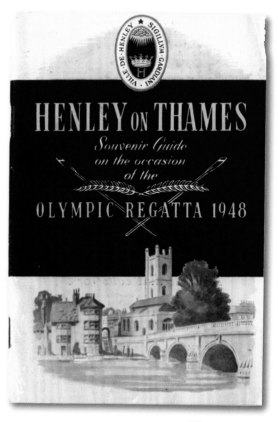

The cover of the 1948 Olympic Rowing guide. (River & Rowing Museum)

Putting Down Roots

After the war, Phyllis Court Club put down deeper roots in its locality. This was not only because an increasing share of the membership lived in South Oxfordshire, Berkshire and South Buckinghamshire. The Club also developed closer links with local organisations. Already in 1938 and 1939, the Henley & District Branch of the Royal British Legion had been permitted to hold its annual dance in the Ballroom. Now the Club itself gave dances for the benefit of such causes as the Thamesfield Youth Association, the Shiplake & Binfield Branch of the Distressed Gentlefolk's Aid Association, and the Andrew Duncan Home for Boys at Shiplake (always at Hallowe'en). The grandest of these charitable functions were the RAF Aid to Greece Ball in 1951, with Lady Katherine Brandram (sister of the King of Greece) as guest of honour, and the Three Counties Ball in 1955 in aid of the National Playing Fields Associations.

The Parish Church Fete was held in the gardens for five summers in a row from 1948. This extended in 1950 to an Elizabethan pageant in which the Hon. Barbara Skyrme, a Club member, impersonated Good Queen Bess. The 1952 fete was opened by actress Celia Johnson, otherwise Mrs Peter Fleming of Nettlebed. A year before, Field Marshal Lord 'Jumbo' Wilson attended a fund-raising event for the Soldiers', Sailors', and Airmens' Families Association. A revival of the Rag Regatta between 1949 and 1951 brought Henley Rowing Club and Henley Sea Cadets into collaboration with Phyllis Court Club; the greasy pole attracted fifty entrants, 'including a number of the fair sex'. In 1953, the paying public came to a Water Carnival to mark the Coronation. The Henley Canine Society held its dog shows in the Paddock, and the Bowmen of Henley set up butts there. Indoors, the Henley Concert Society briefly tried Phyllis Court as a venue in 1950. The Amadeus Quartet played Beethoven and Schubert, and Phyllis Sellick gave a piano recital. Her playing, wrote a critic, 'appeared the more masterly by the way she distracted our attention from what appeared to me to be the uncertain tuning and not very sympathetic nature of the instrument'.

On a commercial footing, Phyllis Court competed with the Catherine Wheel Hotel to host functions for the Henley & District Chamber of Trade, Henley Cricket Club, Henley Sailing Club, the Henley & District Agricultural Association, the Thames Motor Cruising Club and the Thames Masonic Lodge. Two regular fixtures in the calendar were the South Oxfordshire Hunt Ball and the Woodland Foxhounds Hunt Supper. Outside events could be remunerative, but complex licensing laws posed a hurdle. Either the guests had to be elected temporary members at least

The Henley Elizabethan pageant held at Phyllis Court in 1950.

A dinner dance at Phyllis Court in 1949; in the centre is Paul Rosewarne, later Council Chairman 1973–76.

forty-eight hours in advance or else it was necessary to engage an outside licensee to apply for an occasional licence. Sometimes things went wrong. On 2 June 1951, Inspector Morris arrived at Phyllis Court at 4 p.m. to find guests at a wedding reception 'drinking liquid out of champagne glasses' but no sign whatever of the nominal licensee; the bench imposed a £5 fine.

If charity events brought enjoyment, goodwill and favourable publicity, the same could be said of Open Hard Court Tennis Tournaments, once more staged in both spring and autumn from 1947. H.F. Walton, the RAF champion, often triumphed at Phyllis Court, likewise Miss M. Slaney; both several times reached the second round at Wimbledon. New trophies for boys and girls proved so popular that a separate Junior Tournament took place annually after 1951. It was here in September 1953 that twelve-year-old Christine Truman emerged as a first-class prospect; eight years later she contested the Wimbledon ladies' final. Tennis-playing members of Phyllis Court competed with other Thames Valley tennis clubs, and the formal creation of a Lawn Tennis Section in 1950 underlined their distinct identity.

Fragile Finances

The end of petrol rationing that year did not bring about the anticipated resurgence of trade and, after a deficit of £2,520 in 1949, the Council had shed its insouciance about the financial situation. Phyllis Court now had a core of local members who liked coming to the Club for the bar, bridge and billiards in all seasons without spending too much money there. Winter losses were wiping out summer profits, but winter closure might have provoked a mass of resignations, and total membership had recently fallen back below a thousand. A compromise emerged: from Christmas till Easter, the bedrooms ceased to be available and the Restaurant opened only for Sunday lunch. The new Secretary, D.L. Sherwood, was instructed 'to exercise every possible economy in overheads and wages'. He took the Council at its word and faced a barrage of complaints about inadequate maintenance and cleanliness. 'It is true', he conceded, 'that the brackets in the lounge are supported by string in some places. It is also true that when the Secretary took over, every chair and every settee was broken.' Even as austerity relaxed and refurbishment became possible, the Club could afford only urgent repairs. It managed to get a permanent £5,000 overdraft facility in 1951 by offering its surrendered debentures to the Westminster Bank as security. Each year a large segment of subscription income went straight towards paying off the previous year's debt.

An additional modicum of guaranteed revenue came from the sale of a contingent lease of the property. International tensions were high in November 1951 as a result of the Korean War, when the Prudential Assurance Company pledged to pay £3,400 (over a decade) for the right to move its surveyors' department into Phyllis Court during a national emergency. The Council reasoned that the Clubhouse would again be ripe for requisition in any case, so there was probably nothing to lose, and the Prudential would make a more careful tenant than the military. (Renewals of this arrangement in 1961 and 1971 brought in rather less in real terms; détente and the doctrine of 'Mutually Assured Destruction' diminished its value.)

Captain Roy Finlay died, aged seventy, at Shiplake on 20 February 1952. A tribute in the *Henley Standard* recalled that he had 'forever planned greater and greater things' for the Club, where 'at one time it was said that if you sat on the lawns of Phyllis Court you would see on them every living notability'. The elegiac note, it may be observed, related almost as much to the Club as to its Founder. Its finances were known to be fragile, and speculation about its sale resurfaced periodically. The national press printed a Phyllis Court story in June 1952, when jewellery worth £2,500 was stolen from Dorothea Knight and the Hon. Mrs Whitamore; their bedrooms had been unlocked. Then, in Regatta Week, somebody purloined the Club's flag, the one presented by Prince Arthur, from its glass case near the entrance. A polite appeal in *The Times* failed to recover it.

Another new Secretary nevertheless arrived at Phyllis Court with optimism in the autumn. Lieutenant-Colonel Sir Geoffrey Betham had served nineteen years in the Indian Political Service before retiring in 1944 as British Minister at Kathmandu. Now he was promptly asked to get the Nepalese Ambassador to present prizes at the next Boxing Day Fancy Dress Ball (which he did). Betham believed that all-year opening could not succeed while it remained half-hearted. He recommended special *en pension* terms for out-of-season guests who booked rooms for several weeks or months. With residents, 'the Club would give the appearance of being much more alive in the winter' and so attract visiting diners too. As a further inducement, he bought the Club its first television set. Phyllis Court accordingly went into the winter of 1952–53 fully staffed, fully lit and fully heated. By January, losses were running at £500 per month.

The Council informed members of the serious situation and suggested that 'those who can afford it might consider giving donations to "cover expenses".' Florence Bigland became an especially generous donor of crockery, curtains, paint and plants. She declined an invitation to join the Council but latterly accepted honorary membership. 'Some of the happiest days of my life have been spent here', she said.

The entrance fee had been suspended in 1950. Now the Club produced a brochure and sent it to 5,100 selected people with an invitation to join. One month later, only five had applied. In the Council, 'the general opinion was that it was merely a sign of the times'. Economy perforce became the watchword. Phyllis Court in 1954 employed its Secretary, two or three clerical staff, four housemaids, a porter and barman, seven dining-room and kitchen staff, two maintenance men and four gardeners, which the accountants reckoned to be too many. It shocked some members to see the bye-law: 'All drinks purchased over the bar must be paid for in cash at the time of purchase.'

A portrait of Roy Finlay in later life.

The death of the Club's leading creditor in 1954 caused not only sadness but also anxiety. Fortunately, the sons of Sir William Alexander remained highly supportive. One of them, Dr W. Bryce Alexander, was a member of the Council, which no longer held any meetings in London. Commander Glen retired as Chairman in October due to illness. His successor, Captain Harold Pullein-Thompson, had been awarded the Military Cross in the First World War; his wife and daughters were well-known authors of pony books for girls. Spending cuts stabilised the position of the Club, and the accounts 'showed at last a small profit instead of a loss'. But parsimony could not guarantee prosperity, for it starved the fabric of investment.

The Week of the Year

'Phyllis' still kept up appearances in Regatta Week. *The Manchester Guardian* described it as a resort of 'the Very Rich', while Art Buchwald of *The Herald Tribune* joked that 'even the squirrels that frequent it have to wear badges'. No longer was there a public enclosure, but members of associated London clubs could enter for a guinea. On Wednesday and Thursday some other outside bodies brought parties, such as the Institute of Surveyors and Auctioneers and the Henley Chamber of Commerce. Celebrities under the Club's green and striped awnings ranged from Admiral Lord Mountbatten, the First Sea Lord, to Fanny Cradock, the television cook.

The advent of Soviet crews at Henley Royal Regatta (after the death of Stalin) intensified international competition. Newspapers reported the rowing these days; Society gossip was passé. Phyllis Court Club conferred honorary membership on all Ambassadors and High Commissioners in 1946 and again in 1954, though none that year accepted the invitation to lunch on Finals' Day. Traffic congestion was blamed for curbing the interchange between 'Berks' and 'Bucks'. Previously, many spectators in the Stewards' Enclosure had driven to Phyllis Court for refreshment; nowadays they stayed put in order to keep their parking spaces. The Club would have liked a ferry to link the venues, but the Stewards demurred. On the Saturday morning in 1955, Betham discovered on the Phyllis Court lawn a twenty-foot sign saying 'British Railways Parking Place 2s 6d', moved from the station by pranksters.

The Regatta Ball at Phyllis Court retained its place in the calendar of the London Season, an opportunity for débutantes to meet bachelors from the universities and public schools. Often the Club engaged saxophonist Tommy Kinsman and ensemble; nicknamed 'the Deb's Delight band', it played strict-tempo ballroom music for many Society functions.

> When night fell the lawns of Phyllis Court were floodlit. Buildings and terraces gleamed white against the dark back-ground. A girl, swaying her hips like a well-groomed odalisque, wandered into the gold pool with her partner. She looked Rue de la Paix against the High of her companion… no doubt he would eventually discover that every fellow in his year had proposed to her. From the far side of the river came sounds of raucous voices, the wheezy music of merry-go-rounds, and the shrill shrieks of girls on a contraption that almost defied the laws of gravity. The trees were spectral yet the night was warm. Suddenly the sky lit up. The fireworks had begun, and with every flash I saw the crowd standing among the trees or by the water-edge. Henley is a wonderful festival of Youth, with Age joining in with appreciative understanding. If I have to memorize it, I shall murmur, as countless thousands have done before me… punts, strawberries and cream, a foam of lace and silk, pretty faces and blue eyes.

So wrote Louis T. Stanley, correspondent of *The Queen* magazine, in *The London Season* (1955). It was natural by now that most of those who saw it only annually in the early days of July took Phyllis Court for granted as a seemingly eternal element of 'Henley'. Little did they hear of the Club in the other fifty-one weeks of the year.

A Dash for Growth

A prominent and controversial figure at Phyllis Court Club during this decade was Richard Bradshaw. A stockbroker, aged thirty-eight when elected Chairman in May 1955, he openly opined that Phyllis Court had been deteriorating for years. All members' clubs were having a difficult time; many since the war had closed, amalgamated or sold part of their property. To avoid such a fate, said Bradshaw, it was necessary to innovate: 'Phyllis Court had been rather like an aspidistra, rather old-fashioned and sharp at the edges, whereas it was hoped to make it into an exotic plant by attracting new and younger members. Only recently the Council had received a request for a playground for young children, whilst their parents made use of the Club's amenities: it was along these lines that the Council was trying to progress.' Efficiency, novelty and publicity would be required. More conservative members expressed disquiet at the departure of Betham as Secretary. The Council chose Lieutenant-Colonel Basil Ormond Ware to replace him, hired a public relations officer and devised a programme 'to keep a picture of Phyllis Court before the world'.

The BBC televised the 'Queen of Light' ceremony held on 18 December 1955. At nine o'clock, a young woman wearing a crown of cranberry leaves and candles descended the staircase to the darkened lounge, followed by eight girls from the Anglo-Swedish Society, all clad in white and singing the Hymn of St Lucia. (Bradshaw had lived in Sweden.) No longer should winter 'be considered the dead season at Henley's riverside club'. Nineteen fifty-six began exuberantly:

> On the bandstand, Eric Wakefield was kept busy with a constant stream of request items, which varied from Sambas to Eightsome Reels and included a hilarious Gay Gordons in which a battered trombone was used on the dancers to devastating effect. The approaching of midnight was heralded by a sledge laden with prizes, drawn by two shapely blonde showgirls in Santa Claus costume who seemed to meet with the approbation of the male members of the audience. The prizes were presented to the lucky winners to the accompaniment of either cheers or groans, depending upon whether the prize turned out to be a bottle of champagne or a tastefully decorated cauliflower.

Two weeks later came an Anglo-French Evening, where 'mid-winter in England faded into the distance to the catchy continental rhythms played by Norton Colson's Legionnaires who appeared to have stepped straight out of the pages of *Beau Geste*'. Cabaret star Jan Rosol sang 'piquant little songs in his native tongue', and a tumultuous ovation welcomed Yana, the latest glamour-girl sensation, making 'her only appearance outside the West End before departing for greater stardom in the world of film'. A similar Anglo-Italian Evening followed in March. 'International' and 'continental' were becoming buzzwords. Six weeks later, twenty-five cars entered a Grand Concours d'Élégance. Rally-driver Sheila Van Damm and Billy Rees-Davis MP identified a Bristol 405 Saloon and Lesley Stephenson as 'the most attractive car and lady ensemble'. Footage was broadcast in two BBC news bulletins. At a Leap Year Ball on 19 May, the ladies asked the gentlemen to dance. The Central Band of the Royal Air Force played for the Golden Jubilee Ball on 1 June. For fifty years the Club had enjoyed 'a worldwide reputation as being one of the most beautiful landmarks on the English scene'. Still more spectacular, however, was the Scandinavian Midsummer's Eve Ball, held in conjunction with the embassies of Sweden, Denmark, Norway, Finland and Iceland. *Gaffelbiter*, *matjes* and rye bread were washed down with *akvavit* and *punsch*. Hostesses from the Scandinavian Airlines System modelled Stockholm and Copenhagen fashions, while the musicians all dressed as Vikings. At midnight, the red witch of winter was cast upon a bonfire, and six hundred revellers danced until dawn. Finally, the autumn tennis tournament gained prestige when Angela Buxton, the World No.5, won the Challenge Bowl.

In terms of publicity, Phyllis Court Club had not seen any year like it since 1937 (or even 1927), but sadly the dash for growth did not succeed. Income and membership had risen, but insufficiently to offset heavier expenditure. By December 1956, £4,500 was owed to business creditors, so the Council imposed a raft of economies. The Club would close from Christmas to Easter. Charges went up 10 per cent. Raising the subscription to twelve guineas provoked over eighty resignations, wiping out any financial gain. In addition, the Clubhouse roof sprang a leak and the lodge (which housed the head waiter) was judged unfit for human habitation. Bradshaw invited debenture-holders to sell him their bonds for a nominal sum, and disagreements over this action led to a change at the top. The new Chairman, Joseph Burrell, told the Annual General Meeting that 'the loss of £1,569 during the year was due to apathy on the part of the Club's Members'. He continued:

> Ladies and Gentlemen, we have here on the banks of the Thames at Henley, in one of the most beautiful parts of England, an unique Club. Your Club. There is no other like it in the British Isles and it has been in existence now for fifty-one years. Are we going to let it die? All the goodwill in the world, all the cutting and scraping of costs, all the efforts of your Council will be as naught unless you, the Members, support – and continuously support – your Club. Economic facts are unromantic and usually uncomfortable. Ours are damned uncomfortable.…You, who are members, are more fortunate than you know but unless you support your Council and your Club, you will soon have no opportunity to shoot at the one or enjoy the other.…Let me suggest a motto for members: 'The more we use it, the better we can make it.' Stick it upon your mantelpieces and, for the love of Phyllis Court, act upon it!

One of the Council's money-saving measures was a change of accountants to Selby, Dyer & Co. This had an unanticipated result. In November 1957, the new firm stated its view that the Club could not continue to trade without a possible action for fraud for incurring debts without foreseeable means of paying them. The crisis had arrived.

Keeping the Flag Flying
1957–1978

9

FLATS AT HENLEY

Now being erected in own grounds. Unrepeatable situation adjoining historic Phyllis Court, adjacent River and all amenities. Charming superior GEORGIAN STYLE FLATS, complete with all refinements, including electric under-floor heating, luxury bathrooms, shower rooms and fully equipped kitchens (refrigerator, etc.). 2/3 beds, delightful feature lounge. Ideal retired businessmen or City executives. From £7,120 incl. garage. 99 year lease. Ground rent £22 2s 0d. p.a. Apply Sales Office, DAVIS ESTATES LTD., Marlow Road, Henley (open daily, incl. Sunday, closed Tuesday).

This advertisement from the *Observer* in June 1960 basically explains the survival of Phyllis Court Club. The kitchen gardens and orchard to the south of the main drive, comprising about a quarter of the site, were sold to a property company in November 1959 on a 99-year building lease for the sum of £30,000 and a ground rent of £840 per year.

It had taken two years of hard work to achieve this result. At the close of 1957, the outlook had been so bleak that the Council wondered if it were morally justifiable to accept subscriptions for 1958. The Chairman, Joseph Burrell, explained to members by letter the exceptional gravity of the financial situation and urgently appealed for donations, however small. To promote confidence, Council members agreed to contribute an additional 25 per cent themselves (up to a total of £200 each). In the meantime, expenditure was 'cut to the bone'. Members, shocked at the thought of losing Phyllis Court, rose impressively to the challenge. In March 1958, the Appeal Fund reached £5,336. This was enough to pay off the unsecured creditors so that the Club could resume normal trading. While Burrell praised the solidarity of the membership, tributes were paid to his own 'fighting spirit'.

Attention now turned to breaking even – or better. Here an important part was played by Joy Crone. Having joined the staff a year earlier as House Manageress, she became Catering Manageress in March and Club Secretary in August 1958, bringing a new discipline and attention to detail to administration. The Council now sought as many 'outside' bookings as possible, and Miss Crone proved adept at catering for functions that both satisfied clients and made a fair profit. 'Offering good meals at very reasonable prices' simultaneously boosted receipts in the dining room. In 1958, the Club recorded a surplus of £1,050 while suffering a loss of only four members. The following year the surplus grew to £1,744 and membership rose by sixty-seven. 'Entirely due to good team work', stated the Chairman, 'the Club is in a better position than at any time since it re-opened in 1946.' Members credited Miss Crone with 'doing great things'.

Meanwhile, Paul Rosewarne, a Council member since 1954, took the lead in arranging the land sale and negotiating with the successful bidders. Residential development of some part of the grounds had been mooted as long ago as 1934, but post-war shortages of building supplies and the Town and Country Planning Act (1947) together discouraged it. (Up until the abolition of development charges in 1953, the Club could have kept only the existing-use value of any land sold.) Planning permission was obtained, and Robert Cromie, an architect noted for cinemas (who was also a Club member), designed forty-five flats (numbered 1–12 and 14–46) in eight red-brick blocks of three storeys each. The Club suggested that their names reflect the history of Phyllis Court; the developers opted for Temple House (after Temple Island), Charles House, Finlay House, Whitelocke House, Swinnerton House, Grandison House, Marmyon House, and Molyns

Finlay, Charles and Temple Houses, part of the residential development of Phyllis Court Drive between 1959 and 1961.

House. Under the contract, Davis Estates provided the Club with eleven lock-up garages, a dual-carriageway drive, and a new entrance with two pairs of wrought-iron gates (removed in 1982).

After expenses, Phyllis Court Club had £27,000 in hand. It immediately spent £13,208 on 21 November 1959 in order to redeem the mortgage, latterly held entirely by Marlston Estates Ltd. Its directors, Bryce Alexander and his three brothers, reciprocated by donating to the Club the £5,330 of Founders Debentures inherited from their father. 'A truly magnificent gesture', said Burrell, and the four were elected to honorary membership. The other priority had to be remedying the backlog of maintenance. On joining the Council in 1958, civil engineer Gordon Abraham had inspected the structure of the Clubhouse and declared himself horrified. Virtually nothing had been done beyond spasmodic redecoration since before the war: 'In point of fact, it has been a very close run race between ourselves and the roof.' Over £10,000 was expended on its complete overhaul in 1960, making the building watertight and replacing the crumbling parapet and cornices. Club Architect Stephen Bertram oversaw this work. Smaller sums went towards patching up the Grandstand, re-carpeting the Lounge, and removing the roof of the old garage. The skylights in the Ballroom, painted black in 1939, were finally re-glazed.

As an unencumbered freeholder, Phyllis Court Club was now better able to borrow. With a £20,000 overdraft, it demolished the outmoded kitchen block in 1962 and replaced it with one fitted out in stainless steel. An adjoining outbuilding was converted to accommodate ten members of staff, and the former Billiard Room became a second Dining Room. Seating fifty, it could be used for private parties and by members when the Ballroom was booked for functions. Wedding receptions and cocktail parties proved especially profitable.

To celebrate the Club's survival, the Council commissioned an oil painting of Phyllis Court by Max Hofler (1890–1962) – and then expressed dissatisfaction with it. More prominently displayed (by the croquet courts) was a sculpture presented by the Misses Tweed in 1961. Its creator, their father John Tweed (1863–1933), is best known for his statues of Clive of India on the Foreign Office steps and Captain Cook at Whitby. The attitude of this life-size male nude, however, looked anything but triumphal. (It vanished in 2012, presumed stolen.)

In 1960, a vandal daubed 'ASHES TO ASHES DUST TO DUST' in large white letters on Cromwell's Wall. The words remained legible for years, but, if they ever referred to the Club, they soon ceased to be apposite. Membership exceeded one thousand in 1961 for the first time since 1948, and Burrell could report another and larger surplus to the Annual General Meeting. All the same, he tempered the mood of congratulation with a warning against complacency: 'Remember that there are only two alternatives in this life, progress or recession, there is no standing still.'

A painting of Phyllis Court by Max Hofler (1959).

The Sixties

Once the builders had left, the Club could rightly call itself 'an oasis of beauty and peace in a bustling noisy world'. Indeed, whatever may have been going on elsewhere, the 1960s were a quiet decade at Phyllis Court. Amicable stability characterised the nine-man Council (while a nominal tenth member would neither attend nor resign); there was only one change in its composition between 1958 and 1968. A convention emerged that limited a Chairman to three successive years in office. Michael Watson, a director of Thames Plant Hire Ltd, took over in 1961 and yielded place in 1964 to Gordon Abraham, managing director of the highway contractors Sydney Green & Sons (Henley) Ltd. His successor in 1967, Bryce Alexander, had followed his father into the chemicals industry. Arnold Claisse,

Chairman from 1970, was the former manufacturing director of the Gillette razor factory in Reading.

By keeping a close eye on the balance of liabilities and assets, the Council succeeded in keeping the Club in the black while meeting the costs of maintenance. The surpluses were never large enough to clear the overdraft, but they sufficed to service the debt, and, whenever opportunity arose, the Club bought back debentures (usually at 50 per cent of face value from executors). If the mood was cautious and defensive, circumstances made it so. River clubs had become an endangered species, and survivors of the wartime cull now seemed to be dying a natural death along with the generation that recalled their heyday. In 1965, the Brigade of Guards' Club in Maidenhead closed down. In 1967, the Richmond Club disappeared. People were heard to remark, 'Oh! Is Phyllis Court still going?'

In Henley, as ever, the Royal Regatta made a difference, but even this looked like a waning asset. Its sporting prestige remained high, but the internationalisation of rowing was diluting its social significance to the English upper classes. Spectators did not crowd the lawns of Phyllis Court so densely these days, despite the Club inviting RAF Benson, RAF Medmenham and the Administrative Staff College to apply for tickets. The Grandstand had so deteriorated by 1971 that the upper tier had to be dismantled (which worsened the rot in the lower tier by exposing its timbers). That same year the Regatta Ball was renamed a Regatta Dance. Finals happened on Sunday from 1974, while fireworks and festivities stayed on Saturday, which slightly attenuated the traditional carnival atmosphere.

On the positive side, Phyllis Court cemented its reputation as the premier catering venue in the district, especially for dinner dances. Henley Round Table was presented with its charter in the Ballroom in November 1958 and frequently returned there, as did the Rotary Club. Henley Town Council several times hired it for the Civic Ball. Other regular bookings included the Berks Bucks and Oxon Law Society, the Reading Division of the British Medical Association, the regional branches of the Engineering Employers Association and the Federation of British Industry, and the Henley Artisan Golfing Society. The London Transport Executive Board came for a conference in 1964. Among the many local functions held in the mid-1960s were a Teenage Supper Dance for the Henley Sea Cadets Drum Fund, the Ladies Annual Festival of the Henley Royal Jubilee Lodge of the Ancient Order of Druids and an Anniversary Tea for the Henley Branch of the National Council of Women. Charity fashion shows were recurrently arranged by Gladys Falloon of High Wycombe. Despite previously eschewing political groups, the Council permitted South Oxfordshire Conservative Association to hold bridge tournaments and an antiques fair at the Club, but it considered the Henley Branch of the Anglo-Rhodesian Society too controversial.

Miss Crone solved the problem of empty bedrooms by the expedient of renting five of them to permanent residents. Sir Almeric Rich took a room in the bachelor

A collection of Phyllis Court Club Regatta badges (donated by Russell Jones).

wing of Phyllis Court after retiring as governor of Huntercombe Borstal, where he had lived by choice in a cell. The resident members ate in the Club, but they were too few to solve the perennial difficulty of weekday catering. Repeated bouts of trade analysis led only to an acceptance of the impossibility of making a profit with so great a fluctuation of attendance.

The bar was often the liveliest room in the Club. From 1964 it housed a 'one-armed bandit' machine. This affronted some members but, after it made a profit of £541 in three months, the Council resolved to keep it – and hire a second one. Rendle-Mervill reckoned chemin de fer and roulette more appropriate, yet nothing came of research visits to gaming clubs. Gambling at Phyllis Court went no further than the '300 Club' set up by Harold Fender in 1967 as a standing lottery. Each of its members purchased a number by annual subscription and draws for cash prizes were held at social events. The proceeds funded improvements, such as a new stair carpet and a baby grand piano.

The population of Henley expanded during this decade, Phyllis Court Drive being only one of many developments, and a significant proportion of the new residents were retired people from professional and managerial backgrounds. Some of these joined the Club, whose roll had risen to 1,268 by 1964. Public figures among the membership ranged from Sir Michael Perrin, one of the inventors of polythene, to Lord John Hope MP, Minister of Works in the Macmillan Government, and Peter Montague-Evans, the BBC racing commentator. Dame Cicily Andrews was better known as Rebecca West, author of *Black Lamb and Grey Falcon* (1941). Sir Richard Turnbull, Chief Secretary of Kenya during the Mau Mau uprising, belonged to Phyllis Court Club between his terms as the last Governor of Tanganyika and penultimate High Commissioner of Aden. Sir Claude Fenner had been Inspector-General of the Malayan Police. Everyone in the pharmaceutical industry knew Sir Harry Jephcott, long-serving managing director of Glaxo Laboratories. Fighting men included General Sir Andrew Thorne, who had taken the surrender of 400,000 Germans in Norway in 1945, and Admiral Sir Alan Scott-Moncrieff, who commanded Commonwealth naval forces engaged in the Korean War, yet Phyllis Court particularly attracted high-ranking officers of the Royal Air Force. Air Marshals Sir Raymund Hart, Sir Edward Chilton, Sir Paul Holder and Sir Leslie Dalton-Morris all joined between 1959 and 1966, later followed by Air Marshal Sir Denis Crowley-Milling, Air Chief Marshal Sir Christopher Foxley-Norris and Marshal of the RAF Sir Denis Spotswood. It is a tradition that continues. Air Marshal Chilton showed an especially keen interest in the management of the Club, sitting on its Council for eight years from 1963. New entrants still in work most often gave their occupation as company director, insurance broker, chartered surveyor, solicitor, bank manager or sales manager, but diversification is suggested by the arrival of a turf accountant, a model, a social worker, a PT specialist, a dental mechanic and an electro-encephalographer.

The Council started to worry when membership fell after 1965. The trigger for this was an increase in the subscription rate for *new* members from twelve to twenty guineas. Phyllis Court Club had not discriminated in this way before. It was probably intended as a cautious approach towards a general increase (imposed three years later), only in the interim the total number of members dropped by 15 per cent. Pricing, however, could not be considered the sole barrier to recruitment. The Club found itself attracting entrants from a narrowing range of ages. The bulk of the membership had always been mature, but never so markedly. In the past, many members had brought teenaged and grown-up children and grandchildren to Phyllis Court as guests, and the Club had encouraged them to join. Young people aged between fifteen and twenty-one (with a full member in their family) could become junior members paying a quarter of the normal subscription, while intermediate membership at half price was available to persons aged twenty-one to thirty. The Regatta and the tennis courts had hitherto guaranteed a steady trickle of public schoolboys and students, but in the 1960s the emergence of a distinct youth culture widened the 'generation gap' and restricted the flow of young blood to the Club. It was hardly the case that Phyllis Court witnessed inter-generational conflict; younger people simply ceased to frequent it in significant numbers, and so began a vicious circle. The establishment acquired a fuddy-duddy image and became a target for the mocking humour of rowing men on the opposite bank. It is possible to believe that there *were* occasions – Monday lunchtimes in February, perhaps? – when a casual caller might have been forgiven for mistaking the Club for a retirement home, albeit an uncommonly spacious one. Donald Ferguson, the mild-mannered Scot engaged as Secretary in 1967, was 'empowered to take more permanent residents should he wish to do so, but the Council requested that any such members should not be in the older age group'.

In its effort to expand, the Club re-launched a scheme whereby a company could buy 'bulk membership' for its directors. Originally devised in the crisis year of 1957–58, this option had been taken up then only by Sydney Green & Sons and Metropolitan Vickers, the electrical heavy-engineering firm. Now it proved more popular, winning the accountants Spencer Ell & Co., the brewers W.H. Brakspear & Sons, the water-engineers George Stow & Co., and the senior staff of the Administrative Staff College. As Chairman Claisse repeatedly argued, 'With the average age of present members getting rather high, members are resigning because they cannot use Club facilities any more, so the need to recruit new members is important.' It helped that the pool of potential members of working age was growing as a result of the relative ease of commuting between Henley and London. The town retained its branch line, and extensions of the M4 and M40 motorways diminished journey times for cars. Talk of attracting more young families to Phyllis Court did not greatly enthuse existing members, however, with the suggestion of a play area for children evoking 'a general expression of dismay' at the Annual General Meeting in 1974.

An ageing membership naturally influenced the activities of the Club. Demand for dancing was not what it had been, although the abandonment of monthly dinner dances at least had the knock-on effect of making each of the three or four balls held annually seem all the greater an occasion. They were usually very successful. Best remembered were the Italian Balls of 1960, 1962 and 1964, instigated by Renato Guerrieri and Francesco Casale, two members employed by the Italian State Tourist Board and Alitalia (which flew in hundreds of fresh carnations and a serenading guitarist). An Election Ball took place on the night in October 1964 when Wilson displaced Douglas-Home, and a West Indian steel band provided music in 1968. Television doubtless played a part in thinning the programme of evening events. An initiative that flourished, by contrast, was the Ladies' Luncheon Club, started by Mrs Edwards and Mrs Warner and placed on a semi-formal footing in 1967.

The Tennis Section of the Club seemed to be in the doldrums, and levels of usage no longer justified the cost of maintaining seven hard courts to the highest quality, let alone the grass courts. This economy in turn affected the Open Hard Court Tennis Tournaments. In 1959, the *Henley Standard* noted that the entry now comprised 'mainly good club-players and up to county standard, rather than the better-known regular tournament players'. Publicity (and not profitability) had long been the rationale for the championships, so the decline of media interest

An Italian Ball at Phyllis Court in the early 1960s.

was damaging. In an effort to reverse the trend, the Club in 1965 revived the Spring Tournament after a twelve-year gap; Shirley Brasher retained her 1953 title, having won the French Open in the interim. Financial logic prevailed, however, and Autumn 1967 turned out to be the last LTA Open Tournament at Phyllis Court. Fortunately, the burden of maintenance was shared after 1969, when the newly formed Henley Lawn Tennis Club took a lease on first three, then four, and finally five of the hard courts. This link between the two clubs lasted for a decade.

Bridge and billiards retained a steadier following, and their administration was devolved in 1963 to semi-autonomous sections, each with its committee and chairman. Christine Poole, who chaired the Bridge Section, went on to become the first woman member of the Council in August 1973. At this time, the bridge players met upstairs and the billiards and snooker players downstairs. The Billiard Room again exchanged locations with the Members' Dining Room in 1971; the diners gained additional space and the billiard players were spared the distraction of passers-by. Croquet had been little in evidence at the Club since the war, but a revival started in 1967, when Harold Fender initiated a Croquet Section, and Dr Alexander donated hoops, balls and mallets. Phyllis Court affiliated to the

Croquet at Phyllis Court Club.

Croquet Association the following year, and the demise of clubs in Maidenhead and Caversham led to an influx of enthusiasts in the early 1970s. Champion Nigel Aspinall came to coach association players, and the introduction in 1976 of golf croquet (a less complex game) allowed the section to reach a size that merited expenditure on bettering its courts.

The view from the Patio Bar.

The Council had to be hard-headed in budgetary matters. Squash courts and a swimming pool were 'quite out of the question', and even boat-hire ceased to be viable, the Club's fleet of aged punts and skiffs being judged beyond repair in 1966 and not replaced. The boathouse fell into dereliction prior to demolition in 1975. Capital projects were required to recoup their costs in pretty short order, and the only major scheme that met this criterion was the Patio Bar, a single-storey extension to the Lounge, erected in the spring of 1969. The Council correctly anticipated that a bar with fine views of the river would do significantly better business than one with no outlook at all. Alexander made an interest-free loan of £5,000 to the Club and helped it borrow a further £5,000 from the Bank of Scotland. Stephen and Elizabeth Bertram designed the structure, fitted with green carpets and modern white furniture, and Mrs Alexander opened it on 31 May. The Patio Bar was a great success.

The Early Seventies

Property prices were rising in the early 1970s and, although not tempted by overtures from three would-be buyers of Phyllis Court in its entirety, the Council decided that circumstances favoured another limited sale of land. Outline approval had been obtained in 1963 for building on the grass tennis courts immediately north of the drive. Permission for twelve flats followed in 1972, and Rosewarne once again oversaw the tendering process. The plot was sold in February 1974 on a 99-year lease, the purchaser paying £132,000 and a ground rent of £200 per year, though the area was less than a third of that surrendered in 1959. The two new blocks, named Thames House and Connaught House, matched the development opposite. Separate plans for a petrol station next to the Marlow Road never came to fruition.

The Council resisted the temptation to embark on large-scale expenditure. In anticipation of the windfall, it had spent £6,690 in November 1973 on redeeming the last debentures still in private hands, and it also paid off the overdraft and the Patio Bar loans. This left the Club free of debt and fully owned by its members. Capital gains tax siphoned off £22,028, and a certain amount was allocated to furniture, as the annotation 'Very Old' appeared many times in the 1974 inventory. A catering expert, hired to dispel the Club's recent reputation for poor cooking, did so primarily by persuading the Council to pay higher wages to kitchen staff. All the same, £75,000 remained, and Paul Rosewarne, as Chairman 1973–76, could report 'that Phyllis Court Club had a substantial investment income for the first time in its history'.

It was soon going to need this financial ballast, for the British economy had entered stormy waters. Between 1974 and 1977, the annual rate of inflation exceeded 16 per cent, peaking at 27 per cent in 1975. This wrought havoc on Phyllis Court's fragile budget, as costings swiftly went out of date, and a members' club was singularly ill-adapted to making the ruthless price increases required to keep up. Trading losses, which had already started with a modest £2,500 in 1972, mounted to £21,000 in 1975 and £22,000 in 1976, despite urgent retrenchment. It did not help that till 1983 the central heating burnt oil (having been converted from coke in 1947). Winter closing and the withdrawal of weekday catering were both once more considered and rejected, since either 'would result in a crippling loss of members'. In an effort to hold down meal prices for the sake of people on fixed incomes, a snack bar and buttery were opened at lunchtime, even though Rosewarne personally 'felt that it was not in keeping with Phyllis Court to have to wait in a queue'.

One side-effect of rampant inflation seems to have been a more vociferous membership, and Council elections were more often contested. With the end of reserved seats for debenture holders and the retirement of several veterans, its composition changed completely between 1973 and 1977. Another effect was an upsurge in total membership to 1,689 in 1975. Forty-eight per cent of members now lived within five miles of Henley, and another 28 per cent within ten miles of Reading. In real terms, it had actually never been cheaper to belong to Phyllis Court Club. Even after two subscription rises, £37.80 in 1977 signified less than half the purchasing power of £10 in 1946. An entrance fee (of £20) was levied for the first time since 1950. Joint membership for husband and wife now finally supplanted the old category of 'member, plus lady relative'.

On reaching the age of three score years and ten, the Club put up a varnished plaque, listing its previous Chairmen. Revealingly, it was found impossible to go back further than 1935. The death of Jack Rendle-Mervill (Sports Secretary 1928–33, Secretary 1933–37, Council member 1946–47 and 1953–71) had severed five years earlier the strongest link to the pre-war era. John Garton, Chairman of the Royal Regatta, and Denis Moriarty, ex-Mayor of Henley, were guests of honour at the anniversary celebrations held on 5 June 1976, when floodlights from RAF Medmenham and decorations from Henley Operatic Society enhanced the ambience of an open-air ball. It had just been necessary to remove the glass canopy

Phyllis Court c.1976.

The Fire

Phyllis Court suffered a trauma on Christmas Day 1976. In its very first minutes, one of the residents, Cyril Butchart, heard breaking glass. He went over to the window of his room and saw the curtains of the Patio Bar ablaze. The fire brigade, called at 12.08 a.m., arrived to find dense smoke filling the building. In the words of Station Officer John Gosby:

> A quarter of the ground floor was alight. We saw four people on the first floor at the front of the building and another four at the rear. Those at the rear were able to use the fire escape, but the ones at the front were cut off. Two firemen used a ladder to rescue a man from a first floor room and then went back into the room to rescue a woman who was unconscious. Other people were brought down on ladders from the first floor, including a female member of staff who was found asleep in her room. The woman who was unconscious was treated by a local doctor until an ambulance arrived.

Fire-crews from Henley, Sonning and Wargrave fought the blaze until 2 a.m. Hearing the news on the radio at breakfast time, many members came to see if anything could be done. They found the main ground-floor rooms charred and blackened. Much of the rest of the Clubhouse was smoke-damaged, and glass in the windows had melted. Piles of debris and the pitiful remains of Christmas decorations covered the floor. The smell was appalling. At this most dispiriting juncture, the management drew inspiration from the wartime motto of a very different establishment, the Windmill Theatre, Soho, which famously declared, 'We never close.' Local off-

The Patio Bar burnt out, December 1976.

licences made special deliveries to the Club that very morning so a makeshift bar could open in the Reading Room. There shocked members drank seasonal toasts in between giving what assistance they could to the clean-up. What had caused this disaster? The police at once suspected arson, for six days earlier a furniture store at the Club had also been destroyed by fire and part of the kitchens scorched. Within a fortnight, they arrested the hall porter, who had joined the staff less than a year earlier. He stated at his trial:

> The fire in the shed wasn't good enough, so on Christmas Eve I went round to the bar and found the door open. It was one of those moments I couldn't miss. It was too good a chance. I was surprised how quickly the fire took hold. I was very pleased. The reason for all this is because it felt good to be the cause of these things. To be able to control things.

The thirty-six-year-old Australian, already twice convicted of arson in his homeland, was sent to Broadmoor high-security psychiatric hospital.

from the entrance of the Clubhouse for reasons of safety, and only a folding awning replaced it. One sympathetic observer likened 'Phyllis' in this period to 'a gentle-woman in reduced circumstances'. Dutch elm disease, meanwhile, deprived the grounds of several grand trees. In 1968, the County Council had judged Phyllis Court worthy of 120 tree preservation orders, and the Club took seriously its duty to replant for the benefit of future generations.

In the aftermath of the 1976 fire (see box opposite), it heartened Phyllis Court to receive a gesture of support from the Hurlingham Club in the form of a recipro-cal arrangement that has lasted ever since. For the next four months, facilities were limited to the Billiard Room, the Card Room and the temporary bar in the Reading Room, while contractors Walden & Son set about rebuilding the central eastern section of the Clubhouse. The Lounge re-opened in April with a Silver Jubilee fashion show (where all the clothes were red, white, and blue), and the Patio Bar itself was reinstated in time for the Regatta in July 1977, a very impres-sive result, though it took until the following year for redecoration to efface every last trace of smoke damage. Insurers paid out over £90,000. The Club also sold life memberships (for the first time since 1937) and realised £17,500 from the sale of 99-year leases on two small properties, White Cottage and the Marlow Road Lodge, long since deemed inadequate for housing staff. Thanks to these special measures, investment income and donations, it very nearly broke even overall in 1977. At the same time, the trading account registered an alarming loss of £58,500.

Another factor heightened the mood of uncertainty. In the period 1976–78, Phyllis Court experienced four changes of Council Chairman and three changes of Secretary. Rosewarne's successor, Group Captain Bob Brittain, had served in the Royal Air Force throughout the war and then become its first Inspector of Mountain Rescue. He declined a second year in the chair in June 1977, because of differences over staffing policy. Wilfred Sivyer stood down for private reasons in March 1978, having played a valuable role in expediting the insurance claims. Two months later, serious illness cut short the chairmanship of Sir Edward Beetham, the last Governor of Trinidad. As for the Secretaryship, Donald Ferguson retired after nine years in November 1976. Then Wing Commander Laurence Sturt resigned after two months on health grounds. With experience in business consultancy, Christopher Smith was asked to undertake a full review of the Club's operations (during its par-tial closure after the fire). He concluded that members alone would never use the facilities enough to make them viable, so Phyllis Court 'must go flat out for non-member revenue'. He also proposed a sharper demarcation between the setting of policy (by the Council) and its implementation (by the Secretary). Considerable friction preceded his early departure in March 1978. Jack Carson-Bury filled the gap as Acting Secretary for a second time.

By now, the Club was awash with rumours about its imminent sale or merger into a chain of hotels, and a group of members requisitioned a Special Meeting on

Major Harold Harly-Burton, Council Chairman 1978–83.

19 May 1978 'to allay alarm and speculation as to the future'. This gave the Acting Chairman, Harold Harly-Burton, an opportunity to report that the Council had indeed received four enquiries in the past year as to whether Phyllis Court was for sale; it had rejected and would continue to reject, absolutely, all such approaches. He announced the appointment of Ian Bulloch as Secretary Manager, and assured the membership that 'the Council would do its utmost to keep Phyllis Court, a Club second to none, the way it is at present known and loved'.

Between the crises of 1957–58 and 1976–78, Phyllis Court Club had survived in good heart to enhance the lives of its loyal members and guests. This was no mean achievement in years when the mortality rate among members' clubs, even in the West End, stood at an all-time high. That said, the disposing of assets could obviously not be repeated indefinitely. From the multiple misfortunes, anxiety, and even acrimony that marked the end of this period, there began to emerge a general realisation that preserving the Club for the long term would necessarily entail a measure of reform.

10

Reform and Revival

1978–1998

I
n 1980, the exterior walls of the Clubhouse were repainted. From their traditional white, they turned a shade that the colour chart called 'warm sand'
– and this was not the only way in which Phyllis Court Club now presented
an altered face to the world. Once a semi-isolated outpost of London clubland, it
had extended a welcome to charities and social organisations in Henley and district ever since the Second World War. In 1978, the Council decided to go a step
further and offer its facilities to a wider range of visitors.

Harly-Burton, the new Chairman, had experience of the shoe industry and boat-
building as well as holding the rank of major in the Territorial Army. He explained
to members that Phyllis Court was failing to make the most of its assets and emphasised that survival depended upon expansion. A Finance and Forward Planning
Committee accordingly examined various ways of raising more revenue. The first
significant result was a re-organisation of sleeping quarters. Permanent residents

The Clubhouse
in the 1980s.

A bedroom at
the Club in the
early 1980s.

received notice to leave by March 1979 so builders could reconfigure the upper
storey, amalgamating the little old bedrooms into just eleven units with en suite
bathrooms. Unprecedentedly in peacetime, accommodation could henceforth
be booked by non-members (who technically became temporary members, free
to use the Dining Room, Lounge, and garden during their stay). Advertisements
described Phyllis Court as 'a haven for rest and relaxation', providing 'a blend
of old-fashioned courtesy combined with all the comforts of the twentieth century'. As former manager of Hotel Tresanton in St Mawes, the Secretary, Ian
Bulloch, brought polished expertise to this venture.

A second reform was designed to rectify the under-utilisation of reception
rooms. The Club in 1979 sent brochures to 580 businesses within a sixty-mile radius
of Henley, inviting them to hire space at Phyllis Court for conferences, seminars,
recruitment exercises, product launches and shareholder meetings. 'The Thames
Valley's most exclusive meeting place' was reckoned 'particularly well suited to
highly confidential meetings away from the public gaze.' For large functions, companies could book the Ballroom (3,100 square feet, suitable for 250 guests). The
Reading Room (704 square feet, 50 guests) became the Thames Room in
1981. Later the Isis Room, a smaller venue, was made available upstairs. Business
clients soon included H.J. Heinz training its staff, Microsoft marketing information technology, and Henley Management College examining students. Perpetual,

the investment fund managers fast becoming important employers in Henley, held annual general meetings at the Club. Increased awareness of Phyllis Court in the business world also encouraged a growth in block membership (previously called bulk membership, later corporate membership), with the addition of such firms as Black & Decker and Tupperware UK.

In expanding its 'outside' trade, the Club did not aim exclusively at businessmen. Wedding receptions for members and their families had long been a staple activity; now the public also gained access to this 'breathtakingly romantic venue'. The number of wedding parties climbed to a peak of eighty per year, and regular demand for large-scale banqueting revolutionised the catering operation. In 1995, at the earliest opportunity, Phyllis Court obtained a civil marriage venue licence, so actual ceremonies could take place there. To cope with the 'huge increase' in function business, a visitors' car park with sixty-seven spaces was created in 1984, doubling provision.

Judging purely by the bottom line of the accounts, the results of the fresh approach were satisfactory rather than spectacular at first. After a deficit of £3,733 in 1978, surpluses of about £10,000 followed in 1979 and 1980. But the bottom line did not tell the whole story. Turnover increased by 27 per cent, and Phyllis Court Club survived the most severe general recession since the war without slipping into the red. Its 1982 surplus of £46,171 was record-breaking and due primarily to the third component of the new commercial strategy: corporate hospitality during Regatta Week.

The garden-party atmosphere of the event was not sacrificed, ladies being advised that 'the wearing of hats would be appreciated'. Dozens of blue-and-white

Corporate hospitality at the Grandstand.

Corporate Hospitality

In 1976, the Stewards of the Henley Royal Regatta had erected a few marquees on Fawley Meadow and rented them out to companies wishing to entertain clients or reward staff with a day of spectator sport and good cheer. Comparisons might be made to the private enclosures of London clubs and Cambridge colleges at Henley in Victorian times. Their popularity proved so great that the Royal Regatta experienced over the following decade a dramatic social and financial transformation. Non-rowers were back in force and determined to enjoy themselves at 'the most lavish long-running picnic since the Field of the Cloth of Gold'. The phenomenon reached Phyllis Court in 1979, when motor manufacturer BMW offered to pay £2,000 for permission to erect a tent in the grounds and exhibit a couple of its cars. Next year, the Club advertised its own 'sponsored hospitality units'. While the rest of the Clubhouse remained the preserve of members and their guests, companies were invited to hire the Thames Room or one of eight marquees on the south bank of the moat. Crucially for the image of the occasion, the Edwardian Grandstand was brought back into use, with a rebuilt upper floor. Harly-Burton had negotiated with Lovell Construction Ltd., which carried out the work at a discount in return for sixty seats at the next seven Regattas. From 1981, other top-tier boxes served as hospitality units in themselves, with a view of the finishing-line matched only by that of the official press box across the river. The event was turning rapidly into big business. Asked by a journalist the following year about commercial rivalry at Henley, the Club's Regatta Secretary, Heather Green, lightly responded, 'Oh no, there's no rivalry at all. There's no rivalry because there's no competition. We have always attracted the better class of firm to Phyllis Court!' Among its many corporate guests were the Midland Bank, Metal Box, IBM, Flymo, Citibank and Savills.

parasols shaded dozens of open-air tea tables. Outdoor live music returned at the weekend, courtesy of the Ercol Band or Marlow Town Band, and evening entertainments multiplied. At sunset on Friday it became the custom for a military band to stage the ceremony of Beating Retreat, beginning with the Royal Electrical and Mechanical Engineers in 1981. The Regatta Ball on Saturday recovered its lavishness, while the first night turned into Jazz Night; Kenny Ball and his Jazzmen, Digby Fairweather's Half-Dozen, the Humphrey Lyttelton Band and the Temperance Seven all made appearances over the years. In short, there was a sense of occasion, and its effect on 'Phyllis' was memorably described by Tom Hustler in 1983:

> Haven't you felt her getting more and more excited as Henley Royal Regatta approaches? Months before, when the stands start to be erected opposite, she begins to quiver with anticipation; and nearer the great day her mouth waters as the strawberries are carried into her kitchens. She cannot wait to stretch out her arms and give the people a

welcoming hug. 'Fill me up, enjoy me, use me!' she cries. 'Picnic in my car-parks, sip Pimms on my lawns, spill champagne on my terraces, tread my paths, make love under my trees, get drunk with delight in my tents, cheer from my stands, moor against my banks – enjoy and love me!'

The addition of a fifth full day of racing from 1986 meant an even bigger fillip for Phyllis Court Club. In 1988, it employed almost 250 temporary staff during the Regatta and its net income from the event amounted to £139,000. As in Finlay's time, one week in July had come to be 'the cornerstone of the Club's activity'.

Period Charm

The resurgence of Henley Royal Regatta as a social event reflected a broad cultural trend towards 'heritage' and wider popular appreciation of the more attractive aspects of the past. The very notion of a river club appeared outmoded in the 1960s, but by the early 1980s it had acquired a patina of period charm. An advertisement placed in *Country Life* magazine in 1983 announced, 'Elegant Edwardian Phyllis Court offers weekend en-suite accommodation amid garden and lawns sweeping down to the Thames.' Its rarity as a survivor from a bygone era heightened its appeal. Could it justly be called unique? Very possibly, seeing that its

The lawn during Regatta Week 1983.

closest counterpart, the Hurlingham ('the other club' in some members' parlance), differed perceptibly in ambience, due to a heavier emphasis on sport and a metropolitan locale. 'The name has a 1930s ring', wrote a hotel reviewer of Phyllis Court. 'Our room in this lovely house had a balcony, so we pretended we were Amanda and Elyot in *Private Lives*.'

Location finders for film and television companies lighted on the Club around this time. In June 1982, the interior was briefly transformed into a Los Angeles casino circa 1938 for an episode of London Weekend Television's *Philip Marlowe, Private Eye*. The following May, a Regatta tea dance in 1925 was recreated by HandMade Films for *Bullshot*, a parody of Bulldog Drummond. The Clubhouse featured as a contemporary hotel in *Nelly's Version*, an adaptation of Eva Figes' story about a mysterious amnesiac broadcast on Channel Four in 1983. In the realm of fiction, Phyllis Court has many times been mentioned in novels set in Henley in order to strengthen the sense of place. Its moat is declared the most convenient point to alight from a rowing-boat in Duncan Schwann's satire *Molyneux of Mayfair* (1912). In Charles Mason's Cold War thriller *Death in Regatta Week* (1960), that same inlet ('the hole in the wall') leads the hero to guess the significance of a gap in the fortifications of the Iron Curtain. These references seem trifling when compared with the prominence given to the Club in the first two chapters of John Masters' *Now God Be Thanked* (1979), which depict the 1914 Regatta Ball. Similarly desirous of period flavour, David Roberts uses Phyllis Court as a recurrent venue in his 1930s murder mystery *Something Wicked* (2007).

Balloon ascents were a feature of the Club's 80th Anniversary Garden Party in June 1986.

The factual past of the site has also long inspired interest. Letters to *Notes and Queries* in 1931 show Finlay's sister, Laura Norsworthy, researching the ancient manor; she supplied the *Henley Standard* with occasional local history articles. Three decades later, Rendle-Mervill wrote a chronology for inclusion in the Club Rule Book. In May 1966, a relic of the old house unexpectedly came to light, when a lady visitor fell through the ground outside the Ballroom. Happily uninjured, she thus discovered a subterranean ice-chamber, dating from the days of Sir William Whitelocke or Gislingham Cooper – which rather disappointed those who at first envisaged a secret passage to Fawley Court!

The Club in 1981 commissioned a history from Angela Perkins; *The Phyllis Court Story*, printed three years later, heightened

Ian Bulloch, Secretary Manager, with his wife Jo, dressed in Edwardian style for the 80th anniversary.

local awareness of Bulstrode Whitelocke especially. Frances Chidell compiled an updated précis in 1991 and 2005. In 1986–87, members twice donned period costume, marking the eightieth anniversary of the Club with an Edwardian garden party and the fiftieth anniversary of the Members' Club with a 1930s' one.

Along with its history, Phyllis Court Club prided itself on a certain style of unmistakeable Englishness. In banishing French culinary terms from the dining-room menus in 1982, Mrs Adlam declared 'that the Club was very English and any other language was unnecessary'. The Council was not displeased five years later to see that the American telecommunications firm AT&T was using a photograph of Phyllis Court in its advertising for international calls (with a caption that said, 'In the United Kingdom there are only a few things that rival a good game of croquet. A phone-call from you is one of them.').

Prosperity and Its Discontents

When Harly-Burton stood down as Chairman in 1983, the Annual General Meeting gave him a lengthy standing ovation. The finances were in a healthier condition than anyone could remember, and the upward trend continued. His successor, Norah Adlam, remarked that 'this Council should be a very happy one with the Club in a much improving position'. Her own particular contribution to the renaissance had been as overseer of the gardens, enhancing their appearance vastly

Norah Adlam, Council Chairman 1983–85.

without increased expenditure. Phyllis Court Club, it may be noticed, had its first woman Council Chairman when Britain had its first woman Prime Minister.

Membership statistics now made cheerful reading. Subscription rises, aimed at restoring the value in real terms, had initially caused a drop in numbers from 1,701 in 1976 to 1,458 in 1981. Then the tide turned. A target of 2,500 members, set in 1983, was achieved within four years and soon surpassed. The number of permanent staff simultaneously expanded from thirty-eight to sixty-two, while turnover doubled. In 1984, Bulloch persuaded a sceptical Council that the scale of operations justified buying an Apple II microcomputer. Total income exceeded £1 million for the first time in 1987, when the surplus was £91,249. Members of the Council sometimes felt a need to caution each other against euphoria.

Prosperity, however, also gave rise to its own controversies. Back in 1978, the widening of the scope of outside functions had been accepted by members without much complaint as a prerequisite of the Club's survival. Now, the very success of the policy lifted constraints on criticising it. Did the premises of a thriving Club need to be shared so frequently with visitors? When there were multiple bookings or especially large corporate events, members could feel marginalised – and increasingly they said so, sometimes with vehemence. 'It is intolerable to find the Club is *first* a venue for "others" and *second* a Club for members'; so reads an entry in the Suggestions and Complaints Book available at reception from 1985. Of course, rowdy parties caused the greatest dismay. The Council, sensitive to any imputation of aloofness, improved communication with the membership by holding an open meeting each November. It also initiated the *Phyllis Court Circular*, a quarterly magazine (published 1987–90, and later relaunched as *Club News*). There, a member calling himself 'Autolycus' presented this acknowledgment of the problem:

> Throughout all the change, members of Council have never lost sight of what Phyllis Court Club stands for. A meeting place of like-minded persons who may meet with empathy in a place where manners, style, and grace come together. Where iconoclastic vulgarity is not a virtue. The Club is invaded from time to time by a minority of outsiders who are not capable of recognising our values.

The management offered assurances that it was always selective in respect of external clients. It also reiterated certain facts: 'The only profits being made were on the

Regatta event and the functions income' and 'Without the "commercial approach" adopted by your Council over recent years, membership fees would be four or five times the present levels.' Everyone agreed on the need to strike a balance, but exactly what that balance should be remained a moot point. A survey taken in 1989 recorded that 38 per cent of functions in the Ballroom and Thames Room were non-member events.

Some lesser points of friction resulted from change within the membership. By 1989, when the total reached three thousand for the first time ever, nearly two-thirds of members had joined in the previous six years. This significantly lowered the average age, and organisers of social events faced belatedly the problems posed by the earlier revolution in popular music. Contrasting entries in the Suggestions and Complaints Book make the point:

> *Vide* Club Dinner Dance on June 20th – PLEASE NOT A DISCO! As a regular dinner-dancer, I object. Cannot another band be found?

> I may be over 50 but I don't want to dance to music from the 1940s continually, played by inferior musicians. It's BORING!

At the three big annual dances (the New Year's Eve Ball, the Regatta Ball and the Rose Ball), the compromise was to cater for different tastes at opposite ends of the building. In June 1987, for instance, the Roy Young Orchestra played in the Ballroom while Julianna's Discotheque filled the Thames Room – and cacophony reigned in between. Decibel meters latterly became a useful addition to the Club's

A dance in 1987.

equipment. The Bill Robinson Duo and the Embassy Four were among the regular bookings for smaller parties.

Another topic first came to the forefront of debate at Phyllis Court in this decade, and it has never yet entirely surrendered its prominence. This was the dress code. The primary argument possesses great staying power, for both sides can marshal plentiful anecdotal evidence, while conclusive proof remains elusive. One school of thought points to the general tendency to greater casualness in dress, especially among younger people, and argues that the Club deters a substantial number of potential members by preserving antiquated sartorial rules. Opponents retort that the Club derives a crucial element of its special ambience from upholding a higher standard of formality than prevails elsewhere, and they add that this distinctiveness is precisely what attracts new members. Relaxation of the dress code has therefore been slow, contested, and incremental. Where men are concerned, at least the terms of the debate have usually been clear: black tie, lounge suit, jacket and tie, no tie; when is which appropriate?

Arguments over detail really took off in 1988, when the Council permitted 'smart casual' clothes in the Dining Room at Sunday lunchtime. T-shirts, jeans, trainers, and shorts were specified as unacceptable (and men's open-toed shoes were subsequently barred), but it rapidly transpired that members held divergent notions of 'smart casual'. David Brockett, the new Secretary, had to admit that 'with ladies' apparel it is difficult to legislate and the rules are not specific enough in some cases'. A ban on women wearing trousers in the Clubhouse after 7.30 p.m. provoked lively discussion: what about culottes, divided skirts, and evening trousers? By 1998, the rule had been revised: 'Although some Members disagree with this – a lady Member or guest is at liberty to wear trousers, provided they are smart.' Could denim (as distinct from jeans) ever be admissible? Yes, 'but only at certain times and in certain places and of a certain standard'. If the dress code fails (as sadly it must) to please all the members all of the time, it is not for the want of trying.

Differences also emerged over the novel issue of how best to spend the Club's surpluses, once the more obvious priorities had been sorted out. Between 1982 and 1988, expenditure on property repairs and furnishings totalled £1.2 million (including £48,000 from the sale of 37 New Street in 1984). The western half of the ground floor was extensively reorganised in 1985–86. A new Billiard Room was installed upstairs in the former Card Room, which made space downstairs for a larger Dining Room, with French windows opening onto a courtyard, and also a Club Room, suitable for private dining. Renovation of the north-west wing secured new cloakrooms and lavatories, a Reading Room and a Card Room (called the Loddon Room from 1998). The Patio Bar was re-designed and renamed the Members Bar in 1988; the fruit machines departed a year later. Floodlighting was placed in the garden. What next?

The Club
Room at
lunchtime.

The idea of building a leisure centre, with squash courts, sauna and solarium, had occurred to the Finance and Forward Planning Committee as early as 1980 (when the sale of more land for residential development appeared the only way to finance it). Squash courts would attract young professionals, it was thought; Finlay had first proposed them back in 1925, along with a swimming pool. The Council returned in earnest to these possibilities during the chairmanship (1985–88) of Richard Willgoss, a director of the waste-disposal company Grundon. A survey of members in 1986 recorded only 53 per cent in favour of a pool, however; fears about high running costs perturbed a sizeable minority. Before proceeding with these plans, therefore, the Council proposed to focus on increasing revenue by building a self-contained functions suite at the southern end of the Clubhouse. This would allow Phyllis Court to organise many more external events without their impinging so much on members, since the extension was to have its own bar, cloakrooms, and car park. Willgoss spoke of 'a scheme intended to give the Club back to its membership', but critics disapproved of spending £1.3 million on facilities chiefly for 'outsiders'.

Opinion was still divided when accountant John Dore took over the chair. Acknowledging in 1989 that some members thought the Council too commercial, he drew this parallel:

> Margaret Thatcher is now celebrating ten years in office. During that time there have been many changes, not always universally accepted. I remind you of this because our own period of change started a little earlier in 1977, after the fire. At that time we were technically bankrupt; there were no cash resources, the fabric of the building and the interior were run down and – worst of all – the membership was declining. Our older members may well recall how bad the situation was at that time.

An Open Meeting in November 1986. Richard Willgoss, Council Chairman 1985–88, is at the microphone, flanked by his predecessor Norah Adlam and successor John Dore. On the left, Council members Arthur Trotman and Sir Charles Hardie.

Since then, the number of members had doubled, and the entrance fee could now be increased to five times the annual subscription. Phyllis Court Club was booming, along with much of the British economy. A recent television documentary on the 'North-South divide' had presented Henley as the epitome of south-east English affluence. Members were starting to complain of the nuisance caused by helicopters landing in the Paddock. All the same, rising competition in the region's hospitality industry posed challenges, and wage bills were sky-rocketing. New statutory hygiene standards (due in 1992) required heavy expenditure on the kitchens, and the structural deterioration of the Grandstand caused concern; shored up with scaffolding and boarded, it 'looked appalling, like a cardboard box'.

Against this background, the Council reviewed the level of subscriptions and found it 'very much below what is realistic'. Demand for membership was strong, and London clubs charged far more. Rates for 1990 were accordingly increased, from £154 to £230 for a single ordinary member. A decision was also taken to levy charges for games: £20 per year for members in the Croquet Section, £1 per table session in the Billiard Room, £3 per hour for a tennis court, and £1 per head per session for bridge. This provoked an immediate outcry. Dore argued that only ten per cent of members actually played games, so the current system of (rather haphazard and partial) cross-subsidisation needed to change. Critics countered that collectivism was inherent in the very idea of a Club, and they pointed to the financial impact on retired people who played bridge several times a week. Within ten days, the introduction of games charges was deferred, but this did not silence protest. When the Council narrowly resolved to press ahead with the subscription increase, five of its number resigned, and co-optees replaced them. Fifty members then requisitioned a Special Meeting 'to register a vote of no confidence in the Chairman and members of the Council for the time being *in situ*.' Reports of 'the revolt' appeared not only in local newspapers but also in the *Sunday Telegraph* (whose editor was a member) under the headline 'Henley hoo-ha as old and new money clash at club'. Journalists typically reproduced the most provocative quotations to be found. One member attacked plans for a fitness complex as 'the first steps down the road to making the place akin to a municipal leisure centre; track suits and sweaty bodies round every corner'. Another traced the problem to an influx of 'new members with lots of money, who want change. They are not the same class and the longer established members feel they cannot mix with them.' This was certainly not how most dissenters understood the matter, but their grievances did extend beyond the specific points at issue. There seemed to be a perception that the Council had grown too ambitious

Betty Crocker and Elisabeth Wood at the reception desk in 1987.

and perhaps insufficiently mindful of the differences between running a Club for the benefit of members and running a business for the benefit of shareholders.

The Special Meeting on 4 February 1990 attracted an unparalleled attendance of 1,083. It was necessary to erect a marquee in the garden and set up a closed-circuit television link to the Ballroom. The Council offered a concession in respect of subscriptions: people aged over sixty-five who had belonged to the Club for twenty-five years would receive a discount of 20 per cent. The no-confidence motion was defeated by 468 votes to 435, but only after the Chairman gave an undertaking that all ten seats on the Council would be up for re-election at the Annual General Meeting on 1 April. This second turbulent 'tent event' lasted five hours. None of the outgoing Council was returned. Probably not since 1910 had Phyllis Court Club experienced so bruising a confrontation.

'There is a great need for a period of consolidation to make the Club a stable place once more', declared the new Chairman, Victor Adams, a former deputy secretary of the Board of Inland Revenue. He proved an able conciliator. External factors even helped in a perverse way, as the chill winds of economic recession soon took the heat out of certain arguments. A swimming pool? A cut in subscriptions? Neither was a practical proposition in the financial climate of the early 1990s.

Social Life

The range of social activities at Phyllis Court grew ever richer and more varied during the period covered by this chapter. This was due above all to the proliferation of 'sections' – semi-autonomous clubs within the Club. The four original sporting ones all benefited from the overall growth of membership. By 1998, the Bridge Section numbered 115, playing partnership and cut-in bridge on different days, with duplicate added the following year. The Betty Spurling and Ralph Cox Trophies were awarded annually. The Croquet Section had meanwhile expanded to 128 members. Golf croquet thrived at Phyllis Court, a regular venue for the national championships; the Association players faced Hurlingham and Roehampton teams. With four handicap tournaments per year, the Billiards and Snooker Section catered for players of all abilities. The Tennis Section welcomed Richard Knight as coach in 1987; a decade later, four new courts were opened by Bill Threlfall, the television commentator.

Relaunched in 1978, the Ladies Luncheon Club met once a month. Valerie Grove, writing in the *Sunday Times* in 1987, described its members as 'a formidable and forthright breed in whose charge you would happily entrust the running of the world'. It was formally constituted as a section in 1998, at the same time as the Thames Dining Club, whose quarterly black-tie gourmet dinners for gentlemen had commenced in 1985. Among its guests in these years were Sir Evelyn Shuckburgh, the diplomat, and Theresa May, the future Home Secretary. Charitable fund-raising at Phyllis Court Club, by such means as race nights and a Christmas fair, was led from the 1970s by a group known first as the Lady Members' Events Committee, secondly as the Lady Members' Social Committee, and thirdly as the Ladies Charity Committee, before it re-formed in 1995 as the Action Group (rechristened the Charity Action Group in 2004). It supported a different local charity each year. The Boat Owners Association came into being in 1979 as a channel of communication with the Council, when it adopted a new policy on the management of Club moorings (charging more and offering better facilities). Subsequently, the Association blossomed as a social group, holding parties and rallies on land and water.

Three further sections emerged in the 1980s. Beryl Rait founded the Art Group in 1983 for members who painted and drew. They met every Wednesday morning, sometimes with a tutor, and staged exhibitions at the Club. Two years later the Golf Society began arranging matches at a variety of local courses, plus three-day excursions to more distant clubs. At Phyllis Court itself there was a putting green and practice net. The Dance Section, formed on the initiative of Ken Whiteley in 1987, revitalised dinner dances by offering instruction in the waltz, foxtrot, quickstep, tango, jive, rumba, samba and cha-cha-cha.

The next two sections eventually grew to be the most popular of all. The Arts Appreciation Group, founded in 1993, combined trips to galleries and historic

A display by the Classic Motoring Section in 2009. The red two-seater is one of only seven cars made in Henley by the Squire Car Manufacturing Company (1934–36).

houses with lectures on topics as diverse as Mozart, Salvador Dali and medieval manuscripts. Probus, inaugurated in 1994, sprang from the international movement to promote good fellowship among retired and semi-retired professional and business men; unusually, Probus at Phyllis Court welcomed ladies as well as gentlemen from all backgrounds. That same year, Sonia Cox started a Scrabble Section for both casual players and tournament competitors. The number of airmen, military and civil, belonging to Phyllis Court Club ensured a core constituency for the Aviators' Circle formed in 1997, though its meetings and visits appealed to all with any interest in flying. People joked that the two sections created in 1998 needed to be kept separate. The Wine Circle, 'while largely hedonistic in intent', ran to tutored tastings and vineyard tours. The Classic Motoring Section, equally sociable, gathered 'those with an interest in automobiles of a certain age and style'. Its car shows soon became a feature of August Bank Holidays.

Balls and dinner dances often now had a theme, such as Hallowe'en, St Valentine's Day or St George's Day, and summer barbecues became very fashionable. Phyllis Court again hosted classical music – far more effectively than forty years earlier. Australian pianist Ian Munro gave the first concert in 1990. Among his successors were the Allegri Quartet and the cellist Arturo Bonucci.

Celebrity Guests

Guest speakers started to be in great demand. Previously at the Club they had been a rarity; Peter Scott lectured on the Galapagos Islands in 1960. Now, from 1994, a series of literary dinners (open to non-members) was arranged by Blackwell's Bookshop in Reading. From the world of theatre came Peter Ustinov, Sir Harry Secombe, Maureen Lipman and Ron Moody; television cookery was represented by Antony Worrall Thompson, Antonio Carluccio and Rick Stein; journalism provided Jonathan Dimbleby, John Suchet, Sandy Gall and John Cole. Sir Edward Heath, the former Prime Minister, spoke on 16 September 1997, two months before Roy Hattersley, the former Deputy Leader of the Labour Party. The Club introduced its own Quarterly Suppers and welcomed speakers as contrasting as politician Barbara Castle and rower Steve Redgrave, winner of four (later five) consecutive Olympic gold medals. Honorary membership was conferred on Redgrave and Matthew Pinsent, his partner in the coxless pairs, following the Atlanta Games in 1996. Many of the sections held speaker meetings too. Dame Barbara Cartland, the romantic novelist, told the Ladies Luncheon Club about receiving fifty-six proposals of marriage. Outside functions also brought famous names to Phyllis Court, such as Lord Archer, Edwina Currie MP and Terry Wogan. On 22 April 1992, the Duchess of Kent attended a charity fashion show for the Dellwood Cancer Care Appeal; two months later the Duke and Duchess accepted honorary membership of the Club.

David Brockett, Secretary and General Manager, welcomes Maori war dancers to Phyllis Court in 1990 to celebrate 150 years of New Zealand.

The Nineties

The entirely new Council elected in 1990 had predispositions in favour of economy and against expansion, but it could not be accused of inactivity. Kitchen refurbishment simply had to be undertaken; expenditure of £432,000 immensely improved conditions for catering staff. Almost equally pressing, given the importance of Regatta income, was reconstruction of the Grandstand. This posed particular challenges. The timberwork had been renewed in 1980, but the essential structure was cast iron and rusting badly. Furthermore, its status since 1975 as a Grade II listed building restricted the available options. Council member Kenneth Barge had the idea of retaining the existing pillars and arches (to preserve the appearance) while adding a new internal steel framework (to carry the load). At the same time, the ground floor could be glazed and equipped with heating to make it suitable for meetings and parties all year round. Costing £300,000, the restoration project was sufficiently unusual to merit notice in *The Architect's Journal*. Adams opened the Grandstand Pavilion on 2 May 1993.

The combination of high capital expenditure and a general economic slowdown meant that the Club recorded only small surpluses during this time. The tally of members, having peaked at 3,100 in 1990, fell to 2,700 over the next three years. It was necessary to lower entrance fees and recalibrate membership categories. James Simmons, the Chairman from 1993, advocated 'some bold decisions to ensure this members' Club is able to adjust to our changing world'. As the trading climate improved, attention turned to development projects calculated to generate

The Grandstand Pavilion after reconstruction in 1993.

additional income. Both finances and opinion were carefully prepared, and the former received a welcome boost in 1995. Customs and Excise, misinterpreting a European Community ruling, had for four years mistakenly levied Value Added Tax on sports club subscriptions, so, to the extent that Phyllis Court constituted a sports club, it qualified for a refund with interest, which totalled £167,000. This was over and above an annual surplus of £160,019; by mid-decade, the Club had regained its commercial buoyancy.

The Council, now chaired by lawyer Nick Laurie, presented its Millennium Project to the membership for consideration in January 1996. It envisaged a Clubhouse extension to isolate outside functions, a fitness centre with swimming pool, a bowling green and more, budgeted at £2,036,000. Consultation showed considerable opposition to special additional subscriptions and the issue of loan stock, but a referendum in March gave strong support to a new functions suite, financed without borrowing. Provided with its own entrance and separated from the Ballroom by a movable acoustic wall, this set of rooms (called the Finlay Suite) added a thousand square feet to the ground floor of Phyllis Court. It opened on 20 July 1997. Alas, Nick Laurie did not see it finished; he had died two months earlier, aged only fifty.

The Club now had the semi-detached guest facility first held out as a prospect for 'the rosy future' in 1958. Along with new storage and staff rooms, the Finlay Suite cost about £625,000, but it certainly paid its way. Stuart Drew, Chairman of the Membership Committee, explained 'that Members' events always, always took precedence over outside functions even though that could be financially detrimental', because 'the Club only made money to enhance the enjoyment of members and for no other reason'. Phyllis Court Members Club Limited was reclassified as a medium-sized company in 1997, as its turnover exceeded £2.5 million. Richard Edwards served as Secretary and General Manager for nine years from 1995, having resigned from the Council in order to apply for the post. He had previously managed a division of Trust House Forte and later received an OBE for services to the hospitality industry. By 1998, there were 2,920 members served by 74 permanent employees. The staff grew far more international in this era. Poles led the way, initially drawn to Henley, perhaps, by the presence of the Marian Fathers at Fawley Court, and many other nationalities followed. For young people entering the hotel industry, a few years at Phyllis Court presented an opportunity to enhance their English and their professional skills. Few proposed to settle permanently in the district, and property prices in any case discouraged this, so the Club initially rented additional staff accommodation and then bought and converted three houses in Singers Close (1996), Haywards Close (1999) and Western Road (2003). The National Minimum Wage Act and Working Time Regulations required a reorganisation of staffing in 1998 that included engaging a night porter. Closed-circuit television cameras had already been installed as a security measure in 1993.

Nick Laurie, Council Chairman 1995–97.

The appearance of Phyllis Court benefited from two further projects in 1997–98. First, the seventeenth-century brickwork of Cromwell's Wall underwent a thorough restoration. This did entail the loss of the rambler roses from the river frontage, but a soil deficiency had latterly blighted them. More strikingly, in April 1998, the Clubhouse entrance regained its glazed canopy after twenty-two years – or, rather, it gained an excellent replica of the one that had sheltered arrivals and departures between 1907 and 1976. This was financed by contributions from the Action Group and the 300 Club, recently revived as a component of the Heritage Fund, launched by Sir William Barlow in 1994 to 'accumulate money to tackle desirable jobs which fall outside the normal wear and tear'. No one who beholds it is likely to deny that the canopy confers a touch of grandeur. Members would soon

The Finlay Suite was a single-storey building 1997–2003; the occasion here is the Millennium Garden Party in 2000.

be especially pleased to see the Clubhouse looking its best. Its stucco, incidentally, after a cream-coloured interlude, was now repainted a very pale pink.

The Royal Visit

Chairman Grahame Hattam was initially incredulous in September 1998 when Club Manager Laurent Petas telephoned to say that Phyllis Court had been asked if the Queen could visit: 'Is this your Gallic sense of humour?' Petas, quite serious, elaborated. Elizabeth II would be coming to Henley on Friday 6 November to open the new River and Rowing Museum. The most fitting way for her to arrive there was clearly by boat, and officials wondered if she might use the Club as the point of embarkation for her short voyage. The answer was never in doubt. Hattam, a former executive with Marks & Spencer, finalised the details in meetings with the Lord Lieutenant, Sir Hugo Brunner, and the Queen's Private Secretary, Sir Robert Fellowes. The Council brought forward the resurfacing of the riverside path (later to be known as The Queen's Walk) and the police inspected every manhole, drain, boat and bush in the vicinity, as well as making an underwater survey.

The appointed day dawned fine and bright. Gardeners worked against the clock to keep the drive and lawn free from leaves, no easy task in November. Everyone was in their places by 10.30 a.m. Pupils from Rupert House School lined the

Queen Elizabeth II emerging from the Grandstand Pavilion on 6 November 1998. On the left, Council Chairman Grahame Hattam, with General Manager Richard Edwards behind.

road, members waited beside the path and those with moorings watched from the river. As the black Rolls-Royce came into view, the Royal Standard rose over the Clubhouse. The limousine crossed the car park and followed the winding route to the riverbank. There the Queen alighted, amid loud cheers, to be welcomed by the Chairman. She wore a coat and hat of burnt orange and carried a black hand-bag. After children had given her posies, the Queen walked slowly along the tow-path beneath its blue-and-white striped awning to the Grandstand Pavilion, where she sat down to sign the Club's new visitors' book and a large photograph of herself (for subsequent display in the Lounge). The autumnal flower arrangement behind perfectly matched the colour of her outfit. When she re-emerged, Hattam handed her a single red rose, the ancient rent of Phyllis Court, offered today as a token of loyalty and affection. 'That's very nice', said the Queen. 'Thank you very much.' Members of the Council and senior staff were then presented, and more children came forward with flowers. Queen Elizabeth moved down to the landing stage and then *up* a couple of extra steps, constructed by the Club's maintenance staff that very morning, since the river was running exceptionally high. Royal Watermen in red manned *Windrush IV*, the Thames Conservancy inspection launch. As Her Majesty departed, still holding the red rose, the Royal Standard was lowered, having flown above Phyllis Court for twelve minutes. Members then celebrated with a special lunch, and a block of inscribed granite was afterwards placed in a flower bed to commemorate the visit. Roy Finlay would have been delighted.

11

Recent Times
1998–2012

D ozens of gold and silver balloons cascaded onto the heads of revellers in the Ballroom of Phyllis Court in the earliest seconds of the year 2000, as the first of Henley's official fireworks exploded high above the Thames. Long in the planning, the Millennium Masked Ball filled the Clubhouse to capacity (and members with caravans were even permitted to park them in the grounds for the morning after). Six-and-a-half years later, the Club marked its own centenary with three days of festivities. After a thanksgiving service and a piano recital by John Lill on 2 June 2006 came an 'exclusive and exotic' Ball on 3 June, with the Alan Grahame Quartet in the Dining Room, Dave Shepherd's Swing Kings in the Ballroom, and the Scorpio Disco in the Loddon Room. 'The Big Party' on 4 June then extended the fun to children by means of a carousel, hoopla, coconut shy, bouncy castle, dodgems, swing-boats, stilt-walkers, clowns and perfect weather.

Such memorable events were milestones but not turning points, for the beginning of the twenty-first century saw much continuity at Phyllis Court Club from

Millennium fireworks seen from the Clubhouse.

its preceding decades of success. Repeatedly, noticeboards have required enlargement to cope with the expanding calendar of social events and activities. 'More than just a Club, it's a way of life', declares the brochure. The composite structure of the modern Club allows the enthusiasm and initiative of members to shape its programme, and lasting friendships emerge unforced from the bringing together of people with shared interests and common aims. None of the component sections has expired, and several new ones have been born. The Computer Section, created by Tony Robson and John Hicks in 1999, not only advances the knowledge and skill of members but also provided the Club with its earliest website. The popularity of genealogical research via the internet gave rise to a specialised offshoot in 2005, the Family History Section.

The Phyllis Court Club Singers have rehearsed and performed a wide variety of music since 2001. Barry Hardman formed the Classical Music Section (2008) to organise group travel to concerts, much as the Theatre Group (2005) assists playgoers. Professional performers have also come to the Club, mounting stage productions as well as recitals. Swansea City Opera presented *The Pearl Fishers* outdoors in 2006, and Charles Court Opera later gave chamber performances of *HMS Pinafore* and *The Mikado*, while pantomimes have featured in the Christmas programme. The Jazz Appreciation Section, instigated by Stephen Valdez in 2008, holds eight or nine concerts per year at Phyllis Court; saxophonist Scott Hamilton and pianist John Critchinson were among its bookings in 2011. The Garden Club (also 2008) has arranged lectures, demonstrations, and expeditions to such places as Highgrove House and the Royal Horticultural Society. Increasingly valued as 'the lifeblood of the Club', the sections were in 2009 restyled Interest Groups. The two youngest, dating from 2011, are the Real Ale Appreciation Group and the One Club. The latter invites people who hold single membership or regularly come to Phyllis Court alone to attend its suppers, lunches, dinners, book club and walking group.

In 2008–9, the Heritage Fund enhanced the Clubhouse with three significant works of art: a new painting of the Grandstand by Richard Foster and original seventeenth-century portraits of Bulstrode and Mary Whitelocke. Its successor, the Phyllis Court Foundation, presented an exhibition of Zimbabwean sculpture in 2010 and commissioned this book.

Notable visitors to Club functions have been broadcasters Raymond Baxter and John Amis, journalists John McCarthy, Jenni Bond and Sir Trevor McDonald, and cartoonist Bill Tidy. Michael Heseltine, the former Deputy Prime Minister, addressed a Literary Dinner about his memoirs in 2000; MP for Henley since 1974, he had belonged to the Club for four years (1972–76). His parliamentary successor, Boris Johnson, proved a popular speaker; it seems that members had not minded very much his once referring to Phyllis Court as 'a place that looked like something out of the last days of the Raj'. To him, the Club owes its single mention in *Hansard*. Alas, the context was pigswill and the burden imposed on caterers by the

Taking to the Water

The twenty-first century has seen Phyllis Court strengthen its identity as a *river* club, due largely to another new Interest Group. The Rowing and River Section came into being in 2000 (at the suggestion of John Hicks) and affiliated to the Amateur Rowing Association five years later as the Phyllis Court Club Rowing Club. With a focus on veteran novice recreational rowing, it provides professional coaching and access to no less than sixteen boats (including a pink one especially for ladies). Time trials are held twice a year, and a new pontoon was put in place in 2010 to facilitate multiple launches. In the words of Phil Foster, 'What could be more thrilling as a novice than rowing the Henley Royal Regatta course?' For those inclined to gentler sculling, the Club revived its boat-hire facility after an interval of thirty-four years; two skiffs could now be booked by the hour. In September 2010, Phyllis Court hosted the inaugural Henley Regatta for the Disabled. Its prizes were presented by Olympic double silver medallist Debbie Flood, who afterwards became an honorary member and brought twelve athletes from the Great Britain rowing squad to the Club a year later at the Council's invitation. Sadly for Henley, the rowing races of the XXXth Olympiad in 2012 took place ten miles away on a man-made lake at Dorney.

Members of PCC Rowing Club taking part in time-trials in May 2011.

Animal By-Products (Amendment) Order. (In Finlay's time, Phyllis Court had fattened its own pigs on site.) Another star turn at a Quarterly Supper was Ann Widdecombe MP in 2004. Club balls and dances have meanwhile had themes as diverse as the sixtieth anniversary of VE Day and 'Bollywood'.

Phyllis Court retains its importance as a venue for the wider social life of the district. Such events as the corporate dinner of the Thames Valley Chamber of Commerce and the Vale of Aylesbury with Garth and South Berks Hunt Ball exemplify the traditional type of external booking, along with numerous charity functions. There have also been innovations. Thousands of people came to the Paddock in 2009 and 2011 for the Henley Food Festival, and the Club is now one of a dozen locations regularly hired by the Henley Literary Festival. Among authors who have appeared at Phyllis Court are John Mortimer, Colin Dexter, John Julius Norwich, Alexander McCall Smith, Sir Max Hastings and Gervase Phinn.

Twenty-first-century Challenges

Naturally, the running of the Club in this period has not been without its challenges. There were signs as early as 2000 that profits from Regatta Week, so crucial to cash flow in the second half of the year, were ceasing to grow in real terms. This reflected a wider social trend at Henley, where the flock of blazered 'yuppies' in the meadows perceptibly thinned as their style began to fall out of fashion. Around the same time, the only two rowers who were truly household names, Redgrave and Pinsent, came up to retirement, competing for the last time in 2001 and 2003 respectively. The Club responded by revitalising its programme of evening entertainment. The Three British Tenors, Instant Sunshine and Johnny Dankworth provided music; Peter Barkworth and Hannah Gordon gave literary readings; face-painters and magicians diverted children. Undoubtedly, the Regatta remained the liveliest week of the year at Phyllis Court Club, but its days as a sure-fire commercial panacea were over for the present, and the Council saw the danger of keeping too many eggs in one basket.

Under the chairmanship of veterinarian Philip Williamson, the Council had an upper storey added to the Finlay Suite in 2003 at a cost of £400,000. (The ground floor, then six years old, had been designed with a view to this second phase.) The number of guest bedrooms at Phyllis Court thereby increased from eleven to seventeen, enabling the Club to accommodate larger weddings and conferences. This certainly proved beneficial to the business, which obtained an AA four-star rating in 2010. Serious consideration was also given to the idea of constructing a swimming pool, yet the scale of investment again proved daunting. Nor did a bowling green materialise. This had appeared imminent at the turn of the century, when insurance executive Stuart Drew was in the chair. Latterly, however, differences over location, size and surface robbed the project of momentum. The provision of floodlights permitted evening play on two of the tennis courts from 2003.

The first Council Chairmen of the new century: above Stuart Drew 1999–2001 and
Philip Williamson 2001–3; below Adrian Friendship 2003–4 and Tony Robson 2004–5.

Advocates of financial caution pointed to fluctuating membership income. In late 2000, the Club had 3,052 members, but the total dropped by 10 per cent over the next three years, a fact attributed to a general slowing of economic growth. The annual surplus fell by 17 per cent in 2003 (to £186,000), though economy measures promptly reversed this, the number of regular staff being cut from seventy-nine to seventy-one. Electronic Point of Sale (EPOS) cards had been introduced for members in 2002, and the new Chairman, Adrian Friendship, proposed the idea of requiring an annual advance of £100 (in order to encourage dining in the Clubhouse). This scheme was tried in 2004, subsequently abandoned, and

The Orangery, designed by David Salisbury and opened in 2006.

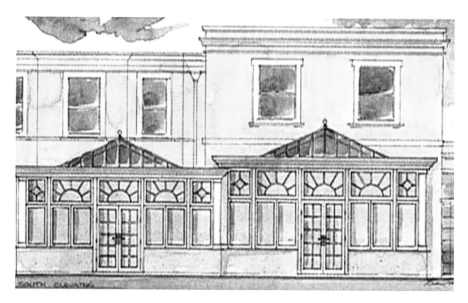

re-introduced in a modified form in 2010. Both Friendship and his successor, Tony Robson, had engineering backgrounds, the former as a maker of interlocking safety systems, the latter with John Brown and Company. A lowering of entrance fees helped bring membership back above three thousand by 2005. There was simultaneously a successful drive to double the number of reciprocal clubs. (Members of Phyllis Court who obtain a card of introduction currently have access to one hundred clubs in twenty-two different countries as far-flung as Canada, Kenya, and China.) For a centenary project, the Council added a conservatory to the northeastern corner of the Clubhouse at a cost of £290,000. It was opened on 2 June 2006 (by the Lord Lieutenant of Oxfordshire) under the name of the Orangery, an extra dining area 'with a bistro-like feeling' and river views.

Terje Johansen, known as 'TJ', a retired investment banker originally from Norway, came to the chairmanship of the Council in 2005 with the instincts of a radical reformer. 'Only one quarter of our income comes from subscriptions and entrance fees', he explained. 'Our Club is no longer just a members' club, but is also a business.' A long-term business plan with explicit goals and strategies was therefore in order, and income growth became a priority. Expansion of the Club to 3,200 members was planned, achieved, and exceeded. Johansen wished to see Phyllis Court grow more like a London club by recruiting wealthy professionals and business people in their forties. Realistic or not, this aspiration contributed to a number of controversies. Eligibility for joint membership was extended from married couples to 'two people in a relationship living at the same address'. A revision of the dress code allowed gentlemen to enter the Lounge, Club Room and Members Bar at any time without a tie or jacket (though 'a structured collared shirt' remained compulsory). Age became a sensitive issue, as some people felt that the focus on attracting new younger members risked making existing older members feel undervalued. In their eyes, the style and ethos of the Club appeared threatened. Changes in senior staff also had an unsettling effect. Laurent Petas, a Frenchman employed at Phyllis Court since 1994, resigned as General Manager (the equivalent of Secretary) after only a year. Stephen Taylor succeeded him. Debate began on modernising the governance structure of the Club, and postal ballots were introduced for elections, but Johansen's proposal that people aged over seventy should never form more than half the Council was rejected at the Annual General Meeting in 2006 (after Baron Stoddart pointed out that he could still sit in the House of Lords at eighty). A year later, concerns that Rule Book revision was progressing without sufficient consultation led 165 members to start requisitioning a Special Meeting. A fresh dispute eclipsed this, however. It is perhaps proof of the devotion that Phyllis Court Club inspires in many of its members that their passions sometimes run high.

In 2007, the Council engaged Nicholas Hollinshead Interiors to refurbish the Lounge, Club Room, Reception, Members Bar and staircase. 'Our brief', wrote the

The Lounge
and the
Members Bar
as refurbished
in 2007.

designer, 'was "elegance and opulence" – a traditional interior with contemporary twists. Crystal chandeliers and white gold gilding complement the vivid fabrics and luxurious furnishings… providing a theatrical and sometimes exotic backdrop.' The green, gold and purple décor proved too exotic for some members, who could not easily regard it as the 'elegant home from home' mentioned in Club publicity. Johansen, reaching the end of his maximum term as Chairman, said that 3,200 members would have 3,200 opinions. Critics protested that so large a project should have been submitted to the membership for approval or more detailed consultation (even though the Club's constitution did not require it). The final cost amounted to £748,465. Supporters argued that this investment would yield a higher rate of return (by attracting new members) than could be earned by keeping the money in the bank. Disagreement grew sharp. At the Annual General Meeting on 13 May, all members of the Council who were not standing down decided either to resign or to withdraw their candidatures for re-election. It was then too late to seek additional nominations, so at the meeting's close, Phyllis Court Club found itself with just three newly elected Council members, none of whom had previously held office. The Council being deemed inquorate, the General Manager served as Acting Chairman for six weeks while further elections took place.

Dinner for ten – the Club Room.

Recent Council Chairmen: Terje Johansen 2005–7, Deon Melck 2007–9, and Geoffrey Fielding 2009–12.

The new Council met on 28 June and chose as its Chairman Deon Melck, a South African who had headed Tupperware UK. At an Extraordinary General Meeting held in September to adopt the accounts, he declared, 'What this Council really wants to do is to communicate with the members. We are members first and councillors second, and we want to make sure that this Club is a happy Club and moves ahead in that way.' An assurance was given that in future any capital project involving expenditure over £250,000 would be referred to the membership for consultation. New advisory committees and focus groups were set up to promote the exchange of ideas. Incidentally, parliamentary legislation laid to rest one thorny issue debated for twenty years and more: private clubs were not exempted from the ban on smoking in enclosed workplaces that took effect in England on 1 July 2007.

Designed to retain the benefits of limited liability, the legal structure of Phyllis Court Club is inherently complex. Technically, its elected Council delegates the running of its activities to the Club Company, whose directors are the members of the Council themselves. In 2007–9, retired barrister Alan Green assisted the Club in clarifying its constitution, aiming to remove any possible conflicts of interest. Henceforth the trustees who held the shares of Phyllis Court Members' Club Limited could not also be appointed its directors. Another revision concerned the tenure of the Council Chairman. Following a narrowly contested chairmanship election and a Special Meeting in 1999, the Council had drawn up a code of practice which recommended that no Chairman serve more than two consecutive annual terms. A decade later, the value of greater continuity was recognised, and a new rule set the maximum tenure at three years and ninety days. Meetings of the Council were renamed Directors' Meetings from April 2010.

Coping with the 'Credit Crunch'

In 2008, an international banking crisis triggered a global economic recession that looked likely to be the most severe since the 1930s. Phyllis Court Club could not be immune to its effects, and Melck at the Open Meeting in November faced the situation squarely:

> The Regatta was down. Abba [a tribute band] with an attendance of 400 made a loss. The bedroom occupancy has been down. Weddings are down. Staff costs are up, food and beverage costs are up well above inflation, service costs are also creeping up. Many of these things are totally outside of our control. Times are tough. We need to buckle down.

The Club that year registered a deficit of £61,167. Following the General Manager's resignation, Council member Geoffrey Fielding stepped into the breach and ran the Club for four months, taking steps to strengthen budgetary discipline that were too urgent to await the appointment of a permanent successor. All discretionary spending was suspended, and the sale of five- and ten-year memberships (known as 'commutation of fees') raised £434,000. The Council thus kept its pledge to maintain a cash balance of at least £250,000 at all times.

More recent figures show how the Club has been weathering the storm. Its pre-tax surplus was £142,729 in 2009, £350,267 in 2010 and £394,165 in 2011

A bedroom refurbished in 2008.

Phyllis Court in January 2007.

– commendable in the circumstances, given that Phyllis Court is (in its Founder's memorable phrase) 'entirely in the nature of a luxury'. The Club could even afford to install a lift in 2010, but the difficulty of its trading conditions should not be underestimated. A precipitous decline in corporate hospitality marked Regatta Week 2009, although tighter control of costs thereafter boosted profitability. Exceptionally low interest rates have meanwhile reduced investment yields, and banqueting does not easily flourish in a period of austerity. 'The Club will have to rely more on member spend than income from commercial activities', explained Fielding, who chaired the Council from June 2009. 'This is no bad thing and will be welcomed by many members.' With previous commercial experience in the timber industry, he developed a five-year Strategic Plan in line with this analysis. Vigorous marketing by means of targeted mailing and open evenings has sustained the membership level, which, having reached an all-time high of 3,358 during 2009, stood only slightly lower at 3,277 at the close of 2011. A new membership recognition scheme awards enamel badges in the shape of a rose to long-standing members. An optional loyalty reward scheme encourages regular buyers of food and drink at the Club. Relative to average earnings, the £678 charged for single membership in 2012 is actually far less than the five guineas demanded in 1906.

With an eye to the future, the Council is aware that the impact of the economic downturn could well be profound and enduring. People are going to be retiring later and receiving lower pensions. It follows that Phyllis Court Club should increase its attractiveness to persons still in full-time work. The development of the Grandstand Pavilion as an occasional restaurant has been one aspect of this approach. Another is fresh interest in the provision of a leisure centre. In 2010–11, negotiations took place with Nirvana Spa & Leisure, a private company proposing to build and run a fitness suite and relaxation pool with jacuzzi and sauna on land leased from the Club; one thousand members of Phyllis Court would receive in perpetuity a 50 per cent discount on membership of the spa. Before this proposal could be put to the vote, however, Nirvana decided to withdraw. The Council continues to regard a leisure centre as an important element in broadening the Club's appeal and thus safeguarding its long-term viability. Only by generating healthy surpluses can the fabric of Phyllis Court be preserved and the enjoyment of its members perpetuated and enhanced.

Graham Owen, Secretary since 2009, takes as his motto, 'Evolution, not revolution'. The 'Credit Crunch' has provided a reminder that the Club's prosperity cannot be taken for granted – but anyone who has read through the last six chapters will have seen that it never could be. The fortunes of a river club depend in

some measure on factors as proverbially fickle as English weather and the public taste. The remarkable aspect of Phyllis Court Club has been its capacity to adapt and endure, thus achieving longevity on which not even its keenest supporters would have wagered in 1906. Only think of the totality of effort contributed over a hundred-and-six years by thirty-five Chairmen, twenty-nine Secretaries, scores of Councillors, hundreds of staff, and thousands of members. People who seek a moral are free to contemplate debts owed to those who went before and duties to those yet to come. It would nevertheless be laughably pompous to end a history of Phyllis Court with a homily on collective endeavour. After all, the primary purpose of a social club is pleasure, and it is hoped that this volume adds a little to the sum of it by stimulating a wider range of associations. Readers passing by Phyllis Court on the Thames Path may be prompted to ponder not only topiary, lawn care and rowing, but possibly also medieval knights, Elizabethan merchants, Civil War soldiers, Stuart lawyers and Georgian bankers, aristocrats and admirals. Readers who cross the threshold of the Club can reflect on the fact that they follow in the footsteps of David Lloyd George, Nancy Astor, Sir John Jellicoe, Nellie Melba, George Orwell, Fred Perry, Arturo Toscanini, Joachim von Ribbentrop, Rebecca West and Peter Ustinov, to name a few of many. Those who reach the Ballroom might fill an idle moment by allowing the mind's ear to evoke the echo of Herr Moritz Wurm's Blue Viennese Band striking up *A Waltz Dream* in 1910, or the syncopations of Casani and Lennard exhibiting the charleston in 1927, or the breathy tones of Yana singing *Climb Up the Wall* in 1957, or the distinctive voice of Edward Heath enthusing about sailing in 1997, or the grunts and exclamations of Japanese wrestlers in 1907, or the whir of RAF model-makers' electric fretsaws in 1942. Awareness of the past enriches experience.

from good to
R??. 1914.

Appendix I: List of Chairmen

The Proprietary Club

Founders' Committee
1906–07	1st Viscount Churchill, GCVO
1907–10	Colonel Sir Douglas Dawson, KCVO, CMG

General Committee
1911–17	Laurence Hancock
1917–19	(Vacant)
1919–31	Commander Sir (Arthur) Trevor Dawson, Bart.
1931–37	Brigadier-General Edward Spencer Hoare Nairne, CB, CMG

The Members' Club

Council
1937–38	Sir Gilbert Eliott, Bart.
1938–45	Brigadier-General Edward Spencer Hoare Nairne, CB, CMG
1945–46	Commander Robert H. Glen, RNVR
1946–47	Henry J. Tapscott
1947–51	Commander Robert H. Glen, RNVR
1951–52	Lieutenant-Colonel R. Ingham Clark
1952–54	Commander Robert H. Glen, RNVR
1954–55	Captain Harold J. Pullein-Thompson, MC
1955–57	(Hengist) Richard E. Bradshaw
1957–61	Joseph A. Burrell
1961–64	Michael K. Watson
1964–67	Gordon J. Abraham, OBE
1967–70	Dr W. Bryce Alexander
1970–73	Arnold J. Claisse, JP
1973–76	(Henry) Paul Rosewarne
1976–77	Group Captain Robert E.G. Brittain
1977–78	Wilfred A. Sivyer
1978	Sir Edward Beetham, KCMG, CVO, OBE
1978–83	Major Harold Harly-Burton, TD
1983–85	Norah Adlam
1985–88	(Ralph) Richard Willgoss
1988–90	A. John Dore

1990–93   (Ernest) Victor Adams, CB
1993–95   James A. Simmons
1995–97   Nicholas R. Laurie
1997–99   Grahame R. Hattam
1999–2001 Stuart B. Drew
2001–03   Philip T. Williamson
2003–04   Adrian F.M. Friendship
2004–05   Tony D. Robson
2005–07   Terje R.G. Johansen
2007–09   Deon Melck
2009–   F. Geoffrey Fielding

Appendix II: List of Secretaries

The Proprietary Club

1906	(Reginald) 'Roy' G. Finlay (Hon.)
1907	Captain Charles E.M. Morrison (Hon.)
1908	Vernon Holt & St John Mildmay (Joint Hon.)
1909	Captain Charles E.M. Morrison (Acting Hon.)
1910	William Onslow Secker
1910–33	Captain (Reginald) 'Roy' G. Finlay (Hon.)
	1916 Captain E. Claremont, RN (Deputy)
	1917–19 Helen Goff (Deputy)
	1919–20 W.A. Ingram (Deputy Hon.)
1933–37	Jack Rendle-Mervill (Hon.)

The Members' Club

1937–39	Colonel Charles J. Pickering, CMG, DSO (Hon. from 1938)
1939–40	Guy Blaker (Hon.)
1940–45	W. Bruce Dick (Hon.)
1945	J.S. May
1945–50	Major Douglas 'Dickie' Dunn
1950–52	D.L. Sherwood
1952–56	Lieutenant-Colonel Sir Geoffrey Betham, KBE, CIE, MC
1956–58	Lieutenant-Colonel Basil Ormond Ware
1958–66	Joy Crone
1966–67	R.E. Owen
1967–76	Donald C. Ferguson
1976–77	Wing Commander (George) Laurence E. Sturt
1977–78	Christopher A. Smith
1978–88	R. Ian Bulloch (Secretary Manager)
1988	Colonel Michael Procter (Chief Executive/Secretary)
1989–95	David M. Brockett (Secretary & General Manager)
1995–2004	J. Richard Edwards (Chief Executive from 2002)
2004–05	Laurent Petas (General Manager)
2006–08	Stephen Taylor (General Manager)
2009–	Graham Owen (Club Director & Secretary)

Appendix III: List of Interest Groups

March 2012

Artists Group
Arts Appreciation
Aviators' Circle
Billiards and Snooker
Boat Owners Association
Bridge Section
Charity Action Group
Classic Motoring
Classical Music
Computer Section
Dance Section
Family History
Garden Club
Golf Society

Jazz Appreciation
Ladies Luncheon Club
PCC Rowing Club
Phyllis Court Croquet
Phyllis Court Singers
Probus
Real Ale Appreciation Society
Scrabble Section
Sunday Cinema
Tennis Section
Thames Dining Club
Theatre Group
The One Club
Wine Circle

Also special visits and events associated with the Olympic Games, London 2012.

Select Bibliography

General

John Southernden Burn, *A History of Henley-on-Thames* (1861)

Richard Burnell, *Henley Royal Regatta: A Celebration of 150 Years* (1989)

Frances Chidell, *A Short History of Phyllis Court Club* (1991, 2005)

Emily J. Climenson, *A Guide to Henley-on-Thames* (1896)

Christopher Dodd, *Henley Royal Regatta: 150th Anniversary Edition* (1989)

Ernest W. Dormer, 'Memories of Old Phyllis Court', *The Antiquary*, November 1905

Roderick Mackenzie, 'Round Henley Regatta Reach', *English Illustrated Magazine*, July 1892

Angela Perkins, *The Phyllis Court Story: From 14th Century Manor to 20th Century Club* (1983)

Cecil Roberts, *Gone Rambling* (1935)

Simon Townley, *Henley-on-Thames: Town, Trade, and River* (2009)

Simon Townley (ed.), *The Victoria County History of England: The History of the County of Oxford*, vol.XVI, *Henley-on-Thames and Environs* (2011)

David C. Whitehead, *Henley-on-Thames: A History* (2007)

The Manor of Filettes

R.W. Bailey, M. Miller, & C. Moore (eds.), *A London Provisioner's Chronicle, 1550–1563, by Henry Machyn* (online, accessed 2011)

J.H. Baker, 'Hales, Sir James (c.1500–1554), judge', *Oxford Dictionary of National Biography* (2004)

Alfred P. Beavan, *The Aldermen of the City of London*, 2 vols. (1908–13)

J.S. Brewer (ed.), *Letters and Papers, Foreign and Domestic, Henry VIII, Vol.II* (1920)

Calendar of State Papers, Domestic Series, Elizabeth I, 1581–90 (1865)

Calendar of State Papers, Domestic Series, Elizabeth I, 1601–3 (1870)

Calendar of the Close Rolls, Edward III, 1341–54 (1902–6)

Calendar of the Patent Rolls, Edward III, 1338–54 (1898–1907)

Calendar of the Patent Rolls, Edward IV, 1461–67 (1897)

Calendar of the Patent Rolls, Henry VII, 1494–1509 (1916)

Charles M. Clode, *The Early History of the Guild of Merchant Taylors* (1888)

G.E. Cokayne, *Some Account of the Lord Mayors and Sheriffs of the City of London* (1897)

John Cooper, *An Account of the Charities under the Management of the Corporation of the Town of Henley-upon-Thames* (1858)

Court of Common Pleas, Oxfordshire: Feet of Fines, Henry VII, TNA CP 25/1/191/31, www.medievalgenealogy.org.uk (accessed 2011)

Thomas Dekker, *Troia-Nova Triumphans* (online, accessed 2011)

Natalie Fryde, 'A medieval robber baron: Sir John Moleyns of Stoke Poges', in R.F. Hunnisett & J.B. Post (eds.), *Medieval Legal Records* (1978)

Anne P. Fuller (ed.), *Calendar of Papal Registers: Papal Letters, 1495–1503* (1994)

P.J.P. Goldberg, *Women in England, c.1275–1525: Documentary Sources* (1995)

John Harley, *The World of William Byrd: Musicians, Merchants, and Magnates* (2010)

P.W. Hasler (ed.), *The History of Parliament: The House of Commons 1558–1603* (1981)

Michael Hicks, 'Hungerford, Robert, third Baron Hungerford and Baron Moleyns (c.1423–1464), nobleman and administrator', *Oxford Dictionary of National Biography* (2004)

F.J. Malpas, 'Roman Roads South and East of Dorchester-on-Thames', *Oxoniensia* vol.LII (1987)

Ivan D. Margary, *Roman Roads in Britain*, 3rd ed. (1973)

Jens Röhrkasten, 'Moleyns [Molyns, Molines], Sir John (d. 1360), administrator and criminal', *Oxford Dictionary of National Biography* (2004)

The Whitelocke Era

Joseph Addison & Richard Steele, *The Tatler – Volume the First* (1804)

Richard Blome, *Britannia, or a Geographical Description of the Kingdoms of England, Scotland, and Ireland* (1677)

Calendar of State Papers, Domestic Series, Charles I, 1644–47 (1890–91)

William Cobbett, *The Parliamentary History of England from the Norman Conquest in 1066 to the Year 1803*, vols. 2 & 3 (1807–8)

Considerations on the Present State of Great Britain, with several remarks upon the Reigns of James the First, Charles the First, &c., Unto the end of the Stuart Race in Queen Anne in a Letter to Sir William Whitelock. By a Country Layman (1717)

David Eddershaw, *The Civil War in Oxfordshire* (1995)

A.A. Hanham, 'Whitelocke (Whitlocke), Sir William (1736–1717)', in D.W. Hayton (ed.), *The History of Parliament: The House of Commons 1690–1715*, vol.3 (2002)

Deirdre Le Faye, *Jane Austen: A Family Record*, 2nd ed. (2004)

George Lockhart, *The Lockhart Papers*, 2 vols. (1817)

Damian X. Powell, *Sir James Whitelocke's Liber Famelicus 1570–1632: Law and Politics in Early Stuart England* (2000)

S.W. Singer (ed.), *The Correspondence of Henry Hyde, Earl of Clarendon* (1828)

Ruth Spalding, *The Improbable Puritan* (1975)

Ruth Spalding (ed.), *The Diary of Bulstrode Whitelocke 1605–1675* (1990)

R.H. Whitelocke, *Memoirs, Biographical and Historical, of Bulstrode Whitelocke* (1860)

Laura Wortley, 'Jan Siberechts in Henley-on-Thames', *The Burlington Magazine*, vol.CXLIX no.1248 (March 2007)

The Freeman Era

Mark Bence-Jones, *Clive of India* (1974)

H.V. Bowen, 'Clive [née Maskelyne], Margaret, Lady Clive of Plassey (1735–1817), society figure', *Oxford Dictionary of National Biography* (2004)

John Charnock, *Biographia Navalis*, vol.6 (1798)

O.F. Christie (ed.), *The Diary of the Revd. William Jones 1777–1821* (1929)

Emily J. Climenson (ed.), *Passages from the Diaries of Mrs Philip Lybbe Powys* (1899)

Randolph Cock, 'Freeman, William Peere Williams (1742–1832), naval officer', *Oxford Dictionary of National Biography* (2004)

G.L. Newnham Collingwood, *A Selection from the Public and Private Correspondence of Vice-Admiral Lord Collingwood*, 3rd ed. (1828)

David Hancock, *The Letters of William Freeman, London merchant, 1678–1685* (2002)

B. Hart, 'A Brief Sketch of the Writings, with a Memoir of the late Strickland Freeman, Esq., of Fawley Court', *The Sporting Magazine* (April 1832)

Lectures on the Results of the Great Exhibition of 1851 (1853)

W.S. Lewis (ed.), *The Yale Edition of Horace Walpole's Correspondence* (1937–83)

Thérèse Muir Mackenzie, *Dromana: The Memoirs of an Irish Family* (1906)

A.P.W. Malcomson, *The Pursuit of the Heiress: Aristocratic Marriage in Ireland* (2006)

C.H.H. Owen, 'Sir George Bowyer, first baronet (1740–1800)', *Oxford Dictionary of National Biography* (2004)

James Ralfe, *The Naval Biography of Great Britain* (1828)

Roger Sayce, *The History of the Royal Agricultural College, Cirencester* (1992)

Geoffrey Tyack, 'The Freemans of Fawley and their Buildings', *Records of Buckinghamshire* vol.24 (1982)

John Wilson, *Agriculture of the French Exhibition* (1855)

G.M. Woodward, *Eccentric Excursions* (1796)

The Mackenzie Era

R.R. Bolland, *Victorians on the Thames*, 3rd ed. (1994)

David Brooke (ed.), *The Diary of William Mackenzie – The First International Railway Contractor* (2000)

Michael Chrimes, Mary Murphy, & George Ribeill, *Mackenzie – Giant of the Railways* (1994)

John Dodd, *The History of Chalfont St Giles* (online, accessed 2010)

Paul Karau, *The Henley-on-Thames Branch* (1982)

D.L. Rydz, *The Parliamentary Agents: A History* (1979)

Neil Wigglesworth, *A Social History of English Rowing* (1992)

The Finlay Era

Mrs Baillie-Saunders, 'The Bachelor in Society', *The Star*, 18 April 1908

Ralph D. Blumenfeld, 'Our London Letter', *Town and Country*, 30 September 1911

Jacintha Buddicom, *Eric & Us*, 2nd ed. (2006)

2nd Viscount Churchill, *All My Sins Remembered* (1964)

R.T.P. Davenport-Hines, 'Dawson, Sir Arthur Trevor (1866–1931), armaments manufacturer', in D.J. Jeremy (ed.), *Dictionary of Business Biography* (1984)

Brigadier-General Sir Douglas Dawson, *A Soldier-Diplomat* (1927)

Hallton East, 'The River of Pleasure', *The Idler*, July 1901

Clive Fenn, 'Society's Rendezvous', *English Illustrated Magazine*, November 1910

[Roy Finlay], 'Letters from the Front', *The Times*, 14 January 1915

Henley Royal Regatta, Minutes of the Committee of Management (1902–12)

Lt.-Col. Lionel James, *The History of King Edward's Horse* (1921)

'The London Sunday', *Poverty Bay Herald*, 8 September 1906

A. Temple Patterson (ed.), *The Jellicoe Papers*, vol.2 (1968)

'River Restaurants of Seine and Thames', *Vogue*, 30 May 1928

Vance Thompson, 'The Royal River', *Outing Magazine*, July 1908

George Wade, 'The River of Pleasure', *English Illustrated Magazine*, July 1904

'A Woman's Letter', *Sydney Morning Herald*, 26 August 1905 & 15 August 1914

Filson Young (ed.), *Trial of Frederick Bywaters and Edith Thompson* (1923)

The Members' Club

Debra Aspinall, 'Courting Favours', *Bucks Free Press*, 3 October 2005

Charles R. Bastien, *32 CoPilots* (2004)

Lindi Bilgorri, 'A Little Piece of England', *This is Buckinghamshire*, July 2005

Robin J. Brooks, *Oxfordshire Airfields in the Second World War* (2001)

Art Buchwald, *I Chose Caviar* (1957)

Paddy Burt, 'A Club We're Happy to Join', *Daily Telegraph*, 4 August 2001

Francis Chase, 'These Childish Things', *The Field Artillery Journal*, July 1946

Toby Helm, 'Henley Hoo-ha', *The Sunday Telegraph*, 4 March 1990

Henley Royal Regatta, Minutes of the Committee of Management (1944–46)

D.A. Lande, *From Somewhere in England* (1991)

The National Archives, AIR 29/227, Operations record book, RAF Medmenham 1941–3

Alastair W. Pearson, 'Allied Military Model Making During World War II', *Cartography and Geographic Information Science*, vol.29 no.3 (July 2002)

Ursula Powys-Libbe, *The Eye of Intelligence* (1983)

Joan Rice, *Sand in My Shoes: The Wartime Diaries of a WAAF* (2006)

Louis T. Stanley, *The London Season* (1955)

Acknowledgements

I thank the Phyllis Court Foundation for the confidence it has shown in me throughout this project, and I am especially grateful for the help and encouragement that I have received from those members with whom I have worked most closely: Deon Melck, Marion Forde, and Mary Kendrick. I would also like to record my appreciation of the co-operation always extended by employees of Phyllis Court Club to this curious repeat visitor who was neither member, guest, nor staff.

The following kindly gave permission to reproduce the images on these pages: River and Rowing Museum, pp. 17, 20, 75, 85, 99, 121, 169; National Maritime Museum, p. 37; © National Portrait Gallery, London, pp. 42, 44, 86, 89; Private collection, p. 59 (Siberechts picture); National Trust Photo Library, p. 79.

Particular thanks are also due to the following for providing information, illustrations, and diverse assistance: Simon Bradshaw (*Henley Standard*), John Cave, Dennis Cox, Simon Davis, Stuart Drew, Geoffrey Fielding, Adrian Friendship, Sue Gill, Daniel Grist (Henley Royal Regatta), Lindsey Guest (River & Rowing Museum), Barry Hardman, Grahame Hattam, Elizabeth Hazeldene (River & Rowing Museum), Richard Hewitt, Charles Hoare Nairne, Terje Johansen, Paul Mainds (River & Rowing Museum), Maureen Marsh, Clare Morris, Graham Owen, Gary Panter, Robert Peberdy, Liz Pentlow (Trinity Hall), Kenneth Rendle-Mervill, Chris Roberts, Tony Robson, Suzie Tilbury (River & Rowing Museum), Dione Venables, Laureen Williamson, Philip Williamson, Michael Willoughby, and Elisabeth Wood.

Quotations from *The Diary of Bulstrode Whitelocke* are by kind permission of the British Academy. The extract from *Sand in My Shoes* is reprinted by permission of HarperCollins Publishers Ltd © 2006 Joan Rice.

Index

This book is an initiative of

The Phyllis Court Foundation

Chairman: Deon Melck
Secretary: Richard Hewitt
Treasurer: David Young
Membership: Richard Fletcher
Archivist: John Cave

Committee:
Simon Davis
Geoffrey Fielding
Marion Forde
Mary Kendrick
Pat Mackenzie

Original Members:

Carel & Colin Barker
Moira & Michael Binns
John Bishop
Alan Collier
Dennis Cox
Beulah & David Cremin
Stephanie & Richard Crosby
Pat Davis
Paula & Malcolm Dillingham
Valerie Ehlers
Sonia Eveleigh
Sylvia Ewan
Liz Feuchot
Veronica Fielding
Margaret & Andrew Flower
Sue & Philip Foster
Jill & John Hale
Moira Hankinson
Ann & Barry Hardman
Inez & Clive Hemsley
Patricia Hewitt

Charles Hoare Nairne
Jo & Richard Howard
Daphne Hutchings
Joan Jenkins
Anne Jones
Anne & John Luker
Gill Melck
Adele K. Miller
Jeanette & Robert Mulligan
Noel Parker
Ann & John Powell
Norma & Peter Read
Pauline & Ruben Sarkissian
Pauline & Roger Simmonds
Patricia & Simon Watson
Elizabeth & John Whitmore
Marjorie & Bill Willis
Pauline & George Willis
James Wilson
June & Sydney Wood
Maggie Young